the urban homestead

Kelly Coyne and Erik Knutzen

the urban homestead

Your Guide to Self-Sufficient Living in the Heart of the City

PROCESS

process self-reliance series

the urban homestead is part of the Process Self-Reliance Series

Process Media
1240 W. Sims Way
Suite 124
Port Townsend, WA 98368

www.processmediainc.com
www.homegrownevolution.com

Design and illustrations by Gregg Einhorn
Production assistance by Bill Smith

ISBN 978-1-934170-10-6

10 9 8

This book is dedicated to the South-Central Farmers,
and the memory of 14 acres that once fed 360 families.

Acknowledgments

First, we would like to thank our amazing contributors for sharing their stories with us: Amy, Taylor Arneson, Severine Baron, David Byrne, Deena Capparelli, Laura Cooper, the Greywater Guerrillas, Eva, John Howe, Suzanne Mackey, Ken & Lorie Mars, Mary McGilvray, Jean-Paul Monché, Nicholas Sammond, Elon Schoenholz, Maya Shetreat, and Claude Willey.

And then we must kneel in gratitude before our keen-eyed, patient and insightful beta-readers: Caroline Clerc, Bryn-Ane MacKinnon and Elon Schoenholz.

Before, during and after the writing of this book we've been inspired by the work of the following people and organizations. We offer this short list knowing we're going to forget a lot of people. Once you put your special glasses on, you'll see there's so many smart people doing cool things out there that it's hard to keep track. But we'd like to at least mention Nance Klehm, David Kahn, Steven Box, Enci, The Culture Club, Sandor Katz, Melinda Stone, Tara of Silver Lake Farms, Paul Mackey, Nick Taggart, the revolutionaries at the Eco Village, the Bike Kitchen and the Fallen Fruit collective. They've all shown us the way.

Thanks also to the visionaries behind Process Media: Jodi Wille and Adam Parfrey, for liking our blog and asking us if maybe we'd like to write a book.

And of course, where would we be without our moms? Thanks, Moms!

Preface

When we began this book in the spring of 2007, we had no idea that we were sitting on the crest of a wave. Traveling around since then, we've met hundreds (thousands?) of wonderful people from all walks of life who are embracing the home arts of gardening, brewing, home cooking and small-stock keeping. DIY living — sustainable, grounded and local — represents a cultural sea change, one that is happily here to stay.

   We've had a heck of a good time meeting you all — and it's been an honor, too.

Thank you.

Kelly and Erik
October 29, 2009
Los Angeles

Contents

This is a project and resource book, complete with step-by-step illustrations and instructions to get you started homesteading right now.

To save you the trouble of typing in long URLs to access internet resources, we're maintaining a managed and updated set of links and recommended reads on our own website: www.homegrownevolution.com

Unleashing The Homesteader Within

Unleashing The Homesteader Within

Let's get together and get some land
Raise our food like the man
People people
We gotta get over before we go under
   —James Brown, *Funky President*

Imagine sitting down to a salad of peppery arugula and heirloom tomatoes that you grew yourself. Or a Sunday omelet of eggs laid that morning, served with a thick slice of fresh sourdough, butter and apricot jam—all home-made, of course. Or imagine toasting your friends with a mead made from local honey. Where would you have to move to live like this? A commune in Vermont? A villa in Italy?

My husband Erik and I have done all of this in our little bungalow in Los Angeles, two blocks off of Sunset Boulevard. We grow food and preserve it, recycle water, forage the neighborhood, and build community. We're urban homesteaders.

Though we have fantasies about one day moving to the country, the city holds things that are more important to us than any parcel of open land. We have friends and family here, great neighbors, and all the cultural amenities and stimulation of a city. It made more sense for us to become self-reliant in our urban environment. There was no need for us to wait to become farmers. We grow plenty of food in our backyard in Echo Park and even raise chickens.

Once you taste lettuce that actually has a distinct flavor, or eat a sweet tomato still warm from the sun, or an orange-yolked egg from your own hen, you will never be satisfied with the pre-packaged and the factory-farmed again. Our next step down the homesteading path was learning to use the old home arts to preserve what we grew: pickling, fermenting, drying and brewing. A jar of jam that you make of wild blackberries holds memories of the summer, and not the air of the Smucker's factory.

When you grow some of your own food, you start to care more about all of your food. **Just where did this come from?** we'd find ourselves asking when we went shopping. **What's in it?** At the same time, we began to learn about cultured and fermented foods, which have beneficial bacteria in them. Few of these wonder-foods are available in stores. The supermarket started to look like a wasteland.

A little history

The idea of urban farming is nothing new. Back in the days before freeways and refrigerated trucks, cities depended on urban farmers for the majority of their fresh food. This included small farms around the city, as well as kitchen gardens. Even today, there are places that hold to this tradition. The citizens of Shanghai produce 85% of their vegetables within the city, and that's just one example of a long Asian tradition of intense urban gardening. Or consider Cuba. Cubans practiced centralized, industrial agriculture, just as we do, until the collapse of the Soviet Union in 1989. Overnight, Cubans were forced to shift from a large, petroleum-based system to small-scale farming, much of it in cities. Today, urban organic gardens produce half of the fresh fruits and vegetables consumed by Cubans.

The United States once was a nation of independent farmers. Today most of us do not know one end of a hoe from the other. In the last half of the 20th century, a cultural shift unique in human history came to pass. We convinced ourselves that we didn't need to have anything to do with our own food. Food, the very stuff of life, became just another commodity, an anonymous transaction. In making this transition, we sacrificed quality for convenience, and then we learned to forget the value of what we gave up.

Large agribusiness concerns offer us flavorless, genetically modified, irradiated, pesticide-drenched frankenvegetables. They are grown in such poor soil—the result of short-sighted profit-based agricultural practices—that they actually contain fewer nutrients than food grown in healthy soil. Our packaged foods are nutritionally bankrupt, and our livestock is raised in squalid conditions. The fact is that we live in an appalling time when it comes to food. True, we have a great abundance of inexpensive food in supermarkets, but the disturbing truth is that in terms of flavor, quality and nutrition, our greatgrandparents ate better than we do.

There is a hidden cost behind our increasingly costly supermarket food. The French have a term, *malbouffe*, referring to junk food, but with broader, more sinister implications. Radical farmer José Bové, who was imprisoned for dismantling a McDonald's restaurant, explains the concept of *malbouffe*:

> I initially used the word 'shit-food', but quickly changed it to *malbouffe* to avoid giving offense. The word just clicked—perhaps because when you're dealing with food, quite apart from any health concerns, you're also dealing with taste and what we feed ourselves with. *Malbouffe* implies eating any old thing, prepared in any old way. For me, the term means both the standardization of food like McDonald's—the same taste from one end of the world to the other—and the choice of food associated with

the use of hormones and Genetically Modified Organisms as well as the residues of pesticides and other things that can endanger health.

— *The World is Not for Sale* by José Bové and François Dufour

So what are the strategies urban homesteaders can follow to avoid *mal-bouffe*? Farmers' markets, co-ops and natural food stores serve as good supplements to the urban homestead, but we've found that growing our own food, even just a little of it, rather than buying it, not only results in better quality food, it has changed our fundamental relationship to food and to the act of eating itself. Now, now not only do we know our crops are free of pesticides and GMOs but we discovered an entirely new world of taste and flavor that big agribusiness had stolen away from us. Growing your own food is an act of resistance. We can all join with José Bové in dismantling the corporations that feed us shit.

We've also shifted from being consumers to being **producers**. Sure we still buy stuff. Olive oil. Parmigiano reggiano. Wine. Flour. Chocolate. And we're no strangers to consumer culture, not above experiencing a little shiver of desire when walking into an Apple computer store. But still, we do not accept that spending is our only form of power. There is more power in creating than in spending. We are producers, neighbors, and friends.

Think you don't have enough land to grow your food? Change the way you see land.

Before you start thinking that you have to move somewhere else to grow your own food, take another look around. With a couple of notable exceptions, American cities sprawl. They are full of wasted space. As a homesteader, you will begin to see any open space as a place to grow food. This includes front yards as well as backyards, vacant lots, parkways, alleyways, patios, balconies, window boxes, fire escapes and rooftops. Once you break out of the mental box that makes you imagine a vegetable garden as a fenced-off parcel of land with a scarecrow in it, you'll start to see the possibilities. Think jungle, not prairie. The truth is that you can grow a hell of a lot of food on a small amount of real estate. You can grow food whether you're in an apartment or a house, whether you rent or own.

Do you have 4' × 8' feet of open ground? If you don't have a yard, do you have room on a patio or balcony for two or three plastic storage tubs? If you don't have that, then you could get a space in a community garden, a relative or neighbor's house, or become a pirate gardener, or an expert forager—some of the tastiest greens and berries are wild and free for the taking.

Think you don't have time? Think again.

We homestead at our own pace, to suit ourselves. Some things, like bread baking, have become part of our regular routine. Other kitchen experiments, like making pickles, come and go as time allows. More ambitious projects, like installing a greywater system, take time up front, but save time once implemented. It's unlikely that we spend any more time on our food-producing yard than we would on a traditional lawn-and-roses-type yard. You can set up your urban (or suburban) farm so that it takes minimal time to keep it going — we talk about ways to do that in this book.

Sometimes, when life gets too crazy, we don't do anything beyond the barest maintenance, and eat a lot of pizza. Nothing wrong with that.

Besides saving time, with the exception of a few ambitious projects, like converting to solar, everything we talk about in this book is also cost-effective. Homesteading is all about reusing, recycling, foraging and building things yourself. Seeds are cheap, composting is free. Nature is standing by, waiting to help. And as oil prices continue to rise along with the cost of food, learning to grow your own may be one of the wisest investments you can make.

The paradigm shift

Urban homesteading is an affirmation of the simple pleasures of life. When you spend a Saturday morning making a loaf of bread, or go out on a summer evening after work to sit with your chickens, or take a deep breath of fresh-cut basil, you unplug yourself from the madness. Many of us spend a lot of each day in front of a computer. Homesteading hooks us into the natural world and the passing of the seasons, and reminds us of our place within the greater cycle of life.

Our style of homesteading is about desire. We bake our own bread because it is better than what we can buy. We raise our own hens because we like chickens, and we think their eggs are worth the trouble. Erik bicycles everywhere because that's a thrill for him. There's mead brewing in our guest bedroom because you can't buy mead at the corner liquor store — and because fermentation is the closest thing to magic that we know.

Maybe you aren't so into gardening, but would like to brew your own beer. Maybe you'd like to tinker with a greywater system for your house. Maybe you want to make your own non-toxic cleaning products. Try it! Start by doing just one project, one experiment, and you may well unleash the homesteader within.

Chapter One
Start Your Own Farm

Start Your Own Farm

Strategies For Growing Food In The Urban Setting

No matter where you live, there is always somewhere to grow food. What follows is an overview of four basic strategies for urban gardening. This is just to get your wheels turning. A little later we will get down to the nitty-gritty of how to grow food.

The four general strategies are:
1 Container Gardening
2 Edible Landscaping
3 Community Gardening
4 Guerrilla Gardening

Urban Growing Strategy 1: Container Gardening

You might live in a high-rise, or maybe your landlord won't let you touch the landscaping. Whatever the case, if you have no access to soil, you can grow your food in containers on patios, roofs or balconies, or even indoors, if you have enough light. For practical suggestions regarding container gardening, please see page 81. What follow are ideas to help you envision different ways you can turn your apartment into a mini-farm.

A Window Garden

If you've got nothing else, you've got a window. Or we hope you do. Grow some herbs in your window. Herbs are a great way to get started on your farming career. They do well indoors, and don't need much care. Store-bought herbs are expensive and never around when you need them. Once you get used to having fresh herbs on hand, you'll never go back to the packaged stuff. Herbs are your gateway plants to a farming addiction.

First and foremost you need a sunny window, because herbs are sun lovers. You might find that herbs that grow well for you in the summer die-off or go into suspended animation during the short, dark days of winter. If that is the case you should view them as a summer crop: grow as much as you can while you can and preserve them the excess for winter use. Just trim off the luxuriant growth, tie the stems in bundles and hang them upside down out of the sun to dry.

But given sufficient light, herbs are easy to grow indoors. Try the reliable window herbs first — chives, parsley, cilantro and thyme. Basil and rosemary prefer to be outside, but can be coerced into living indoors, especially if they get to live outside part-time. Herbs don't need plant food or special care. The only trick is to not over-water them.

If you have a bright, south-facing window, you can go beyond herbs and try some other plants. Try this: coerce your cat out of that sunny spot and plop down a cherry tomato in a great big pot and see what happens. Indoor plants do better if you supplement your sunshine with artificial light in the evenings. A traditional fluorescent bulb or a compact fluorescent will work well — just position the bulb as close to the plants as you can. There is no need to buy fancy grow lights.

Beans can also grow in a south-facing window in a big pot. Use transparent monofilament to make an invisible trellis in front of your window, then plant pole beans and let them crawl up the wire to form a living curtain.

If you are lucky enough to have a giant south-facing window, treat the entire area in front of it as you would a balcony or patio garden. See next section.

Got a head of garlic just beginning to sprout? Break it up and plant the cloves close together, pointy side up in a pot and cover them with about an inch of soil. Keep slightly moist, but not soggy. Shoots will start sprouting up in about a week. Cut the green, garlicky shoots with scissors and use as you would chives or scallions — in salads or in cream cheese or in eggs.

These garlic shoots don't need much light, and are an excellent winter crop to hold you over when your other herbs are dead or just hanging on. Don't be shy about using them up though, because the shoots only have a lifespan of a month or so — they exhaust their bulb, and eventually peter out. As you use the shoots, keep poking new garlic cloves in the pot to keep the whole thing going.

The Patio/Balcony Garden

The key to patio gardens is to maximize all available space in all directions.

- Use a combination of low-growing plants, plants that creep up trellises and railings and fire escapes, and plants that grow in hanging pots.
- You can improvise a trellis by stretching rows of string or heavy monofilament wire between two points, like between the railing of your balcony and the roof. Vines can also grow on fire escapes, and

along stair rails. If you've never grown vining plants before, you will be amazed at how well they grab on to things.
- Group smaller plants on shelves, or arrange them in rows, with the plants in the back rows raised higher than the front, as if they were on a staircase.

Play with growing more than one thing in one pot. There is no reason to waste an inch of space. We are conditioned to seeing plants growing all alone in pots, or in tidy rows in fields, but nature doesn't think that way at all, and neither should you. The only thing you have to be a little careful about is to be sure that you don't combine plants with very different water and light needs. A sage plant and a lettuce plant wouldn't make good roommates, for instance, because the sage prefers some dryness. You can't go wrong matching types: all leafy greens have similar needs, as do most root vegetables. As you gain experience you can grow progressively bolder in your experiments. Try this:

- Fast-growing things can be planted with slow-growing things — radishes and carrots together, for instance.
- Sprinkle green onion seeds in different pots, among your lettuces, your greens, your beans, your tender herbs. A few green onions won't take up any room in a pot, and are good to have on hand.
- Plant two or three kinds of leafy greens together, for variety.
- Plant a cucumber and train its vine to run up a pole or trellis, then plant dill at its base. Then you will be all set to make pickles.

For small gardens you are best off giving priority to fruit-bearing plants, because those just give and give and give, unlike, say, a cabbage, which takes a long time to grow and gives you one meal in the end. So plant all sorts of beans and peas in the spring and tomatoes and melons and cucumbers and squash in the summer. You can get small varieties of zucchini and melons that are no bigger than softballs. Whereas these kind of plants usually need some sprawling room, the small-fruited varieties will do well on trellises.

When you are arranging your containers, you want to give the sunny positions to the plants that are sun-greedy, like tomatoes, peppers and eggplants. The rule of thumb for all food crops is that they need at least six hours of sun a day. But this rule is flexible. Your lettuces and root vegetables will tolerate some shade particularly in the heat of summer, when they actually appreciate it if other plants are running interference for them. Put these tender types under or just behind the sun lovers, or tuck them in shadier corner spots. Keep in mind that plants do not have to be in direct sun to thrive. A plant will pick up sun reflecting off the wall near it, or the concrete beneath it. If your balcony tends to be dark, play with mirrors, white gravel or white boards to capture sunlight and bounce it to dark corners.

Think about jungles. In a jungle every available surface has something growing on it. Nature likes things lush. It does not care for modern minimalist aesthetics. You want your balcony to look like a jungle — kind of like that lady down the way with the 300 creepy spider plants on her porch, only your jungle is all food.

Rooftop Garden: The Holy Grail

If you have access to your rooftop and an understanding landlord, this is the best possible situation for the apartment gardener, simply because it affords you so much space and light. You of course will want to make sure that the roof can bear the weight.

Rooftops are hot in the summer, freezing cold other times, and usually windy. Try to set up the garden in a spot that is buffered from the wind, or contrive some kind of windbreak. Constant wind battering will stress your plants, and interfere with their growth. Self-watering containers (Essential Project 5), which we recommend in all situations, are heavier than normal pots, but do insulate the plants from the extreme temperature fluctuations of the roof. They also save you from having to run up to the roof twice a day to water, and they don't leak like regular pots.

I have lived in New York City for the duration of my residency in pediatrics and fellowship in pediatric neurology. So, it's been a long haul. Living by your values can be really difficult when you're busy and reside in a big urban center.

I have always tried to "reduce, reuse, recycle" but I was still disgusted by the amount of garbage we made each day. So, I began to vermicompost. We use the compost we produce mixed with potting soil on our indoor vegetable garden. While we do belong to a CSA (community supported agriculture) to get fresh organic fruits and vegetables in the warmer months, I still wanted to supplement with my own fruits and vegetables that I could pick fresh myself. I also wanted my children to have the experience of tending a garden and picking fresh food, even if it is a bit unnatural to raise crops indoors. Most importantly, I think that nurturing a garden is a truly spiritual experience. We have turned our bedroom into a semi-greenhouse by taking big five-gallon containers and filling them with mixed soil and compost. We placed them next to windows but found we needed to supplement with artificial light as well. Our harvest has yet to come, but we now have climbing beans, Tom Thumb green peas, tomatoes of all varieties, sweet pepper, and many herbs.

My children have delighted in all aspects of this experience. They love having their worm "pets" and watching how they make our garbage into something useful. They are attentive to the plants, searching for aphids or noting that the leaves are looking dry. We have shown them that waste isn't necessarily to be thrown out, but that it can be used as part of a life-cycle in which all matter has a meaningful role. We are trying to have less of an impact on the planet in our small way. All around, important lessons for city kids.

Maya Shetreat, New York, NY

Urban Growing Strategy 2: Edible Landscaping

Edible landscaping is a good strategy to employ when you are colonizing any space visible to the public, whether you own the space or not. It is simply the practice of choosing landscaping plants on the basis of both looks and edibility. A turnip patch may only be beautiful to the enlightened, but many edibles are attractive as well as tasty and these can be put to use creating a practical, attractive landscape that gives you food in return for your investment of time, energy and water.

This is an ancient form of gardening: think of Roman gardens full of olives and grapes, or medieval cloister gardens that grew food and medicinal herbs for the monks, or colonial kitchen gardens with their climbing beans and apple trees. It's simply a practical way to interact with nature: the crops provide all the lush green and scents and flowers your eyes and your soul crave — and then you get to eat them. We propose that our tended gardens be woven into the fabric of our lives. The artificial separation between city life and nature will disappear.

Just imagine every yard, every median strip, every balcony, every roof and even every sunny window given over to food, healing herbs and habitat. Food can and should be grown in public spaces, along parking strips, in front of office buildings, in public parks. Every nook and cranny should be blooming with life. With a little rearranging any city could keep itself in fruits and vegetables. This grand vision may take time, but we all can begin in our own spaces.

First Steps Toward An Edible Landscape

If you live in a house, or on the ground floor of a building, you likely have the advantage of soil at hand — the area around your front door. Or maybe you have access to some weedy common ground, such as the space between building units, or around the parking area. To an urban homesteader, any empty place means an opportunity to grow food. If you rent, you should work with the building manager or landlord to get permission to colonize these areas. If you own, you have to deal with the neighbors who are not used to seeing food grow in public. In both cases, attractive presentation helps smooth the way.

To overcome possible resistance to your farming, start by surreptitiously planting small, easy things like herbs and radishes or green onions around whatever is already there — usually that would be some kind of spindly, badly pruned shrub or uninspired ground cover.

If you have a flowerbed to trick up, consider some of these strategies for incorporating food with flowers:

- Liven it up with some colorful Swiss chard, bright colored, wrinkly red lettuce, or big purple cabbages.
- Plant strawberries around the borders.
- Nasturtiums have edible flowers, leaves and seed pods.
- Basil is a beautiful plant, and it gives you pesto.
- Chive plants throw up cute purple pom-pom flowers, which are edible themselves.
- Italian parsley is attractive, and so useful to have on hand for cooking.
- Pea plants have flowers just a little less showy then those of their floral cousins, the sweet peas.
- A pole or runner bean can grow up a fence behind a flower bed, or grow up the wall by your front door.
- There's nothing wrong with planting a cherry tomato plant in flowers. Just choose a "patio" variety (i.e. small and well-behaved) so that it doesn't take over the entire bed.

You don't need to slave over starting seeds. All of these plants are easy to find in nurseries and in some farmers' markets as seedlings. If flowers are managing to grow in a location, odds are that the veggies will like it there too. Just dig a little hole and tuck them in there. Keep doing little interventions like this, and no one will notice that you are secretly farming.

Ambitious Edible Landscaping

If you have control over an entire front yard, there are two basic ways for you to go. The first is a larger scale version of what we discussed above: you switch out familiar landscape elements with edible equivalents. Plant fruit or nut trees in your front yard instead of traditional shade trees. Plant berry bushes instead of useless shrubs. Replace your flower beds with beds mixed with edible flowers, strawberries, herbs and greens.

If you live under the tyranny of a neighborhood association and have to keep your front lawn, that's fine. Just encroach on it slowly. Widen the beds around the sides of the yard and pack them with edibles. Keep widening the beds a little more each year. By the time your lawn dwindles to a single square foot of turf, your neighbors will be converted to your side by your gifts of green beans and tomatoes.

The other route is more radical. You make no pretense of your yard being a traditional landscape anymore. You make it into a show garden, an elegant potager made up of several well-arranged and tidy vegetable beds. This is more work than edible landscaping, which relies on perennial plants that are more or less permanent fixtures. It takes work to make an ever-changing vegetable garden look good all the time. But it may be worth it, particularly if your best sun exposure happens to be in your front yard.

To give your garden curb appeal plant colorful things and mulch your beds so they look neat. Add lots of flowers to the mix, and keep the flowers closer to the street. Most importantly, you'll want to keep all your gardening equipment hidden out back. The neighbors don't want to see your compost pile, all your tools and crappy plastic pots filled with seedlings. Treat the front yard as a show place, keep it neat, and the neighbors might surprise you with their acceptance.

Be A Tree Hugger

No matter how you landscape, do not neglect to add as many fruit and nut trees as possible, choosing those that work best in your region. They give you a lot of food for very little input. Maximize the number of fruit trees you can have in your yard by investigating dwarf varieties, and learning the value of pruning. Fruit trees can be kept quite small through vigilant pruning, but will still give a lot of fruit. They can even be grown flat against a wall so they take up no space at all. A tree trained into two-dimensionality is called an espalier. Some fancy nurseries sell young trees that are already trained in that shape, but you can train a young tree all by yourself. Espalier looks elegant, but is not difficult. You just have to encourage growth in certain directions, and clip off anything that grows contrary. Look for how-to's in a good pruning book, like Taunton Press' *The Pruning Book* by Lee Reich.

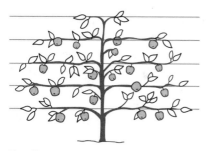

Espalier

Our neighborhood is pretty mellow, but when we planted our parkway with vegetables we wondered if the city or neighbors would have anything to say about it. It is a fairly attractive setup, consisting of two square raised beds, each with a wire obelisk in the center to act as a trellis. Wood chips cover the ground around the beds. After two years we've had nothing but pleasant comments from our neighbors, and no interaction with the city, though technically what we have done is illegal. Our neighbors are curious about what we are growing. We've discovered than many people don't have the slightest relationship with vegetables in their native state — they can't even identify a carrot top or a tomato plant. People come by with their kids so that the young ones can see what growing vegetables look like. We've met many neighbors that way, and have come to consider frontyard gardening a key to our own community involvement.

Whenever we meet a neighbor while we are working out front, we try to send them away with a little fresh produce, but we have not found that people are much inclined to help themselves to the produce in our absence. If they did, they'd be within the law, because the median strip that we plant in is public property, so that food belongs to everyone. But in our experience, tomatoes seem to be the only thing people take. We only grow cherry tomatoes in the parkway, and those are so prolific we can afford to lose some. No one ever touches the root vegetables or leafy greens.

Urban Growing Strategy 3: Community Gardens

A community garden is a large parcel of land — urban, suburban or rural — that has been subdivided for use by individuals in the community. Some community gardens are guerrilla ventures that have slowly become permanent, others are owned by their cities, others are owned by private individuals or foundations. Most are democratically organized, and being truly grass-roots organizations, no two are exactly alike.

When you join a community garden, you will be given a plot of ground to farm. The size of the plots varies a great deal, but something around 10'×15' might be a reasonable size to expect in an urban setting, though some are much bigger. You may have to pay a modest rent, or contribute to the garden in other ways. There may or may not be a waiting list to get a plot. Even if you do have to pay a small rent, it will be well worth it, because you will probably have access to free water, compost, fertilizer and tools.

Joining a community garden is an excellent option for any city farmer; not only will you get space to grow food, you will also become part of a community of experienced gardeners. For a beginner, this is invaluable. Beyond that, it will also ground you in your community. With so few public meeting spaces left to us, a community garden is a great place for neighbors to get to know one another and talk about what matters to them. Community gardens often interact with the greater community through outreach and education programs. They help tie the whole community together.

If there is no community garden available to you, start one of your own. The community garden movement is a vital part of the greening of American cities. If you don't start one, who will?

About six years ago I joined the Altadena community garden, which was started back in the 1970s. It was sort of squatted by a bunch of mostly African-American families, many of whom were from the South. They planted these pea patches or victory gardens and then it became part of the parks and rec. system of Los Angeles.

I grow mostly vegetables—all organic—and for the first year I'm starting to grow some flowers just for fun. My 300-square-foot plot is huge for me, as a single person. I get 85% to 90% of my produce from my garden. A few specialty things I'll go to a farmers' market for. I'm at my garden twice a week. It's all seasonal of course. I'm probably there for an hour or two a week. I could put in a drip system on a timer if I wanted to, but I like to actually go down there and hang out with the folks and get my hands dirty.

We happen to have two master gardeners in our garden who we use as resources. At our general meetings they give us information on how to control pests organically. People seem to be respectful of those who want to use chemicals and others that want to use organic methods.

This 94-year-old gentleman, African-American, whose family was from the South gave me what are called rattlesnake beans. Its like a lima bean, a butter bean that you grow on a pole. They came from his great-great-great-grandfather, who was a slave.

When he gave these to me, he said, "These are special and you're a special person and I want to give you these things." I practically burst into tears right there.

Mary McGilvray, Altadena, CA

Urban gardeners have to be creative to get the most out of the small parcels of land that they can claim as their own. It can be particularly frustrating once you are in the farming mindset to see parcels of land going unused and unappreciated. That's when some people start to question who really owns the land.

Pirate gardening can take many forms, from casual interventions like tossing a few seed balls (see page 30) into the landscaping of an office building, for instance, or in a remote corner of a city park. At the time of this writing, gardening revolutionaries in London just celebrated their second annual harvest of lavender planted along the city roadways (see guerrillagardening.org). Guerrilla gardening may be considered activism, an art form, both or neither.

If pirating vacant property doesn't appeal to you, take over land belonging to your friends, family or neighbors. It's a gentle form of piracy. Plenty of people would be relieved if you took over their yard maintenance for them, particularly if they got some homegrown veggies out of the bargain.

The two of us always look longingly at unoccupied stretches of city land, ones that seem to be begging to be colonized, but we've never pirated a piece of land ourselves. That's why were glad to meet Taylor Arneson, who has planted multiple guerrilla gardens around Los Angeles, claiming land everywhere from the 150 feet of the medium strip of Bundy Avenue (yes, the street made famous in the O.J. trials) to the banks of the L.A. River. On these sites he

plants some of the more sturdy summer crops, ones that can stand up to the punishing Los Angeles sun without coddling: corn, squash and beans, as well as fig and mulberry trees, both of which do well in this climate. He waters his gardens with the water belonging to the property, so one thing he always looks for before he begins planting is a working spigot.

Talking to him has convinced us that pirate gardening is not necessarily a confrontational activity. Though we'd expect that the owners would toss him right off the land when they discovered what he was doing, that has not proved to be the case at all. He claims that sometimes the vegetables do get picked, which he intends, but that he's never had to rip out a garden, nor ever had one ripped out for him.

Taylor's Advice For Would-Be Guerrilla Gardeners:

There's a couple of key things you look for in a guerrilla garden site — any soil is workable but ideally you want something that you can penetrate with a shovel. Preferably water — there should be water in close proximity that's available. Who it's owned by is a minor issue because tap water is so cheap that you can do a large garden for a few dollars a month, especially if you're growing things that are appropriate for the region and you use the water sparingly.

I don't go out of my way to approach the owners and I don't go out of my way to do it undercover either. I wait for the opportune time to have a conversation. So far I haven't had any problems. Usually the owners are pretty flexible and they're interested to help as long as they're not actively wanting to do something with the property.

There's a lot of benefits for both parties. They get their space to look better so they don't have as many complaints from the neighbors and I'm building soil for them for when they go to do landscaping in the future.

PROJECT

HOW TO MAKE SEED BALLS

The seed ball is the Molotov cocktail of the urban homesteader

Peanut-M&M-sized balls made of seed and clay, seed balls are meant to be lobbed anywhere you want to grow something but can't really plant it and tend it in the traditional manner — a fenced-off vacant lot, for instance. Or your neighbor's backyard. You just scatter the balls on the ground and leave them. In their clay coats, the seeds are protected from being eaten or blown away until the rains come. When the rain does come the clay softens and the seeds sprout in the balls, where they are nourished and protected until they get a good start in the ground.

Seed balls are an ancient technology, but they were popularized recently by natural farming pioneer and author of *The One Straw Revolution*, Masanobu Fukuoka. He calls them "earth dumplings" (*tsuchi dango*). They are an important part of his very hands-off methodology of raising crops. And though they are not well-known in North America, they are used all over the world in re-greening projects.

Fukuoka used them to grow grain without invasive tilling and sowing. Others have used them to green the desert or to reintroduce native species to wild areas. In the city, a great thing to do with seed balls is use them to reclaim waste land by introducing wildflowers and other "weeds" that feed beneficial insects and nourish the soil. But you can also try them out with seeds from plants that might feed you.

Be careful how you use these things. In the city it does not matter much where they go, but *never lob them into natural areas.* These balls work, and the seeds you put in them will end up in direct competition with natives.

Check with your nursery where you get the seeds to find out which plants grow best in your area without supplemental irrigation, and which plants are best for your local beneficial insects, and when to plant them. Some classic choices for feeding insects are: mustard, fennel, dill, buckwheat, clover, and wildflowers such as coneflower, goldenrod, yarrow, ironweed and sunflower.

Ingredients:

- Dry red clay, fine ground.

  You can use potting clay or dig clay out of the ground, as long as you dig deep enough so there are no weed seeds in it.

  The subsoil in most of the country is clay, so it is easy to find, especially at building sites or where roads are being built. If you use potting clay, be sure to only use red clay, because the other kinds might inhibit seed growth. Spread it out to dry and then grind it up between two bricks to make powder.
- Dried-out organic compost of any kind.
- Seeds of your choice, one kind or a mix.

Mix one part seeds into three parts compost. Add five parts dry clay to the compost/seed mix and combine thoroughly again. Add a little water to it, just a bit at a time, until the mix becomes like dough. You don't want it soggy. Roll little balls about the size of marbles — be sure to pack them tight — and set them aside to dry in a shaded place for a few days.

To make the strongest impact, distribute these balls at the rate of about ten balls per square yard of ground.

But the greatest change we need to make is from consumption to production, even if on a small scale, in our own gardens. If only 10% of us do this, there is enough for everyone. Hence the futility of revolutionaries who have no gardens, who depend on the very system they attack, and who produce words and bullets, not food and shelter.
—Bill Mollison, *Introduction to Permaculture*

An urban gardener has to be practical, crafty and adaptive. Your motto should be whatever works, works. There are many books about growing food, and many worthy systems that you might want to try, like Mel Bartholomew's *Square Foot Gardening*, John Jeavons' *Grow Biointensive* system or for those with spiritual leanings, Rudolf Steiner's Biodynamic agriculture, to name a few systems that work for people gardening in small spaces. We have always adopted techniques from a variety of sources, but on an overarching, conceptual level we have always been intrigued with the principles of permaculture, and those ideas inform the way we go about tending our garden, and the fundamental principles behind this book.

Now, there's been a lot of buzz among the avant-gardening set about permaculture in the U.S. of late, though in its birthplace, Australia, it is widely adopted and un-exotic. Here there is still a tendency for permaculture to be regarded as an intimidating and somewhat esoteric science, but it doesn't have to be.

Permaculture is a term coined by Australian naturalist and scientist Bill Mollison to describe a philosophy for creating sustainable human environments. The name reflects the intertwined concepts of permanent agriculture and permanent (human) culture. Permaculture seeks to imitate nature by creating interconnected and useful systems with each component complementing each other, forming feedback loops that enhance the health and functionality of the system as a whole.

Permaculture design principles are taken from the observation of nature, and are biased towards creating environments useful to humans, i.e. for providing food, shelter and medicine. While often making use of native plants, permaculturists are not dogmatic and will mix plants from many different regions and combine both wild and cultivated species to achieve their ends.

Though Mollison and his student David Holmgren developed the concept of permaculture in the 1970s, the concept is ancient. When Westerners first encountered indigenous peoples in the tropics, they assumed that such "primitives" did not practice agriculture. In fact many indigenous peoples classified by Europeans as "hunter-gatherers," actively influenced their environments, encouraging wild edible and medicinal plants in subtle ways, letting them grow in a much more ecologically diverse environment than Western farming methods allow.

Living with and encouraging the diversity of a jungle or forest in this ancient way turns out to have numerous advantages. An ecological system where food comes from multiple sources is much less likely to face the kind of catastrophic failure through disease or insect infestations that has caused many a famine in our world — most of which have been predicated by over-reliance on one crop or one system of farming.

The ecosystem of a forest, jungle or desert takes care of itself just fine and does not need to be artificially fertilized or sprayed with pesticides. As in nature, plants in a diverse system provide each other with their own fertilizer and beneficial insects attack another. Permaculturists seek to imitate this balance and create useful and productive surroundings that need as little human input as possible.

An example of such an interdependent system, called a "guild" in permacultural parlance, is the Native American practice of growing the Three Sisters. The Three Sisters are corn, beans, and squash planted together. The corn provides a support for the beans to grow up. The beans, being a type of plant called a "nitrogen fixer," take nitrogen from the air and pump it into the root zone, thereby fertilizing both the corn and the squash. The squash grows on the ground, suppressing weeds and shading the soil, thus saving water. A possible "Fourth Sister," Rocky Mountain bee plant (*Cleome serrulata*), has been found at the site of Anasazi ruins. The bee plant, the sort of super-plant permaculturalists seek out due to its many uses, attracts beneficial insects that protect the other crops while itself providing edible shoots, leaves and flowers, as well as black dye and even a treatment for stomach upset.

Interplanting food this way not only nurtures the plants by providing them with good company, but also makes the most out of the space available, producing the maximum amount of food possible over an extended growing season. More, it ensures that if one crop fails for whatever reason, that same piece of land might still produce others. Overall the threat of losing even one crop to pests is reduced by the biodiversity inherent in the system. Pests love monoculture — planting acres of a single plant is like ringing the dinner bell for bugs.

Permaculture is a way to think about balance and sustainability in our actions and lives. Take the simple act of riding a bicycle as opposed to driving your car. The bicycle gets you from one place to the other, just like a car. But in the same way the interconnected relationships of the Three Sisters benefit your garden, a bike not only provides transportation, but also proves you with exercise, and at the same time helps you develop relationships with your community that you could not initiate while locked inside your car.

So the choice to ride the bike instead of driving makes sense in certain situations, because biking accomplishes more than one thing at a time — it gives you a high return on investment. But permaculture is not about absolutes, it's about doing what works, so we will also acknowledge that there will be other circumstances where taking the bike may not be the best choice. Permaculture is more a way of thinking than something solid you can point to. Don't get hung up on research — just relax, observe and help nature do its thing.

The Practicalities Of Growing Food

Believe us, you *can* grow a whole lot of your own food — even if all you've ever grown in the past is shower mold. But before you dive into the projects later in the chapter, read over our seven principles below.

The Seven Guiding Principles of Successful Urban Farming
(or what we've learned the hard way)
1 Grow only useful things.
2 Region matters. A lot.
3 Build your soil.
4 Water deeply and less frequently.
5 Work makes work.
6 Failure is part of the game.
7 Pay attention and keep notes.

Grow Only Useful Things
You don't have acres of space, so every plant counts. Everything allowed in your growing space has to be edible or medicinal, provide forage for wild or domestic animals, or serve some other function, such as providing mulch or shade. Our general rule of thumb is, "If you water it, you gotta be able to eat it." Water is a resource. Time is a resource. Space is a resource. We no longer squander these resources on merely decorative plants. Food-bearing plants are plenty decorative. Aesthetics is low on our list of priorities, but nonetheless our yard has never looked better, because now there is intention behind everything we plant, and we care for everything we plant.

The first level of priority in our garden goes to our fruit trees, food plants. They get the water and most of our attention. Second in priority are the plants that live around our place in a semi-feral state. They survive without watering and with minimal tending. We let them take up space because they are useful in some way. Perhaps we eat them — this is true for some weeds and our prickly pear cactus — or perhaps they feed beneficial insects — this is true for the wildflowers.

If you take this principle to heart, you will quickly realize that one crop the urban homesteader does not tend is turf. Unless you are a croquet champion, it is time to say goodbye to that waste of time and resources: your lawn. Lawn is the largest crop produced in the U.S., sad to say. It is time to change the thinking that makes that acceptable. One hundred years ago no one would water, weed and slave over something they could not eat. And you know what? They were smarter than us.

Lawn Facts

- Some 85 million households in the U.S. have their own little patch of green — the average size about one-fifth of an acre. All totaled, the U.S. supports 30 million acres of lawn.
- A gas-powered push mower emits as much pollution in an hour as 11 cars.
- Lawns require two to four more water than shrubs or trees.
- Homeowners are using 50% more herbicides than they did 20 years ago.
- The average homeowner spends about 40 hours simply mowing the lawn each year.
- $8.5 billion is spent annually on lawn care products and equipment.

Source: The EPA and the National Audubon Society

Kids and dogs are often held up as reasons why any decent family would keep a lawn in their yard. The truth is that kids love hunting for food in vegetable gardens and climbing low-slung fruit trees and playing in little pockets of wildness, while dogs love sniffing and scratching in all that mulch. Kids and dogs alike benefit from the sensory stimulation provided by permacultural yard. A lawn is a flat void. A little jungle is a whole world to explore.

One of the basic tenets of urban homesteading is that your land works for you — you do not work for your land. This does not mean you do not work your land, but the work you do is productive and meaningful. You do not slave at a job to pay a gardener to maintain a lawn that you do not use. If you own property, think about how much you are paying for every square foot, both in real estate and maintenance, and then consider how very much use or enjoyment you get out of your outdoor spaces. Do you use your yard as often as you would like? What do you do out there?

Would you feel different if your yard held dinner? Beautiful tomato bushes heavy with fruit? Herbs for cooking? More zucchini than you can shake a stick at? What if a couple of chickens were scratching around out there, laying eggs for your breakfast? Would you want to go outside? Would you miss your lawn?

How do you transform your lawn? You lay down sheet mulch right over it. No digging required. See page 55.

Region Matters. A Lot.

Your best source of information about what to grow and when to plant it will come from your fellow urban gardeners, people in your own neighborhood. Fancy coffee-table books and TV shows — i.e. *garden porn* — will most likely lead you to heartbreak. Seed packet information is not universal. This is why it is so important to hook into a network of local people doing what you want to do. They are out there. Once you become interested in homesteading, the magic attractors that rule the universe will bring you together with like-minded folks.

If you can't find any gardeners within shouting distance, you might find them through various community and advocacy groups. Or hook up with other local gardeners through the internet, particularly through vehicles like Yahoo Groups and Meetup. Don't search under gardening — that will yield too broad a spectrum of people. Search under your city names and the terms permaculture, organic gardening, sustainable agriculture, and edible landscaping. Gardeners of a similar mindset might also be found through simplicity groups, slow food advocates and people who are concerned about peak oil.

Beyond that, seek out a knowledgeable local nursery and patronize them, even if they cost more than the big-box stores. Their stock will be healthy and chosen to match local conditions. Big-box inventory tends to be more generic. Small outfits are happy to make special orders for you too. And if you have a question, your local guys are going to be there to answer it for you. Imagine, if you will, bringing a diseased leaf into a big-box store and trying to find someone who can identify the problem. Enough said?

If you are determined to be anti-social and want only the company of books, seek out books written *specifically for your region*. The U.S. is a big place, with lots of climates within its borders. One size does not fit all. You have to figure out how to grow food in your unique climate, whether you live in the desert or the mountains, the far North or the deep South.

And general region is just the start. Even within a single city there will be considerable variation between neighborhoods. Our climate here in central Los Angeles is different than the climate nearer the coast, where the summer temperatures are much lower. For this reason, we are not going to get as good advice from a homesteader living in one of the beach cities as we are going to get from someone living in our own neighborhood. It really makes a difference.

Build Your Soil

An urban garden is pretty much guaranteed to be small—whether it is a back-yard, a community garden plot, or a bunch of pots. In a small garden you have to use your soil very intensely, the same patch over and over again, whereas if you had lots of space you could let parts of your garden lie fallow some years and take a rest. So the ongoing success of your crops is directly related to how well you care for the soil. Soil is not a neutral growing medium. It is packed with nutrients and minerals, worms and other insects, microbes, fungi—more stuff than we understand. Growing food depletes the soil over time. Bad soil causes weak plants. Weak plants attract disease. Disease infects the soil. To prevent this all you have to do is give back to your soil what you take out.

You build soil these ways:

- Compost all your yard and kitchen waste
- Use mulch to protect and build the soil
- Try not to till your soil
- Rotate your crops to prevent depletion and disease
- Never use pesticides or herbicides

Compost

Waste not, want not. Start a compost pile for your yard trimmings and kitchen waste and return all those nutrients to the garden. Your finished compost can be used as soil to fill raised beds, or it can be used as a mulch and spread around your crops to enrich the soil. Either way you are giving back what you took out in your last harvest. Compost is a simple thing (nothing is more inevitable than decomposition), but it is the single most invaluable resource for your garden.

Mulch Your Soil

As we are defining it, mulch is a thick layer of organic matter that you spread all over your yard, particularly around your plantings. You can mulch with compost, but usually mulch is less decomposed: it can be made up of leaves, bark chips, straw, pine needles, etc. This protective blanket helps regulate soil temperature, retains moisture, keeps the plants clean, discourages weeds, provides habitat for beneficial insects and, as it breaks down, improves the quality of your soil. It also has the benefit of unifying the look of your garden, making everything appear polished and organized, even if it is not. This is a real boon in the front yard, particularly if you've torn out the lawn.

Try Not To Till Your Soil

Tilling is the practice of digging deep into your soil and turning it over, mixing up the top layer with the lower layers. It is commonly practiced and recommended in many books, but we lean toward the no-till camp, and this is why: tilling your soil is like a cheap high. First there is a buzz, but after that it's all downhill. By tilling soil you are releasing a quick surge of nutrients by causing the death of large amounts of soil organisms, whose corpses give plants a botanical buzz. Unfortunately, when soil organisms die it takes a long time for them to come back, leaving your plants without the nutrients they need to thrive. Tilling also disrupts the complex symbiotic relationships that exist in healthy soil between fungus, earthworms and soil organisms. That said, sometimes soil is so compromised that it absolutely needs to be broken up and have amendments worked into it. There are no absolutes, we would only recommend that you don't till as a matter of course every time you plant. See page 110.

Rotate Your Crops
"Crop rotation" sounds intimidating, like something taught in agricultural programs, but all it means is that you shouldn't plant the same thing in the same place all the time. Each plant, or more correctly, each plant family draws differently from the soil and attracts its own set of pests and diseases. If you switch your crops around annually it takes some of the burden off the soil and confuses the pests. This applies to pots, too. Say you grow tomatoes in pots one summer. The next summer change the soil and scrub the pots, or grow something else in those pots. See page 102.

Never Use Pesticides Or Herbicides Or Chemical Fertilizers
The urban homestead is organic, make no doubt about it. Organic is nature's way. All the inputs are at hand, and free, part of a grand cycle. You do not want to be beholden to Monsanto et al. in any way, and you don't want to mess up your soil with poisons.

As we said earlier, the soil is an amazing, living mass of many interdependent life forms. When you pour any of these chemical concoctions onto the soil whatever you do not manage to kill will be knocked out of whack.

The alternative is pesticide-free gardening (page 97), and relying on good compost (page 46) and homemade fertilizer teas to feed your soil (page 77).

Water Deeply And Less Frequently
The sight of someone standing in their yard flipping their hose lackadaisically at the end of a long hot summer day is enough to make us froth at the mouth. These people are wasting their time and everyone's water. And their plants aren't very happy either.

Deep watering encourages good root development. As the water sinks into the soil, the roots follow it. Deep-rooted plants are strong and less susceptible to heat and shock and drought. If all you do is sprinkle your plants for a few minutes with the hose, the water will hardly penetrate the soil, so the plants will keep their roots close to the top of the soil as well. If you fail to water them every day, they are bereft and wilt like an abandoned lady in a Victorian novel.

A good watering is deep and slow and lasts an hour or more like...uh...a good massage. Now, you don't have an hour or two or three to stand around with your hose in your hand. What you need is a soaker hose, or its more upscale cousin, a drip emitter system. This kind of watering imitates the benefits of a good rain. The kind of rain that makes the flowers grow in the spring is, after all, not a passing shower but the slow, steady soaking of rainy days. You want to keep the drips system running until the water penetrates deep and is spread in a wide radius around the hose or emitter. The minor effort of laying down a drip system is repaid many times over in easier and less frequent watering.

Another advantage of drip systems is that they keep the leaves of your plants dry. Wet leaves on many plants, particularly tomatoes and squashes and melons and the like, can lead to mildew and other problems. However, plants with edible leaves, like lettuce and cabbage, like a little water on the leaves now and again. It's good to give them a shower once in a while to wash off dust, bugs and pollutants. Just make sure you give them enough time to dry off before the sun goes down: a full two hours of sunshine. You don't want them going to bed with wet leaves.

So how much water is enough water? The answer is it really depends on the plant, on the soil, and the weather, but here is a clue. Don't trust what the soil looks like on top. It might look soggy, but be bone dry one inch down, or the opposite. Get out your little spade and dig down several inches. The soil should be spongy moist no matter how deep you go. Not dripping wet, and not dry. Clay soil (the kind that forms a ball if your squeeze a handful of it) retains water over time, so should be watered less frequently. Sandy soil lets the water drain straight through it, so needs more frequent water. The ideal soil is neither sandy nor clay. Your soil will improve steadily if you keep adding mulch and compost, until it becomes something loose and dark and rich. In the meanwhile, and in general, it's better to let plants dry out ever so slightly between waterings, so they can get some air, than to keep them constantly sopping wet. See page 84.

Work Makes Work

This is a permaculture truism that we've taken to heart. The gist of it is that the fussier you are, the more you try to force your will on the garden instead of working with it, the harder things will be for you. What does this mean in practice? A bunch of different things, but all in all, the end result is that your garden, even if it is just a tiny square of land, even if it just a bunch of pots on your balcony, should feel like a forest. A little wild.

The most sterile zones on this planet are those yards that consist of a sheet of poisoned lawn and a row of rose bushes. What lives in these all too typical yards? Two species: lawn and rose bushes. Maybe a few bugs who eat lawns and rose bushes try to move in once in a while, but they get doused with pesticides, along with any beneficial insects as well. A few weeds pop up, and they get doused with herbicides. Truly, these yards are wastelands. You want your space to be a little messy and humming with life. You want to grow lots of different kinds of plants. You want the kind of garden that is full of birds and bees.

This might sound like a strange analogy, but give it a listen. The bread guru Nancy Silverton, co-founder of the La Brea Bakery, speaks eloquently about how bread dough made from wild yeasts and given time to raise slowly is a living thing. It is not cookie dough. Real bread dough crackles and pulses between your hands, full of invisible life. You want that kind of quality in your garden: full of crackling, invisible life and secret happenings. There's bugs in the soil, bees in the flowers, roots being formed, compost breaking down, all sorts of things you can't see going on, but you feel it. This kind of state comes in one way only — by you doing as little as possible.

When Leaves Fall, Let Them Lay
They're mulching! Or at most, push them to another area of the yard where they're needed more. In other words, don't be obsessively tidy. Don't waste your time collecting leaves to throw in the trash. Leave twigs around for birds to use, leave rocks and logs in odd corners as mini-wildlife refuges. If the floor of your yard begins to resemble that of a forest, you're doing well.

Cultivate A Positive Relationship With Weeds
Some are a pain, yes, and that is what mulching is for. Don't spend your spare time cursing and weeding. And whatever you do, don't break down and use toxic herbicides such as Roundup! Keep on top of your weeds by eating them for dinner. We go so far as to encourage little beds of edible weeds in our yard, though some people just grab them where they find them. See the Feral Greens section for the 411 on foraging. Also, chickens love weeds, so you might also consider weeds animal fodder. Are you getting the idea that your garden is not going to look like Martha Stewart's garden? Good.

Embrace The Wildlife

Birds and bees and spiders and ladybugs do your garden good. Now, wild creatures don't like artificial environments, so the wilder your yard, the more creatures it will host. "Wild" means a lot of things, but it means diversity first and foremost. You want to grow lots of different kinds of plants, so something is always happening in your yard: things are sprouting, things are fruiting, things are seeding, things are rotting. Wild means there are flowers for creatures to feed on, not just roses, but the blossoms on fruiting trees, the flowers on your herbs, the flowers sent up when you let your crops go to seed. You don't have to do extra work to attract birds and insects. Left alone, your yard naturally attracts birds and insects.

Birds eat a phenomenal amount of insects. Nothing warms our hearts more than watching our favorite bird, the phoebe, swoop down on the white butterflies that turn into cabbage worms. The phoebe staked out its claim on our yard after we put in the birdbath. It is just one of many birds that have started dropping by since then, amazing birds we've never seen before. One day a hawk stopped by for a drink. A birdbath doesn't have to be a gaudy Victorian monstrosity (though most baths you find at garden centers are just that). It could be as simple as a hubcap sitting on top of a post. Just make sure it is elevated, because birds like to be out of the reach of cats.

In case you are wondering, we don't have a bird feeder, because we want our bird friends to dine at our splendid insect buffet. But if you live in a cold winter place, they'd surely appreciate food during the freezing months when the bugs are sleeping.

When we first started trying to grow things, we'd find evil-looking red and black bugs on our plants and worry we were infested by some awful plague. Turns out they were ladybug larvae. These tiny alligator creatures are prodigious aphid eaters. They eat more aphids than mature ladybugs. Next time you see one, give it a hug.

Grow Edible Perennials

Perennials are plants that live on year after year (or come back year after year), as opposed to annuals, which spend their entire life-cycle in one season. A grape, for instance, is a perennial plant, whereas a cucumber is an annual. A grape dies back in the winter and sends out new growth in the spring. The cucumber has to be reseeded.

To work less, dedicate a part of your garden to plants that bear food without you having to think about it. All fruit and nut trees fall into the perennial category. There are dwarf and semi-dwarf varieties that do not take up much room, but deliver plenty of fruit. Between pruning and selecting the right variety, we promise you that you can keep a tree, maybe even a tiny orchard, in the smallest yard. With trees you have annual harvesting and pruning duties, which is some work, but less than shepherding annual plants from seeds to harvest. Citrus plants do well in big pots, and you can bring them indoors for the winter. We have a potted kumquat which we adore, because though it is just a little thing, it gives hundreds of sweet fruits every winter.

After trees, there are fruiting bushes, like blackberry and raspberry bushes. These are usually grown on trellises to control their growth and make harvesting easier. As with trees, this is some work when you set it up, but not constant work afterward. Blueberry plants are also excellent fruit-bearing perennials. You don't see them in home gardens much because they need special soil. But for this very reason they are a great container plant — so even patio growers can have blueberries on their cereal in the morning. Grapes are fantastic, as are the almost forgotten berries like the gooseberry or the red currant.

Not all perennials are trees and bushes. Some are more tender plants that die down in the winter, but then come back of their own free will in the spring. A favorite perennial vegetable is asparagus. Once established, an asparagus bed will hand you a bounty of asparagus every spring with little attention from you. Similar plants that come to mind are strawberries, fennel, artichokes, Jerusalem artichokes, rhubarb and many herbs, like chives.

Some annuals or biennials can be made to behave like perennials. Many of your leafy crops — broccoli, collards, kale, lettuces — will give you a second harvest if you harvest them by cutting off their heads, leaving their root system and some stalk intact to send up another flush of growth.

Other plants multiply and can be subdivided. Chive plants are already perennial, but you can make them multiply more quickly. Dig them up and carefully tear the root mass in two, then plant the other half somewhere else. Both halves will expand and thrive. Keep doing this and you'll be up to your ears in chives.

In a similar vein, let some of your herbs and veggies go to seed, they'll show up somewhere else in your garden the next year. This is almost like having perennials. Italian parsley and cilantro and dill weed are very good at popping up wherever they want. So are some greens, like arugula. Let them have their way. Any plant that wants to grow on its own, that will take the initiative for you, is your new best friend. Envision your yard as place where you go out and forage, not a place that you have to control.

Start Small

Most first-time gardeners fail not out of incompetence, but out of ambition. They plant too much and end up overwhelmed. Small problems quickly become big ones, things spiral out of control. Then the would-be gardener tells herself she's not meant for it, and resolves to subsist entirely on take-out. Don't let this be you! The first year start with a small bed or a few pots. If you get a community garden plot, you don't have to plant every inch of it the first year. Leave room to expand.

Failure Is Part Of The Game

You will make mistakes. This is how you learn to garden. Sometimes you are forgetful, or lazy, or misinformed. Other times, shit happens you can't control: frosts, heat-waves, wind, punishing rains. For these things, learn to let go. As for the rest, be ruthlessly Darwinian about your garden. Keep what works and forget about trying to grow anything frail, sensitive or fussy.

Pay Attention And Keep Notes

It does not take all that much time or hard work to grow food, but it does take a little attention, and sometimes that's hard enough to find. Try to make it a habit to walk among your plants each morning — maybe as you drink your coffee. Get to know your plants. When all is well, they definitely have a contented, industrious look about them that you will learn to recognize. "Ah, happy plants!" you'll say, and feel all is right with the world.

When you're watering, look for any problems, especially bug infestations or signs of disease or other problems. When you're growing organic, you need to catch problems early, because there is no nuclear solution. Clip the diseased foliage off a plant. Get that cabbage worm before it does more damage. Putting out little fires like this saves big trouble down the road.

Keep a farmer's notebook, noting what you planted, when you planted it, and where you planted it, when you harvested it, and note whether it worked out or not. Trust us, you think you will remember, but you won't. You will forget what you planted before it sprouts.

> **Your notebook will be an invaluable record to help you:**
> · Figure out what works best in your garden and under what conditions.
> · Time your plantings so your crops come in successive waves, rather than all at once.
> · Plan your crop rotations. This principle is explained on page 102.

Chapter Two
Essential Projects

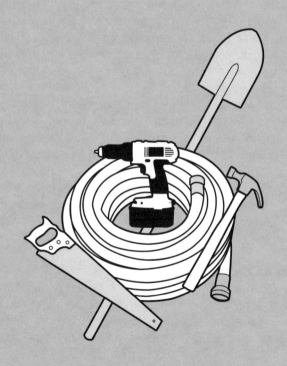

Essential Projects

Urban homesteading is about action. What follows is a compendium of hands-on projects and how-to's that help you grow your own food.

The first five projects we consider indispensable, and so have labeled them "Essential Projects." When friends ask us how they should start growing food, these are the first things we suggest, because they are the basic techniques that make small-scale, intensive gardening possible.

ESSENTIAL PROJECT 1

START A COMPOST PILE

This first project is one everyone can and should do, whether they garden or not. All the space you need is a patch of bare ground large enough to set a garbage can on. If you don't have that, you can still compost.

There's no reason not to compost — it's easy and the benefits are many. If you're growing food you need fresh compost to renew your garden. If you're an urban homesteader you don't want anything to go to waste, and that includes your kitchen scraps, your yard trimmings, and the chicken poop from your hen house. Composting transforms all of this waste matter into new soil.

As unromantic as decomposition may seem to the uninitiated, homesteaders have gushed to us about how much they love composting, the simple miracle of it. There's a lot of b.s. in the gardening world about the "science" of composting and an equal number of expensive devices that you supposedly need to accomplish the decomposition that nature does for free. With a few exceptions that we'll get into, it's hard to go wrong in composting. Yes, there are efficient ways to go about it that will speed up the process, but no matter what you do you will eventually end up with usable compost.

Acquiring A Compost Bin

The easiest bin to start with is simply a lidded garbage can with a few holes punched in the sides. This will keep in moisture which speeds decomposition and will help keep out rodent visitors. Both plastic and galvanized metal cans work fine. The metal lasts longer, but the plastic is easier to punch holes in. Choose the largest can your space allows.

If your bin is going to sit directly on soil (as opposed to your porch or something), punch a lot of holes ¼" or larger in the bottom of your garbage so worms can come up through the soil and help you compost. If you have to keep your bin on concrete, you'd better leave the bottom intact. If you do compost on bare ground, the ground beneath the can will become very rich with nutrients. Move the bin every once in a while so you can plant in that spot.

You can also create an open, circular bin simply by rolling a length of chicken wire or hardware cloth into a tube and securing the ends together with a few twists of wire. Or you could nail four pallets together into an airy box. Open bins dry out fast, so if you live somewhere dry you might want to stick with the more closed system. They also attract more animal visitors. But it is nice to be able to see your compost.

Another possible composting container is a stack of used tires. Every year the U.S. generates just under one used tire for every man, woman and child, meaning that there's a hell of a lot of rubber out there waiting for the industrious urban homesteader. To re-use them as a compost container, simply start with a couple of stacked tires, and add more as the pile grows. The black rubber will help heat up your pile, which is a good thing. If you have the ambition to do so, cut out the sidewalls of the tires so your compost doesn't get hung up in the tire wells.

You can buy ready-made composters. We have one that we got at a steep discount from the City of Los Angeles. It is basically an extra-commodious plastic garbage can with a built-in harvesting door at the bottom. If you want to pay for something like this that is fine, but we'd warn you away from the more complex composting gadgets out there. They simply aren't necessary. They are another attempt by the Man to sell us stuff we don't need. Composting is free!

All you have to do to start composting is set out your can, or tire stack, or whatever, and start tossing your yard trimmings and food scraps into it.

It's good to keep a balance between the types of materials you're tossing on your pile. We like to keep a ratio of about half nitrogen-rich material, what we call "green" stuff, and carbonaceous material, or "brown" stuff. Green materials consist of fresh leaves, kitchen scraps, garden weeds, manure from herbivores, and organic lawn trimmings (even though as a righteous urban homesteader you of course don't have a lawn). Though brown in color, used coffee grounds are an excellent "green" material that many cafés give away for free. The more finely-chopped your green and brown materials are, the faster the pile will decompose.

"Brown" or carbonaceous material is dead stuff like dried leaves, wood chips, sawdust, and shredded newspaper. Avoid using sawdust from pressure-treated lumber or glossy magazine-type paper, as both contain bad chemicals. The brown layers in your compost pile serve to absorb moisture and allow oxygen to reach the interior of the pile since they are generally more loosely packed than the "green" stuff. Without them the green materials go mucky and stinky.

The rule we follow is that each time we add a layer of green stuff, especially kitchen scraps, we cover it with brown stuff. Leaving exposed kitchen scraps is like sending out an invitation for a giant maggot party. We keep shredded paper, newspaper, dried leaves, etc., in a separate, covered bin next to our compost pile for convenience.

If you ever add too many kitchen scraps, you'll know it by the smell and the maggots. Just add some brown stuff and give your pile a stir to bury the maggots. No matter what the ratio is, the simple fact is that everything rots eventually, and in the case of compost, rotting is a very good thing.

Your pile should be kept moist but not soggy. If you live in an area that gets a lot of rain, you may need to cover your pile to prevent it from getting waterlogged. The consistency of the pile should be like a sponge that's just been wrung out. In dry places you may need to water your compost every so often. One way to do this is to take a whiz on the pile once in a while. A compost pile makes an excellent urinal for gentleman urban homesteaders, though we've heard talk of some intrepid sister homesteaders placing toilet seats over their compost piles. The occasional addition of urine is a great way to add both nitrogen and moisture to the pile.

Some people choose to turn their compost piles once a week or so. Turning means stirring—going in there with a shovel and mixing it up. The idea behind turning is that it speeds decomposition. Being lazy, we are inclined to believe the need for turning is exaggerated, so we only do it if we end up with a maggot infestation. This may mean our compost doesn't break down as fast as it can, but speed is just not a high priority for us. So turn your pile exactly as often as it pleases you. The fastest composting system, if you're wondering, is said to be the worm bin, which turns scraps into compost in three months. See project 2.

It is not advisable to add bones, meat, fish, stuff with oil on it, dog or cat poop, or dairy products as these items could attract pests and your pile may not be able to achieve the hot temperatures required to safely decompose that kind of icky stuff.

Compost is done when it looks like soil. Good compost is dark and crumbly and smells nice. The best compost we've seen almost looked like crumbled chocolate cake. You might find a few things that just aren't going to break down in your finished compost, like a stray avocado pit or a stick, but other than that you shouldn't be able to find anything identifiable. Identifiable objects mean it's not done yet. The top of your pile isn't going to ever look "done." The good stuff is found at the bottom of the pile.

You have two ways of inspiring your compost to become that crumbled chocolate cake. One is to empty out your compost bin. Spill it out on some clear ground. Shovel the unfinished top stuff from the top back into the container, then collect the finished compost. It takes up to a year using our lazy no-turn system to achieve compost, so if you don't find anything that looks finished, don't despair, just shovel it all back in and wait some more. Decomposition speed depends so much on temperature, climate, and the materials being composted.

The second option is to cut a little door at the bottom of your bin. A door allows you to reach in and scoop out compost from the bottom without disturbing the top. The downside of it is that if the door is not secured, critters will pry it open and rifle through the compost looking for bugs.

Compost shrinks. So don't worry if you fill your bin with a lot of yard scraps. It will drop down pretty quickly, and you'll have room for your usual kitchen scraps. We call it the equilibrium of the pile: there's always just enough room. However, if you're a composting fiend and you really do fill your bin, just start a new one.

Some forward-thinking people in Oakland put out a humble and wonderful series of publications a while back titled *Eat to Live*. The photocopied newsletters could be found for a brief period during the late '90s in East Bay pizza parlors and laundromats. Issue number two appeared with the headline "You Can't Compost Concrete." The writers of *Eat to Live* hailed the Chicago Pneumatic Paving Breaker as the gardening tool of the future and promoted backyard unpaving parties to get things started.

I can't say that my love of composting stems entirely from the "Eat to Live" directives, but I do gain a keen sense of reattachment to the ground under my feet when I walk across the paved backyard of our Culver City compound and deposit our uneaten food scraps into the compost pile on a small patch of dirt surrounded by so much dead pavement. My compost is a bypass around the concrete sealant that separates me from the living ground underneath my feet.

Composting keeps me from taking things for granted. Should I throw those tortilla crumbs away? If I throw them in the compost they'll feed a bunch of bugs and then some smaller bugs and then become soil. No waste. It's a crazy sort of accounting. We're done with the food, but it's still food. It still matters.

Composting is, perhaps more than anything else to me, a meditation on death. Mine, in particular. Whenever I walk out to my backyard to turn the compost — about every other day — I look into it and think, "That's where I'm going." And it makes me feel all right. Makes me feel as though I belong somewhere. And I'll contribute in a meaningful way, at least after I die.

There are so many lofty reasons to get a compost bin going in your backyard, or apartment porch. But those reasons fall away when you start looking forward to seeing the progress your microbial waste management crew is making every couple of days. It's fun to play in the dirt and watch bugs. Remember the carrot peeling tossed into the compost at the beginning of the week? No orange in sight now. Bad yogurt? Gone. Lawn clippings? They're soil now. It's sort of like making a big soup that's always evolving and always cooking; always changing colors and ingredients. And best eaten once it's worked its way back up through your garden as a new vegetable or fruit.

Elon Schoenholz, Los Angeles, CA

VERMICULTURE
or COMPOSTING WITH WORMS

Worm bins are the only feasible method of indoor composting for apartment dwellers, but this is no second-rate method. Even if you do have a yard and a traditional compost pile, you might want to keep a worm bin for your kitchen scraps, because the compost that comes out of a worm bin is some of the best you can get.

Worms will eat your kitchen scraps for you and give you a black, odorless, extraordinarily rich compost in return. Worm castings (a polite way of saying worm poop) are the gold standard of natural fertilizers: they are packed with water-soluble nutrients as well as beneficial microbes and bacteria. Castings can be applied to the surface of the soil, directly around your plants, or mixed into soil to enrich it, or soaked in water to make an energizing fertilizer tea that you pour over your crops.

You can keep worms indoors in a plastic bin small enough to fit under your sink. Properly kept, they do not smell or attract flies. The worms could also live on the back porch, backyard, mudroom, basement or the garage. Keep them anywhere they are safe from extreme temperatures. Worms can survive down to freezing or up to 100°F, but they work their best at room temperature.

In its simplest form, a worm composter is just a box with some drainage holes poked in the bottom, full of shredded newspaper, worms, and kitchen scraps. The problem with this system is that it is a pain in the ass separating the worm castings from the worms (trust us, we've been there). Far better to have a stacking system, sort of a worm condo, where the worms can be lured away from finished stuff for ease of harvesting. You can buy fancy worm bins online, though some are shockingly pricy. The next project will show you how to make a good bin for the cost of two plastic storage tubs. But first, some basics of worm wrangling:

What To Feed Your Worms

Worms like fruit and vegetable scraps, coffee grounds, tea bags, plain pasta and cooked grains, your basic vegan diet. Don't give them any fats or dairy products or meat. Feed them food prep waste, not plate scrapings.

Grind up eggshells for them once in a while so they get the calcium they need to breed, or give them a crushed Tums if you don't eat eggs.

Worms love rabbit poop and do great things with it, so if you have rabbits, you're in luck. Some people even set up the worm bins directly beneath their rabbit hutches. But no, they will not clean your cat box for you, so don't get any ideas. Pure herbivore poop is all they can deal with.

How To Feed Them

All you have to do is pile the scraps in the bin, and then cover with moist, shredded newspaper. The newspaper is important. The scraps have to be covered up so that they don't attract flies. Rotate your scrap pile to a different corner of the bin every week so that the worms spread their love around.

How Much To Feed Them

How much to feed them depends on how happy and hungry your worms are, how many worms you have and what you are feeding them. When you are figuring this out, remember that your worms are, hopefully, breeding. That means they will eat more as time goes on.

It all comes down to getting a feel for it. Shoot for a pound of scraps a week when you start off, and see how they do with that. Try feeding them twice a week. If the food is just sitting there, the worms are overwhelmed. Give them time to catch up. The cycle from new garbage to completed compost is about three months.

Simple Two-Level Worm Bin

You need:
- Two matching 8–10 gallon rectangular plastic storage bins with lids. They must be opaque, because worms hate light.
- Wooden blocks or bricks for the bins to sit on
- A drill with a $\frac{1}{16}$" bit and a $\frac{1}{4}$" bit
- A bunch of shredded newspaper
- One lb. redworms (*Eisenia foetida*), about 1000 worms

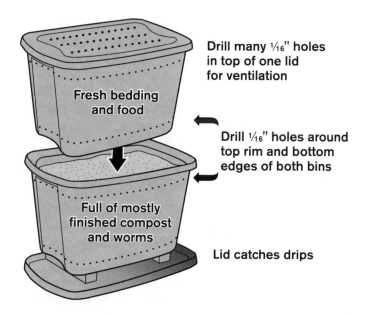

Drill many ¹⁄₁₆" holes in top of one lid for ventilation

Fresh bedding and food

Drill ¹⁄₁₆" holes around top rim and bottom edges of both bins

Full of mostly finished compost and worms

Lid catches drips

1 Using your big ¼" bit, drill about 20 evenly spaced holes in the bottom of each bin. These are for drainage and worm migration.

2 Using the ¹⁄₁₆" bit, drill ventilation holes near the top rim of both bins, and also around the lower edges of both bins. See illustration. The exact location and spacing of the holes does not matter very much. You can add more later if the bin seems too humid.

3 Using your ¹⁄₁₆" drill bit again, drill at least 20 ventilation holes in the top of one of the lids, but not in the other. One must stay intact.

4 Optional: if you have some screening material around, or perhaps some nylon, you can line the bottom of the bin with it to keep clumps of compost from falling out of the drainage holes. This is tidier, but not necessary.

5 Cover the bottom of one bin with about four inches of damp shredded paper newspaper, cardboard, letter paper or brown paper, any kind of paper except shiny paper, such as that used in catalogs and newspaper inserts. Leave the second bin empty for now. Dampen the paper by submerging it in a bucket of water, and then squeezing it out before it goes in the bin. It should never be dripping wet. Worms drown. Its consistency should be like a wrung-out sponge. That said, their bedding must also be kept damp at all times, because a dry worm is a dead worm. Mix in more dry or wet newspaper to get the right consistency.

6 Mix in a handful or two of soil of any kind in with the paper to give the worms the grit they need to digest.

7 Add your worms to their new home. Feed them very modestly at first. Begin by burying just one handful of scraps in a corner of the bin the first week, working your way up to greater quantities as they acclimate.

8 Choose the bin's final location. Lay the lid that has no holes in it on the ground. It is going to be used to catch drips. (There should not be much liquid spillage; if there is, the bin is too wet. But if you do catch some, feed it to your plants.) Arrange the bricks or blocks on top of the lid, and then rest the bin on top of them. Cover the bin with the second, ventilated lid to keep out flies and vermin. A third intact storage tub could be used to collect the drips instead of the lid—just nest the other bins in it.

9 What about the second bin? Use it when you're ready to harvest your compost. In the meantime, you can nest it under the working bin, or store it somewhere else. You'll know it is time when most of the contents of the bin have transformed from food and newspaper to something that looks like soil. Of course your most recent additions will still be recognizable. Don't worry about those. Set the empty bin directly on top of the compost in the first bin. Fill the new bin just like you filled the first one: with damp newspaper and a little soil. Add some nice fresh food scraps and the worms will begin to slither their way through the holes up to the new digs. Continue as usual for one or two months, until your worms have finished the food in the first bin and completed

the migration upstairs. Then remove the first bin and reap the benefits of a whole mess of fresh worm castings.

Escaping worms: If the worms evacuate out the bottom, they are desperate. Either they are drowning or starving to death or suffering from light exposure. If they are dying, maybe they are too dry. The contents of the bin should always be damp and fluffy, not soggy and dank, or dried out.

Bad smells: The bin may be too wet. Add more newspaper, drill more ventilation holes, leave the lid off a little while. You may be putting in too much food for the worms to handle. Stop feeding for a while.

Fruit flies: Keep the food well buried. You can lay a sheet of cardboard directly over the bedding to help with this, too.

Note: Be sure to buy redworms (*Eisenia foetida*) for your bin. These are proper composting worms. You can find them at bait shops, the occasional farmer's market and online. When choosing a supplier choose one near to you so the worms don't have to be shipped across the country.

| ESSENTIAL PROJECT 3 | MULCH YOUR YARD |

MULCH YOUR YARD

No other tip, trick or technique will help your garden more. Mulching is an integral part of the urban farm, and it replaces the lawn in the homestead aesthetic. Mulch generously, frequently, passionately. Think of the rich duff on a forest floor, a soft carpet of fallen leaves many inches deep. When you walk on it you sink down a little and your steps are silent and you smell that rich, peaty smell. You want your yard, your garden beds, even your planted pots to be like that.

Mulched plants are happy, healthy plants. Mulch holds in moisture, stabilizes the soil temperature and represses weeds. As the mulch breaks down it feeds the soil; it actually becomes soil. Because it keeps the soil moist, earthworms move in beneath mulched areas and start doing their own improvements. Other beneficial insects use mulch for habitat. Mulch also looks pleasant — it creates a nice visual unity that makes your yard look tidy. Once you become a mulch convert, you will begin to cringe at the sight of bare soil.

While mulch will improve soil and make for better growing conditions, it can also be used in places where you don't plan to plant anything at all, like walkways, open areas, seating areas. Let it replace the lawn as a sort of a placeholder. Ideally, your entire yard will eventually be mulched anywhere it is not hardscaped.

We are going to describe three styles of mulching in ascending stages of complexity: regular mulching, sheet mulching and lasagna mulching. All three are simply variations of laying down loads of organic matter in your yard.

What Is Mulch? Where Do You Get It?
Mulch can be made up just about any organic material you can lay your hands on: fallen leaves, small wood chips or wood shavings, straw, pine needles, corn husks, even dried seaweed — whatever is cheap and plentiful in your area. Lawn clippings are fine — just make sure they haven't been sprayed. You can mulch with any of your yard trimmings provided they don't have seeds in them. Those seeds will sprout later on; for that reason you should never mulch with hay, only straw.

Many cities offer free wood chips for the taking, as do many tree trimming services. To find out where to get free mulch in your city, do an internet search with your city name and "free mulch" and you should find your answer pretty quickly. Largish wood chips are fine for the outer reaches of your yard, under trees, on walkways, etc., but you will probably find you prefer something a little finer right around your food. You may want try your local equestrian center. Stables will often allow you to haul off truckloads of used horse bedding for free, which makes a fine mulch/compost, though your place will smell horsey for a week or so.

Rocks, polished glass and decomposed granite are mulch, too, and are okay to use in patio areas or on paths, but obviously they are not going to build the soil. Some people also call plastic sheeting and shredded tires mulch, but those, while they do suppress weeds, don't build the soil or improve the beauty of the landscape. And worse, they never go away.

If you have a large area to cover, and you absolutely have to buy your mulch, it is much cheaper to order your mulch in bulk than it is to buy many bags of it from the nursery. Bulk suppliers will dump a truck full of it in front of your homestead. Truckloads might seem like a lot of mulch, but read on.

Bulk deliveries of mulch, wood chips, soil, etc., are measured in cubic yards. To figure out how many cubic yards you'll need, multiply the square feet by the depth in inches you want for your mulch, and divide that number by 324. For instance, to figure out what you need to cover 100 square feet (a 10' x 10' plot) at a depth of five inches, you'd do the following calculation: (100 x 5)/324=1.54, or about 1.5 cubic yards.

Regular Mulching

IMPORTANT NOTE: If you want to lay down a soaker hose, the time to do it is before you mulch. Put the hose against the soil, and layer everything else over it. Drip emitters, on the other hand, need to be on top of everything, or they will clog.

All you have to do is lay down a generous layer of organic matter around your plants. Anywhere you spread mulch you will be enriching the soil beneath, discouraging weeds and keeping nearby plants happy. Hardy weeds will still pop up, but they are much easier to pull than weeds in bare soil. Be sure you lay down at least five inches, more is better. Use less than that and all you are doing is decorating. It might look nice (for a short while) but it's useless.

Mulch breaks down, so you have to add fresh material annually. Fortunately, Mother Nature offers free mulch every autumn. You can probably do all the annual mulching you need with fallen leaves that you collect around your place and from your grateful (but perhaps bewildered) neighbors.

Sheet Mulching

Sheet mulching is just a regular mulch backed up by a weed barrier. A sheet mulch will kill a yard full of weeds — or a lawn — with no digging or tilling. And the best thing is that the weeds or lawn you bury will nourish your future crops. This kind of mulching is particularly good for reclaiming hopelessly weedy yards — or as an insurance policy against future weeding.

Start sheet mulching laying down a weed barrier, something water-permeable and organic. This will either smother existing weeds or prevent new weeds from ever seeing the light of day. The most common barriers are newspaper or sheets of cardboard, though feel free to use your imagination. We hear the Japanese use old tatami mats, for instance, which just seems so much classier than cardboard. Other possibilities are old 100% cotton sheets and towels and throw rugs. Maybe your old straw hat. All organic barriers will break down over time, some faster than others. You can plan that strategically — use sturdy barriers in areas where you know you aren't going to ever be changing anything; they'll serve for a long time. Use newspaper in more active areas. That way if you want to change things around, you don't have to dig up the old sisal carpet that you buried there.

Whatever type of barrier you use, lay it down all over your mulching area, piecing it around the trunks of trees and shrubs as necessary.

If you use newspaper, soak it first in buckets and then lay down sections four to six sheets thick. Avoid using the shiny inserts, which might have toxic inks in them. After you've thoroughly covered the area you want to protect, lay down at least five inches of organic matter on top of it.

You can plant directly into this mulch. Just sweep the mulch aside, cut an X in the weed barrier with a knife or razor blade, and then tuck your plant in the soil beneath. Close the edges of the weed barrier back around the plant and replace the mulch.

A word for people in hot, dry climates: Sometimes dry weather and heat will bake newspaper and cardboard into water-repellent shields. If you find your mulch floating when you water, that's what is happening. You might be better off without the weed barrier.

Lasagna Mulch

This is sheet mulching raised to a high art; a mulch of many layers, thus the name. It is used to remediate poor soil. So you would want to consider doing this in parts of your yard where the soil is hard packed and dry, or recently disturbed by excavation, or too sandy or too clay, or stricken by an ancient curse — whatever the cause, this is a part of your yard where nothing seems to grow at all. Even the weeds avoid it. An area, in short, that needs healing.

A real soil wonk would begin this process by sending a soil sample to the lab for analysis. Then they would design the mulch to address specific deficits or imbalances in the soil. If you want to learn how to do that, you're going to have to read another book. We're going to show you an all-purpose lasagna mulch that will do any soil a lot of good. If you try this, and a year later find that still nothing will grow in your bad spot, then maybe it's time to contact the lab.

Mow or stomp down any weeds, but don't bother pulling them or cleaning them up. They'll help feed the soil. Water the soil if it is dried out. Put a sprinkler on low and let it sit for a good long while until the water penetrates deep.

Spread out a layer of high-nitrogen material—i.e. poop—to accelerate the decomposition process. This could be rabbit poop, chicken poop or horse manure—but not bagged cow manure, which is too salty. Put down 50 lbs. of manure every 100 square feet.

Lay down your weed barrier as described above in Sheet Mulching. Be sure to overlap all of your sheets significantly.

Put down the compost layer. Make this first layer at least three inches thick. It can be made up of any organic matter that does not have seeds in it: aged sawdust, dry leaves, dried grass trimmings, chopped-up yard trimmings, dried seaweed, compost from your bin, or a mix of things. This layer does not have to look good.

Add the top dressing. This mimics the top layer of a forest floor, and is made up of the freshest stuff, the nutrient reserves that will work their way down into the soil bit by bit. It is also the aesthetic layer, what you and the neighbors will look at, so it is best composed of one type of mulch only. This could be dried leaves, straw, bark, wood chips, pine needles, any kind of chafe or husks that might be available locally. This should also be three inches thick, at least. And this layer will have to be renewed annually.

If the soil under this mulch is in poor shape, let it rest, mulched, for one whole year. Yes, an entire year. It may actually be worth planting when you come back to it. Trust us, this is the easiest, and the most natural, way to remediate poor soil. Either build a raised bed on top of it, or make a few self-watering containers to hold your crops in the meantime.

If you live in an area that gets very little rain, you will want to water your lasagna mulch every so often to encourage decomposition, worms and microbial development. Just set up a sprinkler and let it rain. No need to over-water, just put your hand beneath the barrier and check to see if it is moist.

Regarding mulch in vegetable beds: Mulching helps keep veggie leaves clean — no splash up when it rains. It also keeps fruiting plants, like zucchini or strawberries, off the bare soil, so they don't rot. Straw is attractive and clean and often used for that kind of thing.

Caveat about vegetable mulching: Be careful with mulching tomatoes and other heat-lovers because mulching cools the soil. If you live somewhere with mild, overcast summers, mulched tomatoes might not get as much heat at the roots as they want. Use your judgment. If you notice that the soil looks cold, moldy, or in any way unhappy under the mulch, rake it away and let the sun shine on the soil for a little while. When the weather warms up you can rake it back in place.

Slugs and snails like to hide under mulch. Realistically, they'll go after your vegetables whether you mulch or not, so don't let this put you off mulching. Just keep a sharp eye out for them. If the problem gets way out of control, though, you might have to de-mulch the parts of your garden which are most affected.

ESSENTIAL PROJECT 4

BUILD A RAISED BED

Once you have your composting systems set up, the next step is to set up a place to grow your crops. If you have a little bit of ground to work with, put a raised bed on it. If you have no soil, only a porch, balcony or patio, see the next project on how to build a self-watering container.

We cannot overemphasize the benefits of growing your food in raised beds. A raised bed is nothing mysterious: it is just a bottomless construction that holds soil, like a sandbox. Raised beds provide your crops with the fluffy, rich soil they need for good root development, which means much healthier plants and higher yields.

There are other benefits, too. Raised beds are easier to weed than the hard ground, and seem to have fewer pests. The soil in them is warmer, so you can start planting earlier in the spring. Rain drains from them more quickly, so you don't have to worry about waterlogged soil. The soil never gets compacted from being stepped on. They make gardening more comfortable because the plants are closer to you. They wall off and protect your crops from wild dogs, dragging hoses, and running kids. They allow you to garden without digging holes in your yard, which may be helpful if you rent. And maybe most important — sad to say — they lift your crops off your native city soil, which may be contaminated with lead or worse.

When planning a raised bed, be sure it is narrow enough that you can reach all of it from one side or the other, probably a maximum of four feet, or less if you can only come at it from one side. If you have multiple beds, leave room between them for a pathway. Place your bed where it will get a minimum of six hours of good sunlight during your growing season, and try to orient it on a north-nouth axis, so the plants all get their fair share of light.

The height of the bed varies from a minimum of about a foot, up to waist high. The one-to-two-foot range is standard. The reason people build extra-high beds is so they don't have to bend over to tend them, or so they can reach them from a wheelchair. In short, your bed can be built in any size and shape at all, but most often you will see them built as 4 × 8 foot rectangles, a size which arises from standard lumber dimensions.

The walls can be made up of anything that will stand up to water. The style of your bed depends entirely on your imagination and resources. They can be elegant garden furniture or Road Warrior constructions. You can build free-form walls of broken-up concrete, for instance. You could do something more polished with masonry if you have the skill or money. If you choose wood, you should use to use rot-resistant cedar or redwood if you want it to last, but make sure to use sustainably-harvested wood. It's okay to use whatever scrap wood you can find, from found pallets for instance, as long as you don't mind rebuilding every once in while, because the wet and the insects will rot away your boards. Whatever you do, though, don't use railroad ties, as they are soaked with creosote, a wood preservative that is a potential carcinogen.

Don't confuse railroad ties with pressure-treated lumber (the green-tinged stuff). There is controversy over whether or not it is safe to use pressure-treated lumber near food crops — or anywhere at all. It is somewhat safer than it used to be. Until 2003 pressure-treated lumber was soaked with chromated copper arsenate (CCA), which leached arsenic. Now it is treated with other copper compounds which are supposed to be better. We are not convinced, personally, but we'll leave it up to you.

Our raised bed is just a bottomless box with some posts in the inner corners to allow you to easily screw the sides together. What follows are instructions for building a bed measuring 4' × 8', and standing about 16" high. The sides of the bed are made by two courses of 2" × 8" planks. You can use half the wood (three planks vs. six) if you want to make the bed only one course (8") high.

Tools
- Hand or power saw (unless you have your wood pre-cut where you buy it)
- Drill
- Drill bit to drill pilot holes for the #14 screws
- Shovel
- Level (optional)

Lumber
- (6) 2" × 8" boards, eight feet long. Leave four as is for the sides, cut two in half for the ends.
- (1) 4" x 4", six feet long (cut into four equal parts)

Hardware
- 3 ½" #14 wood screws to assemble the lumber
- ½" #8 wood screws to secure the optional PVC pipe hoops
- Hardware cloth or gopher wire (if you've got gophers or moles)

    NOTE: Screws are more practical than nails in many ways, but nails are just fine for this project.

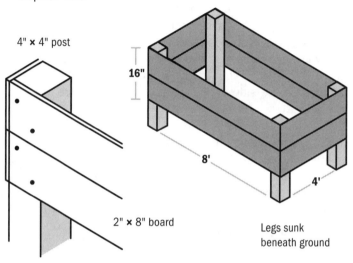

4" × 4" post

16"

2" × 8" board

8'

4'

Legs sunk
beneath ground

It is much harder to describe the building of a box than to just sit down and build a box. Hopefully the illustration will give you the gist of it. Remember, it just has to hold together, that's all that matters, so any sort of walled enclosure you can cobble together will suit the purpose admirably well.

The four corner posts make it easy to assemble. Line up your boards against the corner posts, and affix each board to the post with at least two nails or screws. Build a short side first for the easiest assembly. Pre-drill two guide holes on either end of the plank where it will meet the post. Screw a corner post to both ends of one of the four-foot lengths of board, aligning the top edges and the sides neatly together. Add the second board flush against the first board to make the side of the bed two boards deep. The corner posts will be a little longer than the two planks combined. This is good, because you're going to bury those extra inches in the ground to make the bed extra stable. They're the feet.

Now build the other short end exactly the same way. Then you can join the long boards to the corner posts of the short segments to make up the long sides of the bed. This is easiest to do with the bed upside down — with the legs sticking in the air.

If gophers or moles are a problem where you live, staple gopher wire, which is a kind of galvanized metal screen, or hardware cloth, across the bottom of the bed before you put it in place. How do you know if you have moles or gophers? Do you have any mysterious holes and mounds in your yard? Around the neighborhood? If you see any, err on the side of caution and put in the wire. It will be difficult to add later.

Before you place the bed, use a pitchfork to poke holes into the ground where the bed is going to go. You don't have to turn the soil violently, just break it up a little. It's fine to put the bed down right on top of a lawn. Poke holes in the lawn just as you would bare dirt. All that green matter will enrich your soil.

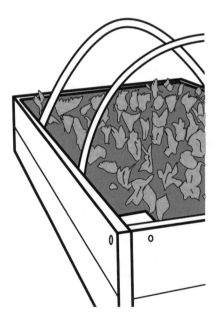

Dig four holes in each corner where the corner posts will sink into the ground. Flip the bed right side up and put it in place.

Fill the bed with good soil. It takes a lot of soil to fill a bed, more bags than you would think. If you compost, you will want to save all your finished compost for this event. You might be able to make a decent soil mix by combining the soil in your yard (assuming it's not too crappy) with compost. Or go the easy route and buy organic soil from a good nursery. Buy the best soil you can afford. Good soil is going to pay you back over and over again in the form of healthy crops. Fill the bed all the way to the top, because the soil will settle dramatically after a few hours.

The Well-Accessorized Bed

The bed can be pimped out so it can easily be covered with aviary netting to keep out critters or plastic sheeting to keep out cold. Screw short sections of 1" PVC pipe vertically onto the inner walls of the bed using 1" galvanized tube straps to keep them in place. Pair them short-ways across the bed. Six, three on each side, should be sufficient. These PVC lengths are used to hold hoops made from the 10' lengths of ½" PVC pipe or thick wire that you bend across the bed (imagine a covered wagon).

ESSENTIAL PROJECT 5

HOW TO BUILD A SELF-WATERING CONTAINER

These containers make it easy to grow vegetables in pots. They are ideal for apartment gardening, but are so useful that everyone should use them to maximize their growing space.

The problem with growing food in pots is that pots dry out quickly and it's all too easy to forget to water. Irregular watering causes all sorts of problems for sensitive fruits and vegetables. Container gardening is also water intensive. During a heat wave it might mean visiting the plants with the watering can two or even three times every day — obviously not a practical scheme for someone who works away from home, or someone with any kind of life at all.

An elegant solution exists in the form of self-watering containers. Rather than having a hole in the bottom of the pot, a self-watering container (SWC) has a reservoir of water at the bottom, and water leaches upward into the soil by various mechanisms, keeping it constantly moist. The top of the pot is covered with a layer of plastic that discourages evaporation. Depending on how deep the water reservoir is, it's possible to go about a week between fill-ups. This arrangement, combined with the plastic layer, prevents both over-watering and under-watering that can occur with conventional pots. In other words, it takes the guesswork and anxiety out of watering.

KELLY SAYS: I'm going to tell you right now that you can buy yourself a self-watering container at earthbox.com. It's great to make SWCs with found materials and all, but if these instructions make your eyes cross, or if you just don't have time, there is no shame in trotting off with your credit card and ordering a couple of these ready-made. They start at about forty bucks.

ERIK SAYS: *Au contraire, ma petite amie!* All it takes is two five-gallon buckets, a few other easily scavenged items and about an hour's worth of time. Those Earthboxes are damned expensive and my time is cheap.

A few years back, an internet hero named Josh Mandel figured out several different techniques for building DYI self-watering containers out of old buckets, soda bottles, storage tubs, etc. His plans are widely disseminated online, and you'll find links to his instructional PDF files at the end of the book, and at our website.

Inspired by his methods, we started making our own self-watering containers. Each SWC is a little different, because each one, being made of found materials, is an improvisation. We're going to show you how to make a simple SWC out of two five-gallon buckets. Once you have the basic principles down, it should be easy to improvise future containers on your own out of whatever you have on hand.

The five-gallon size described is good for one big plant. Try a basil plant in it, especially if you like pesto. Basil thrives with the steady moisture, as does Italian parsley, so both herbs grow huge in SWCs. Or plant a tomato, but be sure it is a small tomato. Look for types designated "patio" or "basket" tomatoes. These are bred to perform well in tight conditions. A five-gallon container seems big, but tomatoes have some of the deepest roots of all vegetables. If you plant an ordinary tomato in a SWC its roots might find their way into the reservoir, and then it will become waterlogged.

We recommend that for your next project you visit Josh Mandel's PDFs for instructions on how to construct a larger, slightly more complex container out of 8–10 gallon sized storage tubs. That size SWC is very good for growing a little salad garden, a stand of greens, or a patch of strawberries, or even a blueberry bush.

Five-Gallon Self-Watering Container

It all starts with providing a water reservoir at the bottom of your container. You can do this either by nesting two containers together (the top one holds soil, the bottom one water) or by making some kind of divider that sits toward the bottom of a single container and holds the soil above the reservoir. However it is constructed, the barrier between the soil and water should be full of small holes for ventilation.

The water is pulled up from the reservoir and into the soil by means of something called a wicking chamber. This can be a perforated tube, a basket, a cup, or anything full of holes that links the soil to the water. The soil in the chamber(s) becomes saturated, and it feeds moisture to the rest of the soil.

The reservoir is refilled by means of a pipe that passes through the soil compartment down to the very bottom of the container.

The last essential element is a hole drilled into the side of the container at the highest point of the reservoir. This is an overflow hole that prevents you from oversaturating your plants.

Materials
- (2) food-grade, five-gallon plastic buckets. If possible, one of them should have a lid.
- (1) 16 oz. plastic drink cup, or a 32 oz. plastic yogurt container, or anything similar that you can punch holes in. A plastic basket of similar size would work too.
- 1 bucket lid (can substitute a plastic garbage bag in a pinch)
- plastic twist ties
- 17 inches of 1" diameter PVC pipe, copper tubing, a bamboo tube, or anything similar
- A big bag of potting mix

Tools
- Drill
- Keyhole saw, safety knife or saber saw

1 Find two food-grade five-gallon plastic buckets. A good source is behind restaurants and donut shops. If they once held food, you know they aren't going to be toxic (but do

wash them). Don't source your buckets off of construction sites!

2 Cut a hole right in the center of the bottom of one of the buckets. The yogurt container or whatever you are using is going to sit in this hole, so it hangs down into the water reservoir below (i.e. the bottom bucket), and act as your wicking chamber. Do this by tracing an outline of the cup on the bottom of the bucket, and then cutting a little inside the line. Use a safety knife, or a keyhole saw for this. It doesn't have to be pretty.

All you have to make sure of is that your wicking chamber will fit in that lower bucket. If the chamber is too tall, you won't be able to fit the two buckets together. This is something that is easy to adjust as you go, but just keep it in mind from the beginning.

To give you an idea of sizes, we have one SWC made from two five-gallon Kikkoman soy sauce buckets. For that one the wicking chamber is a 32 oz. yogurt container, and it hangs down 3 ½" into the reservoir.

3 Cut another hole in the bottom of the same container, anywhere near the outside edge (i.e. anywhere but the center). This hole is for the pipe that will refill the reservoir and should be sized accordingly. Again, just trace around one end of your pipe and cut.

4 Now drill a bunch of ¼ inch holes in the remaining real estate on the bottom of this same bucket. The exact number or spacing does not matter. These are ventilation holes. Go for a Swiss cheese effect, but don't get too carried away. Leave the other bucket intact.

5 Now turn to your wicking chamber — the drink cup or yogurt container or whatever. Punch or drill a bunch of random ½" holes all over the sides of the cup, but not the bottom (the soil would fall out if the bottom was open). These big holes will allow water to seep into the soil in the chamber, and thus be drawn into the soil above.

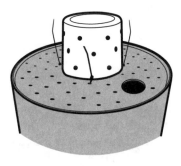

6 Attach the wicking chamber to the bottom of the top bucket. This is a very loose affair, consisting of four twist ties. Just drill holes at the 12, 3, 6, and 9 o'clock positions just below the top edge of the cup and drill corresponding holes near the edge of the large hole you cut in the middle of the bucket. Thread plastic twist ties through these holes to secure the wicking chamber so that it hangs beneath the holey bucket.

7 If necessary, cut the pipe that feeds the reservoir to a good length. You want it to poke out of the top of the container for easy watering. Seventeen inches is just about right for this project. Cut one end of the tube on the diagonal, and put this end down in the bucket. The angled end will allow water to flow freely out of the tube and into the reservoir.

8 Place the bucket fitted with the suspended wicking chamber into the untouched bucket.

9 Make your overflow hole. Figure out where the bottom of the top bucket sits in relation to the bottom bucket. Try holding it up to strong light, or employing a ruler. Drill a ¼" hole in the side of the lower bucket (the previously untouched bucket), placing the hole just a little beneath the bottom edge of the inside bucket. This hole will serve to spill off overflow from the reservoir chamber. You want the top bucket to be wicking water, not sitting in water.

10 Finally, insert the watering pipe through the hole you drilled in the bottom of the inner bucket. Be sure to put the pointy end in the bucket. The flat end will stick out the top.

11 Fill your new container with potting mix. Note that you must use potting mix because regular garden soil does not work very well in SWCs. Fill the container all the way to the top, moistening the soil as you go.

12 Plant your plant, dead center.

13 Make a circular, shallow trough around the perimeter of the plant, and sprinkle about a cup dry organic fertilizer in

the trench. Then cover the trench up with a little soil so the fertilizer is just slightly buried—don't work the fertilizer into the soil. You must be careful with fertilizers and SWCs because they are closed systems. Excess fertilizer doesn't drain away. So always keep it at the top off the container, where it will work its way down gradually.

14 If you've got a lid for the bucket, and your plant is small enough, go ahead and cut a hole in the center of the lid for the plant to poke through, then ease the lid into place, threading the plant's leaves through the hole. The lid will help retain moisture. If you don't have a lid, or if your plant is too big, cut an X in a plastic garbage bag and lay it across the top of the pot, securing it around the sides with a length of tape or string, or if you've got a lid for the bucket, you can cut out the center and use the rim to secure the plastic. A how-to video can also be found at our website www.homegrownevolution.com

A Treasure Chest of Garden Projects and Advice

HOW TO START SEEDS

KELLY SAYS: I am all for skipping the seed stage whenever possible and buying seedlings (i.e. small plants) at the nursery or farmers' market for instant gratification. Your garden will get going faster, and you will avoid the other pitfalls of seed starting. Seeds fail to sprout sometimes, or are just very pokey, and tiny newborn sprouts get nibbled on by bugs and birds. Sure, the per-plant price of seedlings vs. seeds is much, much higher, but you never meant to grow one hundred kale plants anyway, did you?

ERIK SAYS: Seeds are the future! By starting with seeds you can find much more exotic varieties thanks to the internet, catalogs, and seed saving exchanges. In fact that latter category, seed exchange, is one way we can all help preserve endangered varieties. Try letting a few of your heirloom plants go to seed, and share them with other gardeners. And best of all, seeds are cheap. I like cheap!

But we both agree that growing from seeds makes perfect sense for plants that you pull up whole and eat — one-use plants, if you will — like radishes and carrots. This also applies to plants that are good to eat as babies, like lettuce. In the end, starting plants from seeds is not hard, it just requires patience.

You can start your seedlings indoors early in the year. It takes them weeks to get to the point when they are ready to transplant, and in that time the weather will warm enough for you to plant them outdoors. So start them a month or so before your last projected frost. Germination times are listed on the seed packages — they vary quite a bit from plant to plant, so be sure to check. Once the weather warms, you can start your seeds outdoors, but make sure they are in a protected space. They can't deal with harsh sun, wind or punishing rain.

To start seeds you need:
- **A container.** Around here we start seeds in used containers, like empty six-packs. (Seedling six-packs from nurseries, not beer six-packs.) You can buy divided trays made for

the purpose, or use little peat pots. Some people use egg cartons for seed starting, but we find they dry out the soil too fast. If you want to start a lot of seeds you can also sow them in flats, which are big plastic trays about three inches deep.

- **Soil.** It is safest to use a seed starting mix from the nursery, but you can use garden soil if you are sure it is disease- and pest-free.
- **Spray bottle**
- **Plastic bag**
- **Maybe a little fertilizer tea**
- **And seeds**, of course

1 Fill your container with soil, stopping about ¼ from the top.

2 Wet the soil thoroughly.

3 Make holes for the seeds. Read the seed packet's planting depth recommendation, and also open the pack and check out the seeds. Seeds need to go in a hole four times as deep as the seed is wide, unless the seeds are just teeny tiny. Then they just get a little soil sprinkled over them, or sometimes they don't get any covering at all. So taking into consideration the size of your seeds, use your finger, or a pencil, to poke holes into your soil at the right depth. If you are planting in a flat, leave an inch or two between seeds. You can also dig out a mini furrow, a long ditch in the soil, with your pencil and sprinkle your seeds along that line.

4 Drop your seeds one by one into the holes or furrows, and gently cover them up with more soil so they're buried at the recommended depth. Too shallow is better than too deep.

5 Mist the surface of the soil with your spray bottle to settle everything down. While the seeds are germinating, and later when they are just wee little things, you are going to do all of your watering with your spray bottle or a hose set to mist.

6 Label your plants so you don't forget what is what. Write on popsicle sticks or plastic cutlery with indelible marker, or use the marker directly on the pots.

7 If you are starting your seeds indoors, provide them with warmth until they sprout; you can keep them on top of a DVD player, for instance, or the back of a stove. After they sprout make sure they get lots of light.

8 If you have a hard time keeping the soil moist between waterings (this is more the case outdoors than in), seal in the humidity by slipping a clear plastic bag over your plantings. You can leave this on until the seedlings sprout.

9 Keep the soil evenly moist—just moist—all the time, before and after sprouting. Too soggy is as damaging as too dry. If your seedbeds are too wet and cold they will come down with the dreaded damping-off disease, which results in failure to sprout or wilting sprouts. A white mold sometimes appears on the surface of the soil. To prevent it, keep your trays warmish, and don't over-water. If you see any signs of damping off, stop watering for a couple of days, move the pots somewhere warmer, then only water from the bottom. Scrape off any mold, and increase light exposure.

10 Feed your seedlings when the true leaves appear. The first leaves that appear are called cotyledons. They are not true leaves, but food storage cells. They are always rounded and sort of generic-looking. The true leaves will show up next. Those will be miniature versions of the adult leaf. Once the true leaves have unfolded, you can encourage your seedlings with a little food. This is not mandatory, but you can water them one time with a weak solution of fertilizer tea.

11 As your seedlings develop, be sure they get lots of light. Add artificial light at night if necessary—a compact fluorescent will work fine, just put it close to them. A sure sign of insufficient light is leggy plants, seedlings with really long gangling stems. They're stretching their necks out, trying to find the light!

12 Harden them off: Once their real leaves are in and they are looking sturdy and the weather is good, you can begin to acclimate the seedlings to the world outside. This process is called "hardening off." The idea is to keep the plants from going into shock and keeling over from the change in growing conditions. Start putting them outside during the day in a protected spot that's not too sunny, and bring them in at night. Give them a little more sun exposure each day for a few days, then finally start leaving them out all night.

Your seed package will tell you if you have to do anything extra to help your seeds germinate. One common requirement is pre-soaking, which is just setting the seeds in water overnight before you plant them. Another is scarifying. This is to break down the outer coats of particularly strong seeds. All you have to do is rub them between sandpaper or against a screen for a few seconds, or if they are larger seeds, nick them with a knife or nail file.

HOW TO TRANSPLANT
Advice On The Mechanics Of Moving Plants Out Of Pots

Water the plant first to reduce shock, and carefully ease it from its pot. Squeezing a plastic pot around the sides usually loosens it up a bit. You can try to slide a butter knife down the side of a clay pot. Tip the pot over and catch the root ball as it slides out without squashing the plant leaves. The easiest way to do this is to cradle the plant's stem between your first two fingers as you turn the pot upside down. It's considered bad form to yank the plant out of its pot by the neck.

If you're transplanting seedlings from flats, carefully separate one plant at a time from the rest, trying your best to preserve the soil around their roots as you air-lift them to their new home.

Don't dilly-dally when transplanting. You don't want the roots drying out, or the plants going into deep shock while waiting around, naked, for you to get around to planting them. Transplant one plant at a time.

Break up the root ball. When plants have been in pots for a long time, their roots circle around the edges of the pot, looking for somewhere to go. When the circling roots almost make a pot themselves, this is called "root-bound." You don't want to plant a root-bound plant because it will never spread out its roots and make itself at home. You have to help it by loosening up the roots. With small plants (six-packs and the like) this is usually just a matter of gently pulling apart the bottom of the root ball so the heart of the roots is exposed. No need to maul or mutilate. Just loosen. The roots can be tough on bigger plants — too strong to open with your hands without a lot of wrestling and damage. With these you might want to take a sharp knife and make three or four vertical cuts down the sides of the root ball, starting about in the middle, poking in about an inch deep and slicing straight down through the tangled roots to the bottom. Then you should be able to get your fingers in and loosen up the ball.

Planting In An Ordinary Pot

Choose a container at least a few inches deeper and wider than the one the plant came in, and make sure there is a drainage hole at the bottom. Line the bottom of the pot with a layer of rocks, gravel, marbles, little chunks of concrete, broken pot shards, etc. to keep the soil from clogging up the drainage hole. Then lay down a layer of potting soil. The depth of this layer depends on the height of your plant. You want the top of the root ball to be an inch or so lower than the rim of the new pot. You don't want to pot it up to the very top or it will be hard to water. So fuss with this level, adding or subtracting soil from the bottom of the new pot until you get it right. Then settle the root ball in the center, make sure it isn't crooked, and back fill around the edges with soil and maybe a little organic fertilizer. Pack it all down gently and water.

Planting In A Self-Watering Container

See essential project 5 for how to build and maintain one. These do not have rocks on the bottom, or drainage issues like conventional pots. All you have to do in a SWC is gently dig a hole the exact size of the root ball, and tuck the plant in. Easy as pie.

Planting In The Ground

If you are planting in soft, loose garden soil, just dig a hole exactly as big as the plant's root ball and pop it in there. If you are planting a large plant, like a bush or tree, you have no choice but to disturb the soil by digging a big hole. Dig a hole twice as deep and wide as the root ball. Make a little mound of soil at the bottom of the hole. Sprinkle a cup or two of organic fertilizer in there, or worm castings, then drape the spreading roots over the mound. The notion behind this is making sure you don't end up with an air pocket at the base of your plant.

Fuss with the plant to make sure it is the right height and is standing straight. You might have to add to or reduce the mound beneath its roots. The idea is that you don't want the root ball protruding from the soil, because watering will expose the roots. The base of the plant should be flush with the ground. Refill the hole with the same soil you dug out of it. You never want to dig a hole and backfill with fancy soil. The soils will be so different that they will have nothing to do with one another, the hole will become an underground pot, and the plant will never really put down roots and thrive.

For watering ease, make an irrigation basin by forming a little wall of soil in a circle all around the base of the plant, making the circle about the same diameter as the spread of its branches. When you

have a reservoir like this, you can fill it up with water and let sink in slowly. It's very handy. Otherwise when you water the water goes everywhere. These reservoirs are good for smaller plants, too, like tomatoes. After planting, feed the plant by watering with fertilizer tea, and put thick mulch around the plant so that the soil continues to improve.

FERTILIZER TEA

An easy, though slightly stinky, way of delivering nutrients to your plants is to make fertilizer tea — the gentle and healthy alternative to chemical fertilizers. Tea is great for plants in the ground, and great for traditional container plants, which tend to be nutrient-starved, but should not be used in self-watering containers. SWCs do not drain, so the fertilizer levels could build up too much.

Fertilizer tea is just organic fertilizer steeped in water for a day or so. The resulting liquid is super nutritious and easily applied. Any solids left over from the brewing can be mulched around the base of a plant, or added to the compost pile.

Different types of plants have different fertilization needs, so do your research before using the tea too freely, but there are two times where we can categorically recommend its use: 1) a single watering of your seedlings with a fairly dilute tea when they put out their first set of true leaves, and 2) just after transplanting anything, whether it be a seedling or a mature plant, to help with transplant shock.

Tea Recipes

Add *one* of the following to a five-gallon bucket and fill it with water. (Cover it to keep out flies, dogs and toddlers and let it steep for about 24 hours, or at least overnight.)

- A shovelful of finished compost.
- A couple of cups of worm castings.
- A few cups of packaged dry organic fertilizer, like the Dr. Earth brand. The packages will tell you exactly how much to use in tea.
- A shovelful of horse or chicken manure at least six months old. Fresh manure will burn your plants. Steer manure is too salty.
- A shovelful of fresh rabbit poop, and if you've got it around, a spoonful of molasses to activate it. Rabbit poop is the only poop you're allowed to use fresh.

- A whole armload of weeds or garden trimmings. Enough to fill the bucket. Weeds, greens and some herbs are particularly good sources of minerals. Anything green would do some good, but we recommend comfrey, plantain, dandelion, parsley, chicory. Any leafy greens that are good for you will be good for your plants. Just make sure the weeds have not gone to seed yet — or if they have, strain your tea before you use it.
- A few ounces of liquid kelp extract or fish emulsion. Follow the directions on the bottle. (These ready-made liquid products don't require steeping, just mix and use.)

TRASH TALKIN' TIRE PROJECT 1: A TIRE HOSE CADDY

Here's a cheap and easy way to keep that hose from trippin' you up in the back yard. Used tires are one of our favorite junk building materials, easily sourced on any city street.

1 Cut out the sidewall of one side of a tire using a saber saw. You could use a sharp knife, but electricity makes this task a lot easier.

2 Drill a bunch of drainage holes in the remaining wall of the tire (aka the bottom of the caddy) at least one hole every three inches. This is to keep water from pooling when it rains. Tires combined with water make the perfect breeding ground for mosquitoes. Drainage holes keep this from becoming a problem.

3 Coil up your hose inside the tire. Enjoy your tidy patio!

TRASH TALKIN' TIRE PROJECT 2: STACKING COMPOSTER

Want compost but can't build a box? Can't afford a commercial composter? Abandoned tires are always there for you.

Collect a bunch of tires the same size and you can make a stacking compost bin. It's really simple. You're just going to make a tire tower. All you have to do is figure out how to cut out the side walls, because if you stack the tires as is, the compost will get stuck in the tire wells. Without side walls, tires are basically big stacking rubber rings.

You can cut out the sidewalls with firm hand and a utility knife, but an electric saber saw makes it a lot easier.

When you're done, just stack and start filling. Start by putting down a thick layer of dry materials at the very bottom, e.g. dry leaves, straw or dried out grass clippings. Then start to add your food scraps and green trimmings.

The black rubber helps to keep your compost warm and moist, and that's a good thing.

It's okay to start with just a couple of tires, and add more as you go. The best thing about a tire composter is its flexibility. Stack it tall, or break it into two short piles later, play around with different configurations.

Improvise a lid of some sort to keep out the rain and critters. We use a piece of scrap aluminum weighed down by a length of lumber–because we're classy that way.

GROW SOME LETTUCE

This is a good first project for a beginning farmer. Lettuce is easy to grow, and tastes so much better homegrown than from a bag. Better still, it is always fresh when you want it, instead of rotting in your crisper drawer.

It is easiest to grow lettuce in cool (but not freezing) weather. Lettuce is not a sun worshipper. In climates with freezing winters, you should plant lettuce in the early spring. In warm winter climates you can plant it in the fall as soon as the summer heat dies down, or any time over the winter.

You need one packet of mixed lettuce seeds (also called salad blend or mesclun mix) from your neighborhood nursery. There are many variations on this theme, but basically a mesclun mix contains seeds of several different lettuces and salad herbs. If you can't find any such thing, you can buy a few different types of lettuce to mix up yourself. Just be sure you buy loose leaf lettuce, not the ball-shaped Iceberg type.

The next thing you will need is somewhere to plant your lettuce. The best choice would be a self-watering container of the storage tub size. Failing this, any sort of big pot or found vessel would do, as long as that pot has a hole in the bottom of it for drainage. You can even use something permeable, like a basket, if you line it with a plastic garbage bag. Be sure to poke holes in the bottom of the bag for drainage. This general growing technique is suitable for garden beds, too.

If you have a regular pot, put a layer of rocks, or something similarly impermeable, at the bottom of the pot. This will keep the drainage hole(s) from becoming clogged with soil. Fill your pot or self-watering container with potting soil. Not regular garden soil. Add a handful of dry organic fertilizer or worm castings to the pot. If you are using a self-watering container (SWC), leave the fertilizer until later.

- Before you sow your seeds, make sure you've set a little bit of soil aside. You need just enough to cover your seeded area with a light sprinkle of soil.
- Level out your soil and water deeply. Check the pot for good drainage. You don't want your seeds to go swimming.

- Open your seed packet and sprinkle your seeds evenly over the surface of the soil. Do not make rows or poke holes or worry about spacing. Be free — you're sowing seed, man. Just let it fall where it wants. Shoot for a coverage rate that leaves the individual seeds about a finger's width apart, but really, it doesn't matter much if some spots are thicker than others.
- Sprinkle your reserved soil over your seeds in a very thin layer — ¼" or less. It's okay if some seeds are not covered.
- Water again, lightly this time, with a watering can or a hose on the gentle shower or mist setting, or even with many pumps of a spray bottle. The idea is just to secure the seeds and their covering, since you've already watered the pot thoroughly.
- Keep your seeds moist until they sprout, this might take a few days or a couple of weeks, depending on the seeds. The seed packet will tell you what to expect. We use a spray bottle to mist the soil, so that we don't disturb the seeds with big sloshes of water.

Eating Your Way To Equilibrium

Density is the difference between this way of planting and the row method recommended on the seed packet. When plants are close together they shade each other and keep the soil moist and crowd out weeds. This technique makes for lots of baby greens for you, and happy plants, as long as they don't get too crowded. The key is to let the plants be crowded as babies, but thin them by the time they are mature. Your mission is to eat your way into equilibrium. Here's how to do it:

Let the little seedlings grow to harvest height, say two or three inches high. You'll see that as they grow all those identical looking little sprouts begin to take on the unique characteristics of the adult plants. It's good to pay attention to them and learn how to differentiate them from baby weeds, or baby radishes, or baby turnips.

When your plants are the right size, thin out your crop by picking a baby green salad for dinner. Pinch them off at the root — they won't come back. Pulling them up just makes a mess. Try to distribute your picking evenly so you free up a space all over the bed or container. Go after the plants that are growing in tight packs. When you consider that each mature plant will require an area about as big as a soup bowl, you'll understand that you have a lot of salads ahead of you.

Salad by salad, empty out your bed until you have just a handful of full-sized lettuce plants left. They can be pretty close, as long as they are not touching. If there isn't any air between them they will be stunted, and bugs and rot can set in. Six to eight full-grown lettuce plants (which is what would fit in a SWC built from a storage tub) will keep you in salad for the rest of the season. A mature leafy lettuce plant doesn't have to be used whole. Just harvest its outer leaves. It will keep making new leaves for you, and you will keep eating salad.

Your lettuce should grow very well with very little attention from you apart from regular, even watering, and an SWC will do that for you. When you get the plants narrowed down to their final number you can mulch them with a plastic liner or organic matter. Mulch will help regulate the soil temperature, which they will appreciate.

 When it starts to get hot and the lettuce decides it's time to flower, it will send up a funny stalk. This is called bolting. Bolting makes lettuce bitter and tough. When that happens, it is time to plant something new.

TIPS & TRICKS FOR GARDENING IN CONTAINERS

Of course it is more difficult to grow food in quantity in a place without a yard than it is with a yard, but you will be surprised how much you can grow in very little space if you play your cards right. Start with the following suggestions, and once you max out your living space, look into renting a community garden plot.

If you can't put your plants in the ground, you can put them in a pot. Most urban farmers will do some of their gardening in containers even if they have access to land, simply because no space should be wasted. So windows, patios, porches, stoops, balconies and decks all get fitted out with containers full of food.

We recommend using self-watering containers for all food crops, except herbs. Vegetables are greedy for water, and pots dry out fast, especially in the heat. In the dog days of summer you might have to water plants in pots twice a day. Self-watering containers only need their reservoirs filled maybe once a week. So while they do take a little time and energy to build, or money to buy, the investment you put in on the front end more than pays off later on, in saved time, saved water, and in extra healthy productive plants.

The exception to this rule is herbs. Most herbs like to go dry between waterings, which self-watering containers do not allow. A little suffering seems to bring out the best in herbs. This is especially true for the woodier, oilier herbs like lavender, rosemary, thyme, sage and oregano. So plant those in pots. Tender herbs like parsley, cilantro, basil and chives can go either way.

Get the most bang for your buck. Grow produce which is either expensive, unavailable or flavorless at the store. Lettuce is a good example. Growing salad mix is easy in containers. You will have a continuous supply of tender, flavorful salad greens on hand and save a lot of money on bags of bland lettuce. Fresh herbs are great to have on hand all the time, and also expensive to buy. Homegrown tomatoes are a hundred times better than store-bought. Fresh green peas are a real treat, and basically impossible to get — even at farmers' markets — because they taste best if eaten within minutes of picking. On the other hand, some veggies, like onions, are so inexpensive and easy to come by that they would be low on our list of things to grow in containers.

When you choose your plants, remember that it is fine to buy seedlings for your container gardens. It doesn't make a lot of sense to buy a packet of tomato seeds if you're only going to grow two plants. Ditto for herbs. Just buy a little plant. However, seeds do make sense for plants you pull up whole, like carrots, radishes and green onions.

Grow only what you really like. This sounds obvious, but believe us, when you are at the nursery a kind of psychosis will overtake you and you'll want to buy everything you see. Don't waste your time growing stuff you are not thrilled about. Grow stuff you can't wait to eat.

Always use potting soil in your containers—not generic garden soil, but organic potting soil. And buy the best soil you can, or make your own once you've got your compost going. You will be paid back in healthy, productive plants.

Potted plants need food. If they are not in self-watering containers the nutrients in the soil tend to be flushed with each watering. So either feed your plants store bought organic plant food formulated for vegetables or feed them worm castings or fertilizer tea.

Good drainage is vital. When potting a plant in a normal pot, put rocks or broken pot shards at the bottom of the pot before you add soil. This keeps the drainage hole from plugging. This is not true for self-watering containers. Big pots need to be set up off the ground a little, like on a pair of bricks or slats of wood, so that the water can drain out of them freely.

Our Favorite Things To Grow In Containers:

Blueberries, which require special soil anyway, so almost can't be grown in the ground unless you live in blueberry country.

Strawberries, which can be grown in hanging baskets, or strawberry pots, or SWCs.

Cherry tomatoes, just be sure that you choose one labeled a patio or basket variety, so it will be well-behaved enough to live in a pot.

Lettuce, which we've talked about quite a bit elsewhere.

Swiss chard, which is much easier to grow than spinach and not picky about weather.

Stubby little carrots, like the round *Thumbelina* variety.

Radishes, because they're ready so fast.

Basil or Italian parsley, but only in self-watering containers, because they both thrive on regular watering.

THE DIRT ON POTTING SOIL

If you are doing your growing in containers, you will want to renew your potting soil each time you plant something new, or at least once a year. Admittedly, we have occasionally been guilty of pulling an old plant and just sticking something new in. You can get away with that a few times, but if you do that too much your soil will tire out and your plants will suffer. For best results you should renew your soil between each new planting. Some books recommend that you throw out all your soil each time you replant, but we think that's a little extreme, unless you have reason to believe the soil is diseased.

Renewing Your Potting Soil

If you're working on a patio or balcony, or in your kitchen, empty the pot out on newspaper or something to make cleanup easy. Break up the soil and fish out big chunks of old roots.

Add new soil to the mix at the ratio of one part new soil to three parts old soil. The new soil you add can be either straight worm castings or new store-bought potting soil or homemade potting soil.

If you are not using worm castings as part of the blend, mix in dry organic fertilizer at the rates recommended on the box — probably about a handful for a large pot. If you didn't have enough worm castings for the mix, but you do have some, by all means add a handful to every pot, either in the mix or just sprinkle them on top after you plant.

While your pots are empty, take this opportunity to scrub them inside and out with a scrub brush or nylon pad. Salts can build up on pots that are bad for the plants, and other beasties might be there as well. If the last plant in that pot failed, you'll want to be extra thorough with the cleaning, in case it was a disease that caused the failure.

Most sources recommend that you use a solution of one part bleach to nine parts water for pot cleaning, but we don't like bleach and so and use a 50/50 vinegar/water blend that we keep around for household cleaning. Rinse well.

Homemade Potting Soil
Some gardeners really get into mixing their own potting soil, and a quick perusal on the web will show you that there are as many recipes as there are gardeners. We encourage you to experiment — plants are forgiving. Potting soil is different than ordinary garden soil because it has to drain better, therefore it usually has a lot of sand or other additives in it, like perlite.

Basic Potting Soil 1
⅓ finished compost, screened, maybe pasteurized
⅓ garden topsoil, from your yard, or planting mix from a bag
⅓ sharp sand, also called builder's sand

Basic Potting Soil 2
⅓ finished compost, screened, maybe pasteurized
⅓ sharp sand, or builder's sand
⅓ sphagnum peat moss or coir

ADVICE

INSTALLING DRIP IRRIGATION
KELLY'S TAKE: Slow, deep watering is the best way to care for your plants. You should become acquainted with one of two slow watering systems: the soaker hose or the drip emitter system. For years we used a soaker hose. We have dripper emitters now. Both are good, but I like the soaker hose more, actually, because it is so boneheaded easy, and it adapts easily to my random planting patterns.

All a soaker hose is is a black, coarse hose that full of invisible holes that weep steadily when water runs through it, soaking an area several inches deep to either side of it. You can find it at any garden center in different lengths.

Installation is a snap. You just arrange the soaker hose in zig-zags in your garden bed, or run it along a row of plants, or loop it around your trees. Stake it down so it stays put. You can buy special stakes where the hose is sold, or just use bent wire. You don't move it around once you put it down. It just lays there and oozes. Even in a vegetable bed it stays put and the plants grow around it. If you are mulching, the soaker hose should be buried beneath the mulch, against the soil. It is more efficient that way, and it looks better.

Run a normal hose from your water source to the soaker hose. One normal hose can feed multiple soaker hoses if you get one of those branching on/off valve attachments to go between them. These are also sold at any garden store. Then you can choose to water one area while not watering another area by just flipping a valve. Once you've got it set up, all you have to do to water is open the faucet a quarter turn and go do something else for a couple of hours. The only way to know how long is enough is to dig down in your bed and see how far the water is penetrating, but soaker hose time is measured in hours, not minutes.

ERIK SAYS: If you're the type of person who likes to tinker with model trains or robots, and drools over *Make* magazine, you're going to love installing a drip irrigation system. Though Kelly complains that it is too complex, it's simpler than robot building and it's cheap. Anyone can do it. It just takes a bit of planning.

There are two ways to get started: buy a kit, or talk to an actual live human being at your local nursery or at a drip irrigation supply company to help you find the correct parts. If you try to do this at a big-box store with no help you are headed for tears.

To keep your system simple, start with a small area first, such as your raised garden bed, as it can be overwhelming to configure a drip system for a large, complicated space. And when you design your garden think ahead and try to group plants by their water needs as this will streamline the installation and maintenance of a drip system.

A basic system consists of three components, a filter, plastic tubing, and little plastic thingies that drip. The easiest way to start out is to buy a kit, which will cost somewhere between $30 and $40 and will include the aforementioned items along with some other useful parts. Most drip irrigation suppliers have basic kits to get you started as well as add-on kits for particular kinds of plants, such as vegetable beds, shrubs, or trees.

Whether you get a kit or assemble the items yourself, you must have the basics:

- A filter which removes fine particles that might exist in your water supply to prevent drip emitters from becoming clogged.
- A pressure regulator, which lowers your water pressure down to the level that drip emitters use.
- A special hole punch to make the holes needed to insert the drip emitters and branch lines.
- Tubing — mainly ½", but you may also need ¼" depending on the drip components you use.

To this basic kit you will need to purchase drip emitters appropriate to the plants you are watering. These might include:

- Individual drip emitters — to deep water individual plants and trees.
- Soaker drip line for row crops (note this is different than soaker hose). Soaker drip line is a line with drip emitters placed on it at regular intervals.
- Mini-sprinklers for broad areas.
- Misters for special situations.

Timers are also a good investment, since beginning gardeners often forget to water, which leads to stressed-out plants. Real system geeks can even hook up a drip system to sensors in the soil, which automatically sense when your plants need water and to tell the timer to skip watering if there has been rain. Drip systems also work with low water pressure, so you could even hook up your rainwater collection barrel, if you have one, to a drip system. There are also accessories to convert a pre-existing sprinkler system to a drip system so that you can easily convert that bourgeois lawn to your revolutionary victory garden.

Drip Emitter

A warning for those who go fully automated: you still need to regularly check your crops for pests. Vegetables need careful tending and don't do well when ignored.

This year Kelly and Erik have made a peaceable compromise, agreeing to use a thinner sort of soaker hose sold to work with Erik's drip emitter system.

PROJECT

HOW TO MAKE A BEAN TEEPEE
Architecture That Feeds You—
Who Could Ask For More?

A teepee covered with runner beans is beautiful, edible and fun. This is a good project for kids, but if you make your teepee big enough, you can spend time in there yourself. An edible home office, perhaps? A seductive boudoir for the farming set? Alternatively, you can set up several small teepees instead of one big one, and your garden will suddenly look very elegant.

You can make your teepee as soon as frost danger has passed, the earlier the better, because beans don't produce as much when it gets really hot. Talk to the nice folks at your local independent nursery and find a runner bean or pole bean that is suited for your climate. Many runner beans make showy red flowers that attract hummingbirds. All beans have big, heart-shaped leaves that will make your teepee a shady getaway for the entire summer.

As long as you remember to pick the beans, the plants will keep producing more beans. If you neglect picking they'll figure their work is done and close up shop. So pick regularly, and you'll have beans all the way through to fall. Always pick your beans when they are young and tender and tasty. Except toward the end (when you're probably sick of them anyway) leave some on the vine to mature, and save these as seeds for next year's teepee.

To make the teepee, you'll need:
- One or two packs of beans, or a whole lot of bean seedlings (three per pole).

- A bunch of pole-like objects. Verticals, we'll call them. These can be bamboo poles, tree branches, lengths of plastic piping, lathe, anything like that. Six to ten will do. They should be six feet long, minimum.
- Some wire or string to tie the verticals together.
- Compost and a pitchfork or spade.

Mark out a circle in a level spot that gets lots of sun. Say the center of your lawn. Circle size is variable. Who's playing in the teepee? How tall are your poles? The shorter they are, the smaller your circle must be. Hold a couple of poles up and play with the dimensions. You can use a hose or a piece of rope to lay out the circle.

Once you've got your circle marked out, place your poles at equal intervals around the circle, leaving a wide space between two for the door. Sink your poles at least six inches into the ground, more if you live in a windy place or you expect the teepee to get a lot of kid abuse. Unless your soil is soft, you will probably have to loosen the soil first with a pitchfork or spade, and remove any turf which is in your way.

Bean Teepee

Lash the poles together at the top with some twine or wire.

Ordinarily we don't turn over soil to amend it, but since you probably had to dig holes for your poles anyway, go ahead now and mix in some nice compost into the loose soil at the foot of each pole. Beans like loose, rich soil.

Plant three or four beans about an inch and half deep around the base of every pole. Follow the seed packet instructions.

Keep the seeds moist until they sprout, then water regularly, and then soon you'll see why there might be some basis to the story of Jack and the Beanstalk. Beans seem to grow by the minute. You don't have to tie the vines to the poles, by the way — they'll cling and climb all by themselves. It's a beautiful thing to watch.

HOW TO DESIGN A POLYCULTURAL VEGETABLE BED

We've been experimenting with something called polyculture in the garden. We read about it first in *Gaia's Garden* by Toby Hemenway, an introduction to permacultural principles.

Polyculture is the practice of planting a community of interrelated, interdependent plants, mimicking in your garden bed (or hedges, or backyard or wherever) the complex relationships that are found between plants in nature, as opposed to the monocultural practices (all lawn, all corn, etc.) that characterize traditional gardening. A diverse community of plants will support and protect one another in different, often subtle ways. The bigger ones will protect the smaller ones from harsh sun or rainfall. One plant will attract a beneficial insect which preys on the bugs that eat a neighboring plant. One type of plant takes nitrogen from the soil, another puts nitrogen back in the soil.

This project proposes to establish a polyculture in your vegetable bed. Vegetable beds are notoriously orderly — neat lines of carrots and lettuce are what we imagine when we think of a garden bed. This is a radical departure from that model. Our lettuce bed described in an earlier project is based on this idea, but more simple.

A polycultural veggie bed holds more varieties of plants you commonly see in a bed at once, and the plants are allowed to grow much more densely than usual, and in random arrangements. The result is that a polyculture bed is a riot of dense green, with no discernible order. But underneath the apparent chaos there's a lot of good going on. The faster growing plants protect the tender ones from the sun. The thickness of the planting virtually eliminates weeds, and also functions as a living mulch, keeping the soil moist and cool beneath a carpet of green.

There is no hard and fast rule about what to put in a polyculture bed. Growing a polyculture is a living experiment. You give up the traditional methods of growing in rows, of letting one crop mature, pulling it out, and then planting the whole bed with a new crop. Instead, you start by sowing a dense mix of seeds over an empty bed, and let the plants take over. They will grow at different rates, you manage them, but as little as possible. As you harvest, you fill in the empty spaces with seedlings, so that the bed is always full of something.

The benefit of polyculture for you is variety. As an urban homesteader you don't have much space, but need variety in your crops. You don't need bushels of any single vegetable, and you certainly don't need all of it to come ready at once. Polyculture solves this by offering a sort of buffet of veggies for the picking each evening

The idea is to plant a whole lot of stuff at once, very densely. What you plant depends on what you like to eat, but you should choose a mix of things with different maturation rates. The maturation rate is noted on the seed packets where it says "days to harvest."

You would not want to plant space hogs that would take up the whole bed, like corn or melons. Stick with the well-behaved garden bed standards: lettuces, greens, root vegetables, beans, and maybe for fun some tender herbs or edible flowers.

As the summer goes on, you will clear space in the bed by eating your way through it, and refill the empty spaces with seedling plants you have started on the side in little pots. Once a polyculture bed is in full swing it is hard to grow new plants from seed because it is so dense, but you can tuck seedlings into empty spaces and they'll do well. You want the bed to be full and producing throughout the entire growing season.

A polyculture bed is an improvisational process, and yours will be as unique as you are, planted with the things you like to eat — maybe all hard-to-find Asian vegetables, or all rare heirloom varieties. For the sake of explanation, though, we are going to give instructions for a sort of generic polyculture bed designed for a typical spring-fall growing season, inspired by Ianto Evans' bed, which you will find described in *Gaia's Garden*. You need one packet each of the following seeds. Choose whatever variety appeals to you or seems suited to your local conditions.

Lettuce (preferably a "salad mix" of different types in
one packet)
Radishes
Carrots
Green onions/scallions
Parsnips
Swiss chard
Kale
Cabbage
Bush beans (not pole beans — bush beans grow more compactly)

The success of your bed depends to some extent on you being able to recognize these plants while they're seedlings, so you know what to pull, and what to leave. For this reason this project is best suited to someone who has grown at least some of these plants before.

As soon as the danger of frost has passed, prepare your bed for planting. As always, we recommend a raised bed for best results. The size of the bed is up to you, but we would recommend nothing larger than a 4' × 8' to start with, so you don't become overwhelmed. Pull out any dead stuff that is there from the winter, and lay down a fresh layer of compost on top of the bed. Or if it is a brand new bed, fill it with fresh garden soil. Also lay down your drip irrigation system if you're going to use one.

Gather your seed packets and decide what you want to grow. We think of crops passing though the garden in three basic waves:

1 The classic spring crops: lettuce, radishes, carrots and baby greens
2 Crops that transition into summer: some lettuces, greens, beets, beans and peas
3 The plants the carry on into the cold weather like kale, cabbages and parsnips

Sow the entire surface of your bed evenly with all of the following seeds: Lettuce, radishes, parsnips, carrots, green onions and Swiss chard.

Don't premix the seeds, just scatter them one kind at a time. You want each type of seed distributed equally across the entire bed, and premixing can result in an uneven spread. Cover them with a quarter inch of soil (this really means just sprinkle handfuls of soil over the bed until the seeds look more or less covered) and water carefully with a watering can or a hose set to a gentle sprinkle until thoroughly moist, until the water penetrates beneath the surface. Keep the bed moist while you are waiting for them to sprout.

In the next couple of weeks, start some cabbage seeds off to the side in little pots. Later on you will plant the cabbage seedlings in the bed. Don't start too many, because they are very large when full grown.

The first seeds to sprout, and the first plants you can eat, will be the radishes. All sprouts look a lot alike, but radish sprouts have red stems. Later on they'll have hairy leaves, unlike the other plants. You can start pulling the radishes and eating them in as little as four weeks.

The lettuce will arrive at baby lettuce stage in about six weeks. Now you begin to eat tender baby lettuce salads every night to thin the bed. At this stage the garden bed is a carpet of tiny greens. Since each one of them wants to grow up to be a big plant, you have to eat many of them while they are small. You don't have to pull tiny greens up whole, you can just pinch them off at their base, and they won't grow back.

The carrots and parsnips will be slow to develop. The green onions will come along, but it will be a while before they are ready to pull, but you can throw immature ones into your salads. The young Swiss chard can be eaten as a baby green in salads, or you can wait until it is bigger and eat it as a cooked green.

As your eating of radishes and lettuce begins to clear empty spaces, fill the empty spots with cabbages and bean seedlings. Place your cabbage seedlings in empty places. Remember, cabbages are big, so don't plant two right next to each other. Cabbage grows really slow, so it won't be ready to eat until the end of summer, or into the fall, depending on the variety. Distribute the bean plants evenly across the bed. Beans are good for the soil. They add back in the nitrogen that the leafy greens are sucking out.

As the spring transitions to summer, your bed should be just full of plants at different stages of development. You are pretty much guaranteed lettuce all season long. As you get down to fewer, more mature lettuce plants, harvest only their outer leaves instead of the whole plant. This way just a handful of lettuce plants will keep you in salad.

Your radishes will be gone by this time, and your carrots will still be growing (you can pull up some baby carrots if you want) and your Swiss chard will be coming into its own. Like lettuce, you can eat the baby chard plants whole, and just keep a few big ones around. Harvest only the outer leaves and they'll keep making more.

Around midsummer start your kale seeds in little pots. Kale does very well in the cold, and becomes sweeter after a frost, so it is going to provide you with greens into the winter. This is also the time you might lose your lettuce. It really doesn't like summer heat, but some types do better than others, and the tight conditions of a polyculture bed also can provide it with extra shade and cooler soil. But nonetheless, when your lettuce starts to bolt — shoot up flower stalks — you know it's time to pull it.

As you pull and plant, remember you are trying to keep a balance. You don't want to see much bare soil. You are trying to maintain a cooling canopy of green. But you don't want the plants packed so tightly together that their leaves go rotten and soggy. Balance. This might mean that you leave your lettuce plants in after they start bolting, so they function as green mulch. Pull them only when you have something to put in their place, like the kale.

When your beans start bearing, it is important to go out and harvest them all the time. If you leave the pods sitting, the plants will stop producing. If you don't have enough beans to make a side dish, use them as more of garnish — steam them and throw them into salads, or toss them with noodles.

When your kale seedlings have their second set of leaves they can go into the bed.

As the summer turns to fall, your lettuce and beans will fade out. Your cabbages will be getting big. Your carrots and parsnips will finally be coming into their own. Your kale will be taking its place as your primary green, though Swiss chard is hardy in all temperatures, and might still be doing well.

The kale will be the last thing you pull from your bed. Even snow will not kill it, so don't pull it prematurely. Spread a thick layer of mulch around it, and see how long it can last into winter.

When your bed is empty, feed it with some fresh compost, and put down a layer of mulch over that, and let it have a rest over the winter.

Despite the many steps above, remember there are no rules. The fun of polyculture is the experimenting. Plant whatever you want. The worst that can happen is that something will not grow, or the timing will be a little off and everything will mature at the same time. Just plant generously, water regularly, harvest continually, and most of all, have fun, and you can't go wrong.

In our California polyculture beds, we plant much more at once than what is described here. A typical winter bed (winter is the best time for greens for us) might hold green chicory, red chicory, radishes, carrots, wild fennel, common cress, arugula, lettuce mix, beets, garlic and green onions. There's so much going on that we have to eat salad every day or the bed will spin out of control, but they are the best salads, the best greens imaginable.

HOW TO MAKE TATER TIRES

A stack of tires allows you to grow a ton of potatoes in a small amount of space. The trick is forcing the potato plants to produce deep roots by slowly burying them alive. You need:

- Three or four car tires, preferably all the same size, to build one tire tower.
- Three or four seed potatoes per tire tower (see below).
- A whole lot of compost, garden soil or potting soil — or a mix of all three — whatever you can put together, because potatoes aren't picky.

Potatoes are not grown from seed, they are grown from other potatoes, called "seed potatoes." You might want to try this with good organic potatoes that you buy at farmers' market, but the most reliable way to grow potatoes is to mail-order seed potatoes. The reason for this is that eating potatoes might have been treated with growth inhibitors, or may carry some disease. The seed potatoes are certified as disease-free. More compelling than that, though, they are also available in a dizzying array of exotic varieties, and growing heirloom varieties is one excellent reason to grow a vegetable as common and inexpensive as a potato. So do an internet search for "organic seed potatoes" or call your local nursery at the beginning of the year. They might carry seed potatoes, or be willing to order them for you.

In temperate climates late March–April is the earliest planting period. In the southern climes, you can start in February. Seed potatoes do not like to sit shivering in soggy, cold soil. Potatoes form best when the soil is between 60°F and 70°F. When the soil reaches 80° and more, tuber production stops. The black tires warm the soil, so you could push your planting a little earlier, but you should never plant at the height of summer. If you have to cool the stack a little, paint the tires white.

Start with choosing your "seed." Whether you are using bought seed or one of your own potatoes, the routine is the same. Choose potatoes with two or three big eyes. If it's a little tater, plant the whole thing. If it's bigger and has lots of eyes, you can cut it up into two or three pieces; be sure there's at least one eye on each piece. Let those pieces dry out for a couple of days before planting, otherwise they will rot in the soil.

Cutaway View of Tater Tires

Pick a sunny spot. If the ground is packed hard, stab the soil beneath the tire a few times with a pitchfork to help with drainage.

Fill a tire with soil. (You can cut the sidewalls out if you want, or leave them; cutting them out saves work in the long run.) Potatoes don't need fantastic soil, but they do like loose soil. You can even use unfinished compost. Just don't add any fresh manure because it will burn the plants.

Plant three potatoes (or potato chunks) with their eyes facing generally upward and cover them with a couple of inches of soil. In a couple of weeks you should see sprouts. Potato vines resemble tomato plants, their genetic cousins. As they grow, you'll see they are a quite handsome plant.

After they have sprouted and grown tall enough to clear a second tire, add another tire to the stack and bury the plants until only their top sets of leaves are unburied — in other words, leave a few inches free. You may bury some of the smaller shoots, and that's okay. You can keep adding compost, or loose soil, or you could even stretch your soil by mixing it with hay or dead leaves. Potatoes will grow in almost anything. Just make sure it's loose.

Repeat this process as the plants grow, adding soil and tires as necessary until your stack is three or four tires tall. You are forcing the plant to grow an extra-long taproot, which means that the plant is making many more potatoes than it would if not encouraged in this way.

Water consistently but moderately. Container plants tend to dry out fast, and that includes plants in tires. Water is particularly important once the vines begin to flower. But if you water your potatoes too much they will fail to produce, or even rot. Be sure the entire stack is watered through, not just the top.

We recommend using a drip system, or turning your hose as low as it will go and leaving it on the stack a half hour for a slow soak. Deep, infrequent waterings are preferable to frequent, shallow ones.

Two or three weeks after the flowers die there will be tiny baby potatoes ready for eating under the soil. You can root around under the plant gently and pull up the newborn potatoes close to the surface. The potatoes in the lower tires will grow into full-sized potatoes.

After the flowering is over and the vines turn yellow or die back, the potatoes are ready for harvest. Stop watering and let them sit for a week or so, then you can harvest. You can do this by removing the topmost tire and harvest the taters at that level, leaving the rest for later. They store best in the dark, dry soil, so they will be very happy waiting for you in their tires. Or, punk rock style, you can just kick the whole stack over, revealing the entire tater treasure within. That method has its merits too. Harvest amounts will vary, but reports of 20 lbs. per stack are common.

Never wash your newly harvested potatoes (until you're ready to eat them, that is). The moisture will cause them to rot. Never leave potatoes in the sun. They will turn green, and it is not a schoolyard rumor—green potatoes **ARE** toxic. Your potatoes will improve in flavor if you let them cure (i.e. sit around) for a week or two before you eat them. Cure and store potatoes in a cool, dark place. Basements and root cellars are ideal. A refrigerator is not. It's too cold, and alters the starches in the potato.

CONTROLLING INSECT PESTS

ADVICE

We have to admit there is not much to our active pest control methods beyond our monkey fingers and the garden hose. See pests, pick them off or hose them off. That's about it, but it works. Healthy plants don't have too many insect problems, to tell the truth. Bugs and diseases move in on a plant when it is already going down, the same way you'll catch a cold when you're stressed. That said, there are more sophisticated methods than your monkey fingers, and we will talk about those in a bit.

Your first line of insect control is just keeping your plants happy. That means giving them good soil and slow, deep watering. It means keeping your soil healthy. It means planting the right kinds of plants at the right time of year.

If a plant looks sickly, we'll make sure there isn't a technological problem first—like maybe the drip system isn't working. If it is not that, it may just be the wrong plant for that space. Or we planted it at the wrong time of year. Or it has some disease. We pull it out before it before it can spread disease or attract pests. If a type of plant proves consistently difficult or vulnerable, we will not grow it. So many great plants grow with almost no care whatsoever that it is senseless to nursemaid fussy prima donnas.

Another idea to consider is that loss to insects is just part of doing business organically. You'll learn what to get alarmed about and what to let go, and when to plant extra to compensate for loss. For instance, something might snack on the leaves of your bean plant, but if it does not go too far, it won't harm the plant, and won't affect the bean crop at all, so why get your panties in a twist? When it comes to insect worries, remember: Healthy Plants, Healthy Attitude. Beyond that, here's some things you can try.

Hand Picking

Get used to touching bugs. You can pull off cabbage worms, tomato worms, snails and slugs. At these times you will really wish you had hungry chickens or ducks to toss them to because — ugh! — what are you going to do with them? But if you don't have chickens, the least gross thing to do is toss them in a bucket of slightly soapy water. The soap is what kills them. You can throw the grisly contents of this bucket onto your compost pile afterward, providing your soap was natural soap, not detergent.

Perhaps the best way to control snails and slugs is to keep ducks. If that's not in the cards for you, hunt them yourself at night with flash-

lights. Water in the afternoon to draw them out, then go hunting at ten or eleven at night. No earlier. A couple of consecutive nights of hunting should get squelch any outbreak. Wash your hands with vinegar afterward to cut the slime.

The Hose

Smaller insects, like the pernicious and always annoying aphids, can be blasted off with a hose. A spray nozzle with multiple settings will become your favorite garden tool.

Spray Nozzle

Control Ants To Control Aphids

Ants husband aphids for the honeydew they produce — aphids are the cows of the ant world. We would not have much against ants if it weren't for this, as we understand that they do good things for us as well, such as fighting turf wars with termites and eating flea eggs. But we will occasionally discourage them in selected areas by flooding their nests with a hose. If you do this enough, they'll move to where they are not bothered.

Boric acid, which is easiest, and cheapest to buy under the label of "roach powder," can also be used to control ants in a more deadly manner. It is not as vile as most insecticides, but it is not good for kids or pets, so handle it with care. For garden ants you make up a mix of 1 tsp. boric acid to one cup of bait. Your bait is whatever ants will go after, such as sugar syrup, jelly, applesauce, etc. Not all ants are sweet freaks. If they ignore sugary bait, try peanut butter or grease instead. Stir the boric acid into whatever you choose. Don't use more than this ratio of 1 tsp. boric acid: 1 cup bait, because higher concentrations will kill too fast. You want the ants to live to carry the boric acid back to their nest. Divide your bait between small jars. Poke a single hole in the lid of each, and lay the jars on their sides in the garden, or bury them up to their lids wherever you see ants. Within a couple of weeks your ants should be gone.

While these baits are fairly contained, we can imagine a determined dog or toddler getting into them, so keep an eye on them.

Don't Forget Your Bird Friends

Birds eat enormous quantities of insects. Make your yard a bird's paradise and your bug problems will diminish drastically. But be aware that some types of birds like to eat brand new seedlings, and others like fruit, so you might have to protect your newly planted beds with a little aviary netting until the plants are couple of inches high, and your fruiting plants with it once fruit sets. Aviary netting is a good idea for a newly planted bed anyway, because it keeps out cats and squirrels as well as birds.

If you've got them, corral chickens or ducks around a bed that is between plantings. They'll decimate the bug population, and leave some fertilizer behind.

Wolves Of The Garden

We all like to see lots of ladybugs and lacewings around the garden, because they are pretty, and they do eat lots of bugs. But garden spiders are also real bug gluttons, and there are lots of them in a healthy garden. The hunting kind (as opposed to the web-spinning kind) will make their homes in the thick mulch that you are going to lay all over your yard. Now, if you're a bit of an arachnophobe, don't freak out. The mulch will not be teeming with giant black widows like some 1950s horror flick. These are mostly tiny spiders you cannot even see, and, whether you like them or not, they are your very special friends and helpers. They are truly the wolves of the garden.

Some organic gardeners purchase predatory insects and set them loose in the garden, hoping they'll stick around and eat the undesirable insects. We've heard mixed things about the efficacy of this (they often wake up and fly away *en masse)* and have not yet found it necessary to buy bugs.

Better to attract them naturally than to buy them, again by having a pesticide-free garden with lots of places to live and things to eat. If you have space to do it, it is well worth growing some things that beneficial insects like to dine on. If you have use for the plants yourself, all the better. As a rule of thumb, plants from the cabbage family, the carrot family and the sunflower family are known for attracting beneficial insects. Consider finding a place for a few of these plants in your garden: angelica, bee balm, buckwheat, calendula, carrot (left to flower), ceanothus, chervil, cilantro, clover, daisy, dill, erigeron, evening primrose, fennel, goldenrod, lovage, mustard, parsley, Queen Anne's lace, rue, snowberry, sunflower, sweet alyssum, sweet cicely, thyme, valerian, and yarrow.

We do 95% of our insect control using the simple methods above. What follows are other organic methods we might resort to if we were desperate.

Sprays

If plain water is not enough, try spraying with soapy water. Soap suffocates insects — beneficials as well as non-beneficials — so be careful where you spray. If you consider that an adult ladybug eats about 50 aphids a day, the you'll see that the accidental poisoning of even one beneficial sets your cause back a good way. So don't do this casually, and move with caution. Use only detergent and phosphate-free soap. You can also buy something called insecticidal soap at the nursery, which is a combination of soap and oils, and is approved for organic use.

Bt

If you have huge problems with caterpillars or beetles eating your cabbage and broccoli, you might try spraying or dusting with Bt, which is short for *Bacillus thuringiensis*, a natural bacterium in the genus *Bacillus*. Bt kills the bugs after they ingest it, basically by interfering with their digestion, and eventually busting open their guts. Mmm. It is considered safe for humans, but it will kill butterfly larvae, so consider it an extreme measure.

Traps
If you can't deal with touching bugs, trap them.

Slug And Snail Traps

Lay down a board on the ground near a slug or snail infestation. They'll go beneath it in the morning to hide from the sun. All you have to do is smash them under the board the next day.

Fill a shallow container like a tuna can or cottage cheese container with beer and bury it up to its rim in the dirt in the middle of slug and snail territory. The next morning it will look like the aftermath of a tragic fraternity party.

Earwig Traps

Earwig traps are similar to slug traps: bait 'em and drown 'em. Take some kind of deli/cottage cheese-style container that has cover, and poke holes big enough for earwigs in a circle all around the upper rim, just beneath the lid. Fill the bottom with an inch or so of soy sauce and cooking oil, and bury it so that entry holes are level with the soil.

Physical Barriers

The sticky commercial substance called Tanglefoot can be painted around tree trunks to keep insects from crawling up the trunk and infesting your trees and shrubs. Bands of copper keep snails and slugs from doing likewise by shocking them — the copper somehow induces an electrical charge in their mucous.

Floating Row Covers are super light fabric barriers that you spread over your garden bed. It is so light you don't even have to prop it up, you just lay it directly on your plants, even on tiny seedlings. The gauzy fabric will let the sun in, but keep birds and flying insects out.

Companion Planting

This is a complex subject, and one that goes beyond simple insect control. In this limited context, though, companion planting refers to the practice of pairing plants with the hope that one will deter insects from attacking the other. Cabbages are said to do well paired with mint, strawberries with chrysthanthemums, and so on. It certainly makes for pretty gardens, but it is definitely an art, and not backed up by lots of science. We don't practice it (consciously) ourselves, we simply haven't had time to delve into it, but we understand that success or failure has much to do with the ratio of the pairings and spacing of the pairing. Gardening is always a local process, and one size doesn't fit all, so if you wish to try companion planting, do so knowing it will be an ongoing experiment. If they do nothing else, companion plantings will keep your garden beds diverse, and biodiversity is a powerful insect deterrent in and of itself.

ADVICE

ROTATING CROPS

Each plant draws differently from the soil, and attracts its own set of pests and diseases. If you switch your crops around from year to year it takes some of the burden off the soil and confuses the pests. It is an elegant, common-sense way to avoid all sorts of cultivation problems.

In larger-scale yards, the traditional method is to have four large growing beds and to rotate crops through these beds so that ideally there is a three-year interval before one crop returns to the same bed. On an urban homestead you probably do not have that much space. What we do, and what you can probably do too, is rotate them around in every possible growing space you have available: in beds, along walkways, sharing space in the herb bed, planted in containers, etc. If your garden is all in containers, this is easy: it just means changing out containers and soil every year.

Don't worry if crop rotation sounds confusing at first. For the first year or two you don't have to worry about it—your soil is fresh, and the pests and diseases are not likely to find you. As time goes by, and you know your plants better, start taking these rotation ideas into account as you plan your garden.

As we said in our Principles in the beginning of this section, keep notes! A journal, even just a couple of notes scratched in a calendar, is critical to planning your crop rotations.

Plants in the same families tend to be prey to the same diseases and pests. They also like similar growing conditions, so once you learn about one member of a family, you already know quite a lot about the other members. You'll also begin to recognize familial similarities from plant to plant. For instance, all members of the carrot family have similar flowers: flat clusters of small flowers shaped like little umbrellas. Once you know that shape, having seen it in dill, and in the carrots you let go to seed, you might recognize the same shape in fennel blossoms, and realize (perhaps even with some excitement) that it must be a member of the same family. You will be well on the road to botany geekdom.

In its simplest form, rotating your crops is just a matter of avoiding using any one bed, pot, patch of ground for the same family year after year. Try to stretch it out so that you don't plant that family in that spot for two or three years.

These are the families:

Tomato family (*Solanaceae*): tomatoes, peppers, potatoes, eggplants

Onion family (*Alliaceae*): onions, leeks, garlic

Beet family (*Chenopodiaceae*): beets, spinach, chard

Cabbage family (*Brassicaceae*): cabbages, mustard, broccoli, cauliflower, kale

Legume family (*Fabaceae*): all types of beans and peas

Squash family (*Cucurbitaceae*): squash, melon, cucumbers

Carrot family (*Apiaceae*): carrots, dill, parsley, fennel

When you get comfortable with rotating by family, you can add to the challenge taking into consideration how the crop you're growing affects the soil in addition to its family designation. You'll note in these groupings the plants of the same families don't always stick together, since this is about behavior — how they feed.

The Way Plants Feed

The three principal nutrients that plants require in soil are nitrogen (N), phosphorus (P) and potassium (K). The labels of both chemical and organic fertilizers are marked with their N-P-K ratios expressed in numbers, like 4-8-2. You don't need to worry about those ratios, or NPK levels, too much when you don't have to go to the store to build your soil. A little store-bought organic fertilizer is fine now and then — particularly for container plants — but the old-fashioned way with great compost, worm castings, fertilizer tea, and mulch is a more desirable way.

You should know about NPK to understand how plants feed, because you are going to strive to balance your planting so that you don't put plants that are hungry for the same thing in the same place over and over again.

Fruiting plants, e.g. tomatoes, melons and squash, require lots of phosphorus (P). Phosphorus is essential for root, flower and fruit development.

Leafy plants, e.g. spinach, lettuce and cabbage, eat up lots of nitrogen (N). Nitrogen promotes dark green growth, and helps plants grow quickly. People flood their lawns with nitrogen to "green" them.

Root crops, e.g. garlic, carrots and radishes, like lots of potassium (K). Potassium protects plants from the cold and gives them resistance to disease. It also helps them keep from drying out too fast.

Legume crops, e.g. all beans and peas, actually put nitrogen (N) back into the soil, which is very handy.

Say you plant tomatoes in the summer. You don't grow anything over winter, then the next spring you plant melons in that same spot. You have done right by not planting another member of the *Solanaceae* family in the same place — thus discouraging pests and disease — but by planting two fruiting crops in a row, you are depleting the phosphorus in your soil. It would have been a better choice to plant something that did not fruit, like leeks. Beans and peas are always a good choice too, because they add more to the soil than they take away. A good rule of thumb is when in doubt, plant beans. And what about your depleted soil? Just give it some fertilizer tea, mulch with some fresh compost, and it will be okay.

ADVICE

ANIMAL PESTS
Gophers and Moles

Gophers, also called pocket gophers, are found all over North America and some of Central America, while moles cover the Americas, Europe and Asia. In places where they are both found, they are sometimes confused. For a gardener, the important difference between a gopher and a mole is that moles are insectivores. They dig tunnels, which can ruin a lawn (and ruining lawns is a good thing in our opinion!), but other than inadvertent root damage, or possible ankle twists, moles are not your enemy. In fact, moles tend to eat all the bugs in one area, and then move on, so mole problems are often transitory.

Gophers, on the other hand, are herbivores and hence much more annoying for someone trying to grow their own food. They eat both the roots and the tops of plants. They will pull entire plants down into their burrows by their roots. They can devastate a vegetable bed in short order, and damage young trees by gnawing on their roots. So if you have gophers, you have to go to war. If you have moles, we'd advise you not to get too excited about it. But if they prove a problem, gopher-type controls work for them as well.

How do you know which critter you have? Moles make volcano-shaped mounds, whereas gopher mounds are crescent or horseshoe shaped. Moles tunnel so close to the surface that you can sometimes see the tunnels themselves raising the soil, whereas gophers dig much deeper. Moles are nocturnal and elusive. Gophers are active all day, and do pop out of their holes to nibble on surface greens, so you'll probably spot them.

Gopher Cures

There are a ton of folksy gopher deterrents that people swear by, everything from feeding them Juicy Fruit gum, which supposedly clogs their intestines, to various high-pitched-noise-making electronic devices. Then there's the practice of shoving wads of hair, cat poop and various foul-smelling concoctions down their burrows. Unfortunately there's no science behind any of these schemes.

Some people make a blood sport of gopher control: they flood the burrows and play Whack-A-Mole when the gophers try to evacuate. We prefer a less theatrical form of control. Basically you approach a gopher problem as you would a rat infestation. It's a two-pronged approach: you prevent them from getting to your stuff, and if they don't move on, you kill them. The methods that work reliably are poisons, traps, barriers and predators.

Poison we rule out for urban homestead use. It's too dangerous to pets and other wildlife to have poison laying around, and you don't want it tainting your soil.

Traps are brutally efficient and probably the most humane way to kill gophers. There are specific gopher traps, and they have to be set up exactly right to work, so pay close attention to the directions. There are mole traps too. Gopher traps don't work for moles and vice versa.

Barriers prevent the gophers from getting at the crops you value most. This is another case where a raised bed is a great idea, because you can line the bottom of your raised bed with gopher wire and lock the critters out. Gopher wire is sturdy, galvanized wire similar to aviary wire, and can be purchased online, or you can substitute ½" hardware cloth. Don't use chicken wire because the holes are too big. Aviary wire can be used, but it rusts and will eventually break down. You can also buy baskets made of gopher wire for planting individual plants, like baby trees — or fashion them yourself.

Predators such as cats and dogs can be quite effective for controlling moles. Cat smells alone are said to be somewhat of a deterrent to gophers. Dachshunds are ruthless vermin killers (yet so cute!), as are most of the small terriers. If you don't have a bloody-minded little dog, perhaps you could borrow one for a weekend.

Squirrels, Raccoons, Possums, Skunks

All four of these are omnipresent in the urban landscape and fairly intractable. Barring gunplay, the first step in dealing with these larger pests is not providing food and habitat for them. Don't leave out plates of pet food. Make sure that all entrances to your basement or garage are closed at all times, and that you don't have any holes in your roof, your foundation, or accessible old sheds. If they start breeding on your property, you will be worse off than ever. Most importantly, harvest all fruits and nuts and keep them from accumulating on the ground. Also realize that if you have a water garden, you will have raccoons. No question about it.

Squirrels are just going to happen no matter what you do. They really are intractable, and as far as we can tell, nothing really repels them. Trapping them and relocating them is problematic for two reasons; first, it makes your problem someone else's problem. Second, all creatures, including squirrels and mice and raccoons, carve out niches in the places they live. When they are trapped and moved, they become unwelcome intruders in someone else's niche, and will have a hard time surviving there. It would be more humane to kill them. So short of hunting them, you're just going to have to learn to live with them.

Skunks are somewhat easier to deal with. Thankfully they don't climb very well and can be excluded from most yards with a fence. Bury some chicken wire a foot or two deep and connect it to the bottom of the fence — this should keep them from digging under to get into your yard.

Yes, you can hire a professional to trap these critters, but they'll either kill them or relocate them, which, as we just said, just means a slower death.

Rats And Mice

For rats and mice, we use the classic wooden trap, one of those inventions that, like the bicycle, is elegant, simple, cheap and effective. Place the business end of the trap (the part with the food) against a wall, where rats and mice tend to travel. Put it in a place that can't be accessed by nosy dogs, cats or kids as these things can be dangerous. We've had the best success using dried fruit and peanut butter as bait. Rat poison is a really bad idea. First of all it is deadly to pets and native animals that might find it. Secondly it can kill a predator, such as a hawk or owl, that might prey on a poisoned rat and so end up poisoned themselves. Lastly, poisoned rats have a tendency to die in your walls, and thus have their stinky, posthumous revenge.

With few exceptions, birds are your friends and should be encouraged to visit your garden on account of their insatiable hunger for insects. Occasionally they will get into new plantings and eat your seeds, or eat berries from your bushes. This is easy to prevent by covering tempting plants with inexpensive ½" mesh netting, called aviary netting, that can be found at your local nursery.

WHY YOU MIGHT TEST YOUR SOIL

ADVICE

There are two reasons to test your soil. The first is that since we are dealing with urban—therefore polluted—environments on our city homesteads, it may be a good idea to make sure that the soil does not contain any toxins that could make their way from your crops to your kitchen. It depends on the history of your property. Possible sources of contamination could include previous tenants who stored or repaired cars in the yard, or toxic runoff from streets and alleys finding their way into your yard. If your dwelling is a repurposed industrial building, there is all the more reason to be cautious. And no matter what the setting, paint chips from careless stripping jobs are a big source of lead contamination. Lead is a highly stable substance that has a nasty tendency to stick around for years. It is especially a concern if you will be feeding young children with home-grown vegetables, as they are much more susceptible to lead poisoning than adults.

Your local health department should be able to point you to a certified testing lab that can handle soil. All you have to do is send in a sample of your soil for analysis. It will probably run you around 30 bucks.

Lead contamination does not just come from the soil, it also comes from the air. If your yard is near a busy street or highway, or you are near any big industrial operation, lead might be clinging to the surface of your food. Peel away the outer leaves of leafy vegetables. Scrub and peel root vegetables, and wash everything thoroughly. The University of Minnesota Extension recommends washing your veggies in water containing 1% vinegar to remove pollution.

If your soil does come back with high lead levels, do not despair. Plants do not readily pick up lead. You can safely eat the fruiting parts of plants, like apples, tomatoes, corn, squash and the like. Lead will cling to the surface of root crops, so scrub those thoroughly. Leafy greens pick up the most lead, so we'd recommend you grow those in containers or raised beds.

One interesting thing we discovered in our research is that adding a heavy concentration of organic matter — mulch or compost — in the soil has the effect of "reducing lead availability." It interferes with plant uptake of lead. Like we've said all along, mulch is great stuff.

Lead is a common urban contaminant, but should your yard be contaminated with anything else, our best advice in any case is to grow above the ground in high raised beds or in containers.

Troubleshooting your soil: Aside from checking for contaminants, the other reason to test soil is to troubleshoot bad crops to see if persistent problems could be due to a lack of nutrients or a high or low pH level. If your food is growing fine you don't need to test it. What works, works. But if you're having problems, knowing the soil pH and/ or the nutrient levels might give you some clues as to how to amend your soil for better yields.

Soil pH is the degree of acidity or alkalinity. Most plants thrive in the 6.0 to 7.0 range. Some, such as blueberries, like an acidic soil around 5.0. Most nurseries sell an inexpensive and easy to use home test kit that will determine the pH level of your soil. You can then adjust the pH by the addition of sulfur to make the soil more acidic, or lime to make it more alkaline. In general the eastern United States tends towards the acidic, while the west tends towards the alkaline.

It's also possible to test for nutrients, i.e. the levels of nitrogen, potassium and phosphorus in the soil. There are more expensive home kits for this or you can send samples to a lab (ask for a reference at your local nursery). For most folks, except for the geekiest of urban farmers, it's probably not necessary, but if you do it remember to take samples from multiple locations because nutrient levels can vary widely.

ADVICE

NOT DIGGING IT

As we discussed earlier, we advise against tilling or turning over the soil in your garden, because of the damage it does to soil quality over time, especially to valuable microorganisms. Nature does not till, after all, and as much as we can, we try to imitate natural systems in our garden. In a forest, nutrients are delivered by the slow decomposition of plant and animal materials on the forest floor, and by the action of undisturbed worms working deep in the soil. So we improve our soil from the top down by constantly mulching and applying compost and other organic amendments to the tops of our beds. This is far easier than working amendments into the soil every year, and so highly recommended for lazy people.

The no-dig method is dependent on the use of garden beds, either raised beds or dedicated beds on the ground with paths between. The soil must be loose and untrampled for this to work. Just keep adding compost and worm castings to the top of it — at the beginning of your growing season, in the middle, at the end. Whenever. Don't mix them into the existing soil. Just lay it down and leave it alone. It all becomes one in the end.

If you are trying to colonize a dried-up, compacted nasty piece of ground, you have a choice to make. We aren't going to be dogmatic about this no-dig system. You might want to start by digging up the soil and amending it heavily with organic matter. That is one legitimate route. The other is to put a sheet mulch over it, and let it rest for a year.

Chapter Three
Urban Foraging

Urban Foraging

The tropical rainforest is a rich environment that provides abundant food, clothing and shelter for those who know how to navigate its depths. The urban jungle we occupy is no less generous, provided you know how to forage in it. There is no need to run to the backwoods to appease your inner hunter-gatherer. You can gather wild plants in the city, harvest fruit by the bucketful, and hunt down free food, clothing, and building supplies. And while you do so, you become more aware of your immediate environment, more present, more active, more alive. Open your eyes to the abundance around you.

In this chapter we cover three forms of urban foraging, practices that can augment your agricultural activities and fill your pantry. Foraging is a great way for people who do not have land to live off the land nonetheless. We're going to look at harvesting wild plants (a.k.a. eating weeds), gathering neglected fruit, and last but by no means least, hooking into that bottomless reservoir of wealth — the American Dumpster.

Feral Edibles

Pot-herb is an old-fashioned term meaning leafy plant that can be cooked and eaten as a vegetable. Its existence seems to imply that at one time we considered more green things edible than we do now. Many of the plants which we now consider weeds were once considered edibles. In fact, some of our most common weeds here in the U.S. were brought over from Europe intentionally as pot-herbs, the much maligned dandelion among them.

The word weed means a plant growing where it is not wanted, particularly when it is competing with plants under cultivation. So to our way of thinking, weed control is not so much a matter of eradicating them, but of changing our attitude toward them. Consider these feral edibles low-maintenance crops. They taste good and are packed with the nutrition of wild things. Admittedly, some of them are strong flavored. A forager is not a culinary conservative. If you like arugula, kale, endive and other flavorful greens, you will love eating weeds.

The fun of weed eating is learning to hunt them. In the city, weeds are everywhere, growing in lawns, planter boxes, parkway strips, abandoned lots, city parks, and not least, in your own yard. They specialize in colonizing disturbed areas, so you'll find them growing riotously around building sites. But once you learn to identify one or two, the urban landscape takes on new meaning, and once you develop a forager's eye you never lose it.

Your best weed harvesting might happen in your own yard, or your neighbors' yards. This makes sense in the city, because you don't want to eat greens coated with diesel exhaust and the pee of 3000 dogs. Consider weeds a crop, a very casual crop. Let them grow here and there, harvesting them whenever you want some greens, or be a little eccentric and actively cultivate a patch of your favorites. If the greens you want don't pop up voluntarily in your yard, wait until the ones you've noticed on your walks go to seed in the summer, collect the seed and throw it in your backyard. They'll take it from there.

Whatever you do, a little love goes a long way with weeds. When the fussy heirloom vegetables let you down, the weeds are always there for you.

The Six Things To Know About Eating Wild

1 **You need professional help.** A good book is a great place to start, but a live teacher is invaluable. This is because plants are so darn variable. They don't always look like the illustrations in books. They change a lot as they grow, and even on the same block one plant will vary from the next just because of specific growing conditions.

   In most places you can find people offering wild food walks. See the resources below, or search under "wild food" and "survival skills" and your city name or area. You can also try local nature centers, anywhere that wildlife education is a theme. Check community college and university extension classes, too.

   Your local chapter of the Sierra Club probably offers hikes that focus on identifying plants and wild foods. While it is true that you want to learn about city plants, the truth is that these weeds are everywhere — city, suburb, roadside, country and forest. Learning to identify common weeds is just as much wild food harvesting as learning to identify the lesser-known native plants.

2 **Plants are best identified by scientific name.** Common names are just not specific enough. There are about one hundred "chickweeds," for instance, because the name just means a green chickens like to eat. Chickens like all sorts of greens. The chickweed you want to eat, though, is *Stellaria media.*

3 **Start off easy.** Lots of plants are easy to identify. Get to know a handful of plants very well and watch them over the course of a year to see how they change, then add to your repertoire one new plant at a time. Be cautious and sensible, but don't be afraid. Considering how many plants there are in the world, few plants are poisonous,

but even if they are, they may not be completely inedible. The tomato plant is poisonous, for instance—but luckily for us its fruit is not.

A good beginner's strategy is to focus on learning your local poisonous plants before anything else, preferably before you start tramping around in overgrown lots and by road sides. Can you identify poison ivy spring, summer, winter and fall? Because even in the winter, its dead stalks will give you a rash.

4 Seek out the best places to gather. You want to source your weeds from places that haven't been sprayed with insecticides or chemical fertilizers, as plants suck up toxins. God bless them for doing it—but you don't want to eat them. So a vacant lot is a better collection zone than the edge of a golf course, for instance, and the grounds of that old gas station might not be the best place, either. City parks, on the other hand, are great—just stay away from the areas with tended lawn.

5 Always gather respectfully. Unless you are dealing with prolific annual weeds like dandelions, treat wild plants with gentleness. Don't pull up the whole plant unless you are harvesting the root. Try to harvest no more than a third of a plant at a time if you would like to come back and harvest from it again. Careful gathering pays off in another way—it ensures you only harvest what you mean to harvest. If you are going hog-wild and gathering greens by the fistful, you might be pulling in a few plants you don't want to eat, and that could be downright dangerous, or at least leave you with a bellyache.

6 Trust your instincts. Even though we don't use these instincts much anymore, we evolved to be clever omnivores. Our tongues and our guts are more savvy about food gathering than our higher faculties. If something tastes bitter, or smells bad, or turns your stomach, or repels you in any visceral way, just don't eat it. Never force yourself to eat a weed. This should be fun, not a trial. You are not starving. You have nothing to prove. If it doesn't taste pleasant or if your ID is not so positive that you would fist-fight with someone over it, just don't eat it.

Along these lines, always proceed cautiously when eating new foods. If it passes the first taste test, go ahead and cook it up, but don't eat more than a bite or two. Wait and see how it sits. It may not be poison, it might even be fine for other people, but it may not agree with you. After this trial period, you can up your quantities.

What follows is a list of some of the most liked, most widespread edible weeds in the continental U.S. We're not telling you how to identify them here, because we are not set up to be a field guide. This is just to give you a sense of the variety of food that is out there for the gathering. See our resources section for a list of good wild food guides.

Amaranth or Pigweed (*Amaranthus retroflexus*): The low-class relative of the fancy grain-bearing amaranth. Unlike the rest of the weeds we're talking about here, this one is a native to the Americas. This tough survivor doesn't mind drought or heat. It has coarse stalks and leaves that can be steamed or boiled into a spinach-like green. This is what it is valued for most, but the seeds are also edible. Collect seed heads in the fall, and winnow them to separate the chaff from the seed. Add the seeds to hot cereal, or baked goods.

Chickweed

Chickweed (*Stellaria media*): An excellent starter weed. Easy to identify, tender and mild, and high in vitamin C, the tiny leaves of chickweed are great additions to salads. When it is taller and carries more of a stem, it can also be steamed or sautéed, just chop it up because the stem can be a little chewy.

In our local hills, chickweed almost always grows alongside another tender, innocent-looking plant: poison hemlock, the same plant that killed Socrates. Hemlock leaves look a little like carrot tops. You don't want to eat even a bite of hemlock accidentally with your chickweed salad. This is an example of why you should always be careful when gathering, and also why you should know your local poisonous plants.

Dandelion (*Taraxacum officinalis*): This one you can probably identify without difficulty, particularly if your parents ever made you weed the lawn.

Dandelion is a bitter green, there is no getting around that, no matter how young the plant. That does not stop it from being one of the best known and loved wild edibles. Just think of the bitterness as being powerful medicine for your jaded urban liver. You should eat it when it is very young, just coming out of the ground. If it has flowered, it is too late. So you have to learn to identify it by its leaves alone.

Eat the young leaves raw in a salad or cook them as you would any green. They are super-nutritious. You can reduce the bitterness in cooked dandelions by boiling them just until they wilt, changing the water, and cooking them again.

You can eat the flowers, but only the yellow parts. The flowers are also used to make dandelion wine. The taproot is an edible root vegetable. It is, of course, bitter, so is best roasted along with sweeter vegetables.

> Jumped Greens — a fast and easy way to cook any green, feral or not. Start by pre-cooking the greens, either steaming or boiling them briefly, until bright green and tender, then draining. Heat olive oil in a skillet and throw in some minced garlic and a pinch of red pepper flakes. Sauté just until the garlic softens. Throw in the greens and cook a little more, tossing them in the oil to distribute the flavor. Add salt to taste.

Lamb's Quarters or Goosefoot (*Chenopodium ssp.*): A big favorite among weed eaters, due to its mild flavor reminiscent of spinach and pea shoots. It is also packed with vitamin C and minerals. Collect tender, low-growing young plants whole, or pinch off their tops. Older plants will grow into shrubs five feet tall. Use the leaves exactly as you would spinach.

Apparently some people dry the leaves and grind them into flour to stretch wheat flour when baking. We haven't tried this yet, but will remember it when the zombies come. The seeds can be also be collected and used like poppy seeds.

Don't confuse this plant with epazote, which it does resemble. Epazote is an edible herb, but should not be eaten in quantity. Just sniff to make the distinction between the two: lamb's quarters is odorless, while epazote has a very distinct odor.

Common Milkweed (*Asclepias syriaca*): The principal food of the Monarch butterfly, and another big favorite among weed eaters. Unfortunately, milkweed is not found all over the U.S., but we felt its popularity merited its inclusion. *Asclepias syriaca* is not found in the West, or the dry plains. Other plants called "milkweed" might be available in these areas, but do not be tempted to eat them unless you have verified they are in fact an edible species.

It is a particularly good plant to know if it does grow in your area, because unlike some weeds that are only good in the first flush of spring, you can eat milkweed throughout the summer. You eat the tender milkweed shoots when they first come up, the flower pods when they first form, and the seed pods which are left when the flowers fade. Milkweed has uses beyond the culinary as well. The fluff that comes from its seed pods is highly insulating — it is a vegan down that can be used to stuff pillows or coats. Native Americans used the mature stalks to make rope. And its sap (the "milk" part) can be made into a kind of rubber. This is the kind of plant you want to know when the shit hits the fan.

There is a persistent myth that milkweed is bitter and toxic, and to be palatable must be boiled in several changes of boiling water before eating it — which makes it sound hardly worth the while. You'll find this advice all over the Internet, passed about as common wisdom from one source to the next, but our favorite forager, Samuel Thayer, debunks that idea soundly in his book *Edible Wild Plants*.

Common Plantain (*Plantago spp.*): A handsome plant, a prolific lawn weed and the bane of the golf course. It is edible when the leaves are small and tender, but not worthwhile when they get bigger. We like to eat the little leaves on sandwiches, or toss them with other greens in salads. They are strong tasting — kind of like arugula. As the leaves get bigger, they get stringy and tough. But don't give up on the plant yet — wait for the seeds to come.

The plantain sends up tall skinny seed stalks. It is easy to strip these seeds off their stalks when they are dry. The seeds come off along with their husks, which are very light. By blowing gently over the seeds, you can send the husks — or chafe — flying, and keep only the glossy little seeds. That is what you call winnowing. Seeds of the *Plantago* family are known as *psyllium*, which is an ingredient found in high-fiber cereals and in bulk laxatives. You can use these seeds like you would wheat germ, sprinkling them on cereal, stirring them into pancake batter or whatever you please, to up your daily fiber intake.

Another good use for plantain is as a salve. If you have an insect bite, or any skin irritation, even poison ivy, bruise or chew a plantain leaf and rub the mash on your skin. It does have soothing properties. It is most effective on mosquito bites if you rub it on when the bite is fresh.

Purslane (*Portulacca oleracea*): Sometimes this highly-prized weed is found in gourmet markets or farmers' markets. The young fleshy leaves are used in salads — just strip them off the stem. This plant also cooks up well. It has a slight mucilaginous texture like okra, which adds thickness to soups. Think gumbo. Some people pickle purslane.

Sheep Sorrel (*Rumex acetocella*): Also known as sour grass. Sheep sorrel, like its larger domesticated cousin garden sorrel (*R. acetosa*) is sour in a lemony, mouth-puckering way. It is too sour to be eaten in quantity on its own, but it does great things in salads and soups and sandwiches. Look for its distinctive spade-shaped leaves in sunny places and in sandy soil. Also look for its tasty, yellow flowered relative, *Oxalis acetosella* or wood sorrel. It's a common urban weed, and the flowers are as good as the leaves.

Stinging Nettle (*Urtica dioica*): The sting of this plant is strange and unpleasant. Woe to the forager who falls into a patch! But if you do get stung, no need to suffer. Smear the juice of plantain, or dock or jewelweed leaves on the rash. If you're near home, use a paste of baking soda. Then take your revenge and eat the plant, because it is very good.

To be fair, nettles do seem to vary a bit in "stingyness" — it's probably a regional and seasonal thing. Many foragers don't even wear gloves while harvesting, trusting instead their calloused fingers and expert gathering technique. To start, you will want to wear gloves. Pinch strip or snip off the first few sets of leaves from the plants — taking only the newest growth. They are best early in the spring, and become tougher as the season wears on.

Cooking, even just a brief steaming, takes away the sting. The best way to cook nettles is to wash them, then put them dripping wet into a hot pan to steam. Then dress them as you like.

Nettles are full of iron and potassium and vitamin C. People make tea out of dried nettles that is hearty, almost like a broth, and said to have strengthening properties. Drying, by the way, takes away the sting too, so no worries there. Tea is a good way to use nettles later in the year when they've gone tough.

Invasive Edibles

While all of the plants listed above are found all over North America, the following are plants that may or may not be in your area, and may or may not be considered weeds, but if they are well adapted for your climate, then they are probably invasive. By eating them you will be doing your part toward keeping them under control.

Fennel (*Foeniculum vulgare*): Brought over by the Italians, no doubt, and we don't blame them a bit for doing it. This delicious plant naturalizes and spreads like crazy. The foliage tastes like licorice, but even better, dig up the anise-flavored white bulbs and eat them raw to get the most out of their delicate flavor (try slicing them and pairing them with oranges in a salad). They roast nicely too.

Nasturtium (*Tropaeolum majus*, and others): A delicate flower in some places, a garden-swallowing monster in others. All parts of this plant are edible. The peppery leaves can be added to salads or sandwiches. They are reminiscent of watercress, which is a relative. The bright orange flowers are great in salads, or used as garnish. We've made orange pesto with the flowers. We've also stuffed the flowers with flavored cream cheese. The seed pods can be pickled to make poor man's capers.

Blackberries (*Rubus fruticosus*): Mean, tough vines covered with scrumptious fruit for the taking in late summer. Blackberries are fast growing and will colonize any waste area, so look for it not only in the woods, but also in the aftermath of any construction or demolition. When out picking, be careful not to stumble into a poison ivy patch while looking for a berry patch. They look similar if you're not paying attention.

Spearmint (*Mentha spicata*) or **Peppermint** (*Mentha x piperita*): Nothing is better than tea made with a handful of fresh mint. Like real eggs, real tomatoes and real bread, fresh mint tea is a revelation — delicate, slightly sweet, the color of spring. Once you get hooked, you will have no problem keeping on top of any mint outbreak in your yard. When dried, foraged or home-grown mint is better than store-bought mint tea, so be sure to pick some extra to dry so you will always have it on hand. To dry mint, just hang it upside down in bunches until the leaves crumble easily between your fingers. Then strip the branches, put the leaves in jars, and store in a dark place.

Kudzu (*Pueraria lobata* (*syn. P. montana, P. thunbergiana*): The scourge of the South, growing as fast as one foot a day, is said to taste like kale. The roots are high in calories, and if ground into powder make a cornstarch substitute — arrowroot powder. It is also plentiful and nutritious livestock fodder. We've never had it ourselves, but we say to our Southern brethren, "Soup's on!"

Prickly Pear Cactus: The young, skinny pads are *nopalitos*, prized in Mexican cuisine. Wearing gloves, use a paring knife or a vegetable peeler to scrape off the thorns and "eyes." They taste a little like green pepper — slimy green pepper. Chop them up for salsa, or scramble them in eggs to reduce the slime factor. Eaten raw, they are reported by Mexican folk medicine to have numerous health benefits. The fruits, or tunas, are delicious, tasting a little like watermelon, but be sure to skin them, or singe them for a few seconds over a flame, before you eat them, or their tiny pricklers will get under your skin and torment you. And just FYI, if you are ever in some kind of grim outdoor survival situation, the big, unpalatable cactus pads are a good source of water.

Fruit Foraging

One day the branch of a fruit tree is covered with pretty blossoms, and then the next time you look at it, the branch is groaning under the weight of more fruit than you can eat or give away. And as with all homegrown food, this fruit is of better quality than anything you can find in the supermarket: plums running over with juice, crisp apples full of subtle flavors, honeyed apricots that have nothing to do with mealy things offered in stores — fruit that would be pesticide soaked if you bought it in the supermarket, or expensive coming from the organic stall at the farmers' market. Despite this fact, a lot of neighborhood fruit goes unpicked, and ends up rotting at the base of the tree.

Why? Anyone who has tried to grow their own food knows there is nothing inconvenient about a plant that needs little care and yet produces bushels of food without prompting each year. Every home should have at least one. If you know some basic preservation techniques, dealing with that bounty does not need to be daunting. All it takes is a day or two to harvest the tree and preserve the fruit — whether that be by drying, canning, fermenting, making jam or even making cider.

It goes against homestead principles to let food go to waste — whether it be on your land, or someone else's. A homesteader keeps their eye open for food-gathering opportunities at home and abroad, because any food you find is food you do not have to grow, and this includes other people's trees. The law states that any fruit growing in a parkway strip, or on branches hanging over a sidewalk or alley is in public space and therefore fair game for you to pick. Of course it is better to ask permission when you can, and of course we don't need to tell you not to break branches, climb on fences, or otherwise behave like a hooligan when you are picking fruit.

If you spot an overloaded tree in someone's yard on your wanderings, and if your surreptitious sampling proves it to be tasty, inquire with the owner and see if they'll let you harvest the whole thing. Odds are they will be grateful to you if you would relieve them of this burden, and will just tell you to take what you want.

As far as we are concerned, there cannot be too many fruit trees in any neighborhood. Unfortunately they are not as common as they should be, perhaps for the aforementioned "messy" reason, or because a couple of generations of bad supermarket fruit has made us suspicious of fruit eating on the whole. With any luck this will change as a new wave of homesteaders, community activists, permaculturists and forward-thinking landscapers begin to transform the urban landscape with food-bearing trees.

No one voices the importance of fruit trees in the urban landscape better than the activist art collective Fallen Fruit. They encourage both fruit foraging and the planting of more fruit trees in public spaces for shared use. We offer you their manifesto for your consideration.

A SPECTER is haunting our cities: barren landscapes with foliage and flowers, but nothing to eat. Fruit can grow almost anywhere, and can be harvested by everyone. Our cities are planted with frivolous and ugly landscaping, sad shrubs and neglected trees, whereas they should burst with ripe produce. Great sums of money are spent on young trees, water and maintenance. While these trees are beautiful, they could be healthy, fruitful and beautiful.

WE ASK all of you to petition your cities and towns to support community gardens and only plant fruit-bearing trees in public parks. Let our streets be lined with apples and pears! Demand that all parking lots be landscaped with fruit trees which provide shade, clean the air and feed the people.

FALLEN FRUIT is a mapping and manifesto for all the free fruit we can find. Every day there is food somewhere going to waste. We encourage you to find it, tend and harvest it. If you own property, plant food on your perimeter. Share with the world and the world will share with you. Barter, don't buy! Give things away! You have nothing to lose but your hunger!

Read more about fruit foraging, the practice of fruit-mapping, and Fallen Fruit's other projects at fallenfruit.org.

Tools For The Fruit Harvester

Properly managed fruit trees are pruned so that their branches do not grow out of easy reach. But the truth is very few trees are managed so well, so when you go foraging (or when you face up to that tree in your own backyard) you are confronted with clusters of tempting fruit dangling just out of reach. A ladder is not convenient to carry around when you are foraging, and even in your own backyard it can be a little perilous swaying around on the top rung trying to reach every last fruit. Far better to stay on solid ground and use a couple of clever tools to bring the fruit to you.

Fruit Picker
This is basically a long hand on a pole that you can stick up into the tree. The business end is a wire cage with claws at the opening. It looks like the skeleton of a catcher's mitt, or maybe like a particularly aggressive light bulb cage. The claws dislodge the fruit and the basket catches it. Fruit pickers are easy to find in garden centers, and you can get one for under 20 dollars.

Berry Hook
This is a more obscure tool, one used for wrestling fruit out of monster bushes or trees with soft, bending branches. We know of it from Samuel Thayer's *Forager's Harvest*. It is simply a stick with a hook on one end and a rope on the other end. Using the hook, you catch a flexible branch and draw it down gently to your level. So you can have your hands free to pick the fruit, you stand on the tail of the rope. You could make one of these easily out of just about anything: wood, bamboo, wire, metal. For instance, you could bend an old ski pole sharply at the tip, and then tie a rope to the handle. Or you could screw a big hook onto a broomstick — then it would be very much like a dive hook you use in dumpster diving. In fact, you might be able to use the same pole for both purposes.

Fruit Picker

Collecting Bin
For efficiency and safety you want both of your hands free as you work, and you don't want to be running back and forth to a stationary container. So you need to either use a shoulder bag — an old messenger bag would work well — or tie a light tub or basket around your waist. A smallish tub is the ideal collection device for berry picking.

How To Eat Acorns
Why should the squirrels have all the fun?

To our way of thinking, acorns fall between wild food gathering and neighborhood fruit foraging. Unlike most fruit trees, acorns grow in the wilderness, and the semi-wilderness, but you are also going to find plenty of them in the city.

They are so ubiquitous, so easy to identify, and so bountiful come fall, that we thought we had to give them their own section.

Acorns have a bad reputation as being inedible, or fit only for animal fodder. This is not so. Acorns were among the primary staples of the Native American tribes. They are an excellent survival food, being rich in calories, complex carbohydrates, good fats, and a fair amount of protein. All you have to do make acorns edible is process them to remove the tannin, which makes them very bitter. Actually, ingesting too much tannin can cause kidney failure, but tannins are so darn bitter you'd be hard pressed to eat enough to kill you. Acorns are not a nut to be eaten out of hand, but they can be made into a nutritious mush or flour.

All varieties of acorns are edible, but some are better than others. It cannot hurt to try any acorns that you can find growing near you, but in general acorns from white oaks, which are the kind with rounded leaves, are preferable to red oaks, the kind with pointy-tipped, many-lobed leaves, because white oak acorns are larger and sweeter. If you are presented with the choice of a few different kinds of oak trees, open up a few nuts. You're looking for big nuts with plump, pale meat showing no sign of bugs. Taste the raw acorns — a little nibble won't kill you. All will be bitter, but choose the tree that produces the least bitter nuts.

Preparing Acorn Mash And Flour

Harvest the nuts in September. If they've been on the ground, they may have bugs in them. Look for tiny boreholes in the shell and discard those. When you bring your acorns home, put them in a bucket of water and discard any that float.

You can let your acorns sit out in the hot sun a few days to dry, and then you can store them out of the way of rodents until you need them. Or you can process them right away.

Acorns have soft shells. Rather then cracking them, you pop off their little hats and then peel them. A pair of pliers helps. As you work, discard any that look dark or dusty inside. The next step is to grind them up. Unless Armageddon is upon us and you have to use two rocks, the easiest way to do this is in a blender. Fill it with whole acorns then add water. Buzz it to form a creamy mash.

This mash needs to be leached to rinse away the bitter tannins. The original method for doing this would be to put the mash in a running stream. Instead, you are going to line a colander with an old dishtowel or a piece of cheesecloth, pour the mash in and let the excess liquid drain away. Tie up the corners of the cloth, and transfer the bundle of mash to a big bowl of water. Let it sit a while until the water goes cloudy/dark, then dump that water and refill the bowl. Put the mash through several changes of water over the course of the day. How many changes depends upon how much tannin was in your acorns.

It is okay to let the mash sit in a bowl of water overnight, and then continue the changing in the morning. Some sources will tell you to put the mash through several changes of boiling water. This is not necessary, and it may lessen the nutrient qualities of the mash, so don't bother.

The mash is done when the water in the bowl no longer goes cloudy, and when the bitter taste is gone. Tannin has a particular mouthfeel that is quite recognizable — it sort of puckers the tongue. When it tastes clear, squeeze all the excess water from the bundle with your hands. It's ready to use.

After processing, the mash can be used right away, frozen for future use, or you can spread it on cookie sheets and dry it in a low oven or dehydrator until it resembles corn meal. Once it is dry, you can whirl it in a food processor for a finer texture.

Acorn meal/flour does not keep as well as normal flour, so keep it in the fridge and use it fairly soon. Try substituting or blending with corn meal in any corn bread/corn muffin recipe. Toss a little acorn flour into any baked good — cookies, bread, pancakes — to improve the nutritional profile of whatever you are baking.

Using The Mash

Acorn mash can be cooked up with water like you would oatmeal. Just add a little more water to your freshly strained mash and simmer it over low heat until it is at a consistency you like. This is a traditional Native American way of eating acorns. The porridge will be on the bland side, and will need to be tricked up either into the sweet realm with fruit and sugar, or the savory realm with salt and butter. Or perhaps toss in parmesan cheese to make a wild polenta. Another traditional use is to stir the mash into meat stews at the very end of cooking to thicken them.

Dumpster Diving

We live in a land of plenty — and in a land of great waste — as any peek in a dumpster will tell you. Behind every apartment building and retail business in this country sits a harvesting opportunity. Dumpster diving is a class of urban foraging akin to fruit gathering. You are simply taking advantage of what others would let go to waste. It combines the thrill of poaching with the heady satisfaction of finding a really great sale. If you like hunting in thrift stores, it is only one small step from that pastime to diving, since dumpsters are full of stuff that people are too lazy to drop off at Goodwill. Selective diving will yield selective results, whether your scavenging interest is food, building materials, books, clothing, or furniture, you can find dumpsters to serve your needs. On top of all these personal benefits, you will also be lessening the load on the landfills. And that is a very good thing.

The Legality Of It

Dumpster diving is not illegal except where is it specifically prohibited. In 1988, the Supreme Court ruled in *California vs. Greenwood* that there is no common-law expectation for privacy of discarded materials. Your local laws may be different, and you do have to pay attention to obvious things like "No Trespassing" signs and locks. These things indicate that the owners are likely to be irate to find you poking around. Never break a lock or jump a fence to get into a dumpster — that is definitely illegal.

Keep it in mind that building owners fear dumping more than diving. They pay to have their dumpsters emptied, and hate when people fill their dumpsters with trash. They also hate people strewing trash when picking through the dumpster. As a sophisticated diver you'll want to give them no cause for concern.

If you dive retail, your first decision is food or not-food. If it is food you are after, then bakeries and markets are your best bets. Bakeries unload day-old bread and pastries every day. Slightly past-prime baked goods can be revived, or used in many ways.

Markets unload food in huge quantities. If you are diving markets, your food preservation skills will come in handy, as markets throw out ripe/bruised/just-expired foods in bulk. Not a single bunch of grapes, but a whole crate of them. Not a quart of milk, but several gallons at a time, a bounty if you know how to process it. Dry the grapes into raisins. Make fruit butter out of a box of apples or peaches that are slightly bruised or past their prime. Make sauce out of soft tomatoes. Make yogurt out of milk that has just hit its expiry date. Yogurt keeps for a long time in the fridge.

Nursery dumpsters are full of perfectly good bags of soil (they can't sell ripped bags, after all). Candy store dumpsters are filled with heart-shaped boxes of candy on February 15th. Any time a product line is discontinued it ends in the trash, whether this be canned soup, shampoo, or a type of wrapping paper. Waste is built into the cost of doing business.

To start, we recommend you read *The Art and Science of Dumpster Diving* by John Hoffman, which not only lucidly explains everything you need to know about this species of urban foraging, but is also so engaging and passionate that even if you are skeptical, it will make a diver out of you. There are few "how-to" books which are so persuasive that they will change the way you think forever. This is one of them.

Revive Day-Old Bread

Our ancestors knew what to do with stale bread, and we should too. Sliced bread does not revive well, but loaves, pastries and bagels can all be revived if they are a day or two old. Wet the bread just little. Dip a loaf under a running tap for just one second, or wet your hands and rub the loaf. A pastry or seedy bagel might have to be misted with a spray bottle so as not to lose the toppings. Pop the bread into a pre-heated 350°F oven. Smaller things will warm in about five minutes, a big loaf will take ten minutes. The bread will be best while warm.

The Classics

There are plenty of recipes out in the world for these things, we just thought we'd remind you of all the dishes that demand stale bread for best results.

- Consider the humble crouton, which is best made with stale bread, as is stuffing, which should not be limited to Thanksgiving, or to meat eaters.
- Never forget that stale bread is ideal for French toast, as well as its more decadent cousin, *pain perdu.*
- Bread pudding is made with stale bread, but it truly is spectacular (if artery-clogging) when made with croissants or cinnamon rolls.
- Bread crumbs, toasted and spiced with whatever you like (hot pepper flakes? lemon zest? basil?), are a largely forgotten but amazing addition on top of cooked vegetables, casseroles and even pasta, as a Parmesan cheese substitute. Frugal Italians have been doing this forever.

Bruschetta

Stale bread is perfect for bruschetta because it makes sturdier toast. Slice up that dumpster loaf and toast the slices in the toaster, under the broiler or on the grill. Drizzle them with olive oil and rub the surface of the bread with a raw clove of garlic. Then add any topping you like: olive paste, pesto, sautéed mushrooms, chopped tomatoes and basil, herbed goat cheese, etc.

Panzanella

In the summer when the tomatoes are in the garden, use stale bread to make a classic summer dish, a bread and tomato salad called panzanella. Being a salad, there is no real set recipe for panzanella beyond the essential combination of bread and tomatoes and basil. Some people make it more substantial by adding hardboiled eggs or tuna. And additional vegetables, like cucumbers or olives. You can rub the bowl with a garlic clove if you want a little flavor kick.

There are no quantities here, because you should just use whatever you have on hand.

Stale bread cut in one-inch cubes
Ripe, delicious tomatoes chopped up
Sweet red onion, sliced or diced
Chopped parsley
Torn-up basil leaves
Red wine vinegar and/or lemon juice
Olive oil
Salt and pepper

Some people like to dip the bread in cold water to soften it up a bit before it goes in the bowl. Others go the other way and toast it until it is crunchy. You might want to leave it as it is, stale and dry, the first time.

Toss together the bread, tomatoes, onions, parsley and basil. Whip up a vinaigrette by mixing the one part vinegar or lemon juice with three parts olive oil. Drizzle this over the salad, add salt and pepper to taste, toss again, and let it rest for 10 minutes so the bread has time to soak up the flavor. Toss once more and serve.

Chapter Four
Keeping Livestock
In The City

Keeping Livestock In The City

Just as it is possible to grow produce in the city, it is also possible to raise your own livestock — it is just a matter of figuring out what you need livestock for, and what kind of stock fits best into your life. We are confident that in the coming years urban livestock is going to become more and more common, because the current situation with our food is just untenable. Food should be a simple pleasure to buy and prepare, the act of eating with family and friends a respite from the worries of the world. But when we are in the supermarket, a vague anxiety haunts our decision-making — where did this food come from? Is it safe? Was it responsibly raised?

These questions apply to all of our food, but they become particularly charged in regard to animal products, for one because it seems animal products have been monkeyed with more than anything else (antibiotics, growth hormones, irradiation, ultra-pasteurization, brine plumping, etc.), and then there is the awful specter of factory farming, which is enough to give even the most determined carnivore a moment of pause. So each trip to the supermarket becomes a minefield that we have to negotiate with our wallet in one hand and our ethics in the other.

One way to opt out of this anxiety is to grow your own. Just as you grow your own vegetables for flavor, convenience, and quality, you can also provide yourself with eggs and meat. You might not be able to cover all of your needs on your little city lot, but it feels good to do even a little in this direction. Raising your own stock is a way of pushing back at the creeping desensitization of the industrial lifestyle, a way of reconnecting with the cycles of nature, a way of tasting just what it is that we have lost.

Animals Make Your Garden Better

Gardening produces green waste. Your household produces food waste. Farm animals eat this waste and make fertilizer out of it, accomplishing overnight what would otherwise take weeks of decomposition in a compost pile. Then you add their manure to the compost pile, and its "heat" (nitrogen content) speeds along the decomposition of everything else you've thrown in there. You end up with more compost faster, and better crops, which in turn feed the critters better, and they give you more poop. It's a happy feedback loop.

Animals Give You Gifts

The pleasant compost feedback loop may be enough of a reason to keep a few animals in itself, but the benefits are extended if you use animal products.

Chickens will give you fertilizer *and* eggs, angora rabbits will give you fertilizer *and* hair for knitting. And yes, then there is the meat.

In the city we are so far disconnected from our food sources that the idea of raising animals for meat is a little shocking. But of course, if you are a meat-eater, meat does get to your table somehow, and that somehow is usually not a story you want to hear.

If you raise and slaughter your own meat you'll know the animal was raised in the best conditions imaginable — with air and sunlight and stimulation and healthy food. You'll know that it is organic and you'll know it was slaughtered humanely. Your awareness of this animal's life and its sacrifice for you will give significance back to the act of eating. You will also know that you have reached an impressive level of self-sufficiency for a city slicker. Should it be necessary, you could expand your flocks and feed your family.

It is easy to spend all of your time in an electronic bubble. The moment you step into the animal realm, they invert your frequencies. Just being near them hooks you irresistibly into the natural world. You observe their life cycle, and you become aware of your own life cycle, and your place in things. All this aside, it is fun to have them around.

The Chicken is the New Pug

The laying hen is the indisputable queen of urban stock. Chickens are so easy to raise and useful in so many ways, it is easy to see why they are popular. Anywhere you find people, you are likely to find chickens — they are nearly as ubiquitous as dogs — and have been for thousands of years since they were first lured out of the jungles of East Asia and into domestication.

Chickens are a great starter animal for any urban homesteader. They are not exotic or hard to come by. They don't require much space. There is a large knowledge bank both in print and on the web about chickens. While raising animals for slaughter is a big mental step for us urbanites, it is not at all hard to get accustomed to eating fresh, free-range eggs.

Nothing is quite so relaxing as sitting around the backyard, watching chicken TV. Time stops and the blood pressure drops. It is satisfying just to catch a fleeting glimpse of them out the window, running around your yard doing their chicken thing. Up close, chickens are fierce, funny, strange creatures, stupid and smart at the same time. With their bright eyes, sharp beaks and huge claws, they seem more like tiny T-Rexes than anything else.

Chickens are formidable bug catchers, earth scratchers and eaters of weeds. If you put chickens on a fallow garden bed or a sort of weedy, desolate part of the yard that you would like to plant something in, the chickens will handily clear that space of weeds and bugs and fertilize it for you while they are at it. They will eat your kitchen scraps. They will eat the stuff you have to pull out of your garden bed. They'll gobble up the slugs, snails and tomato worms that you are too squeamish to squish.

The nitrogen-rich droppings from their coop do great things for your compost pile. But you never want to put their poop straight on your crops. Instead, when you clean out their henhouse, you add their dirty bedding into your compost pile, and all that nitrogen heats up your pile and makes it decompose faster.

Homegrown chicken eggs are a revelation. They are beautiful, come in all kinds of shapes and sizes and colors, and are fresh and tasty, with the rich yellow-orange yolks telling you that the hen is eating well. Eggs from pasture-raised hens have better nutritional profiles than the prison-raised eggs from the grocery store. For the October 2007 issue, *Mother Earth News* analyzed eggs from 14 pasture-raised flocks and came up with these impressive numbers:

Compared to confined hens, pasture-raised eggs may contain:
- ⅓ less cholesterol
- ¼ less saturated fat
- ⅔ more vitamin A
- 2 times more omega-3 fatty acids
- 3 times more vitamin E
- 7 times more beta carotene

Read the whole article at **motherearthnews.com/eggs.aspx**

As far as practicalities go, the number of eggs a hen will lay varies by breed, diet, hen age and season, but you can expect a good layer will give you about an egg a day at her peak. Three a week is pretty average.

The single most common question people ask us about our hens is "Do they need a rooster to lay eggs?" The answer is you only need a rooster if you want chicks.

Chickens For Meat

We bow to you, intrepid carnivorous homesteader, for even thinking about it in this day and age! It is a brave and honest thing to butcher what you eat. If you eat your own chickens you can be sure that your meat is free of hormones and antibiotics, and that your chicken lived the best life a chicken can hope for, and died with dignity.

As ideal as this sounds, raising chickens for meat in the city is going to be difficult. Once in a blue moon you might have to cull a chicken from your backyard flock and give it a respectful stewing. But to consistently feed your family with your own backyard chickens — this is tough. Birds need to be raised in quantity and on the cheap to make it worthwhile. You most likely cannot keep enough of them in your small, expensive, urban backyard for it to pay off on a dollar per pound basis — and even if you can, keeping that many chickens might well be classed a nuisance activity. Most cities have laws against operating backyard slaughterhouses. When all is said and done, you may as well go to Whole Foods and buy the most expensive, pasture-fed, free-range, spa-raised chicken you can find and save yourself trouble and money.

All the more sensible chicken books offer advice on slaughtering and cleaning birds. *Chickens in Your Backyard, Living with Chickens* and the various Storey Guides to Chickens and Poultry offer how-to's to the curious.

Egg Pie

This is one of our household staples. It is basically a crustless quiche. It is easy to throw together, uses up eggs, and can be tweaked to accommodate any leftovers or garden produce you have on hand.

6 medium leeks, cut into rings and rinsed, tender parts only
3/4 cup whole wheat flour
1 teaspoon salt, pepper to taste
4 eggs, beaten
1 cup milk
1/3 lb feta cheese
9" pie dish or cake pan, greased

1   Preheat oven to 375°F.
2   Sauté the leeks in olive oil until tender, about 5 minutes. Let it sit while you do the next step.
3   In a big bowl combine the flour and salt and pepper. Add the eggs (which are already slightly beaten) and the milk. Using a whisk, blend until smooth. It will look like pancake batter. Stir in the cooked leeks and crumbled feta.
4   Pour it all into the greased pan. Bake for 45 to 50 minutes. Poke the center with a knife to see if it is cooked through. The knife should come out clean.

Chicken Q & A

Where Do You Get Chickens?

A feed store. This is the instant gratification option. If you want chickens and you want them now, go to a feed store and buy some chicks. You can find these stores on the fringes of the city, out in the suburbs, or anywhere horsey, where they might be called "Feed & Tack" stores. You may never have seen one in your life, but if you get chickens, you're going to become a regular customer, because this is where you get your chicken feed, bedding and accessories.

Not all feed stores sell chicks, so call ahead.

Spring is prime chick time, and the best time to buy. Come summer, the stores might not be ordering chicks anymore because of the stress of shipping them in the heat. They tend to carry the popular utilitarian breeds, like Rhode Island Reds and Plymouth Rocks. These are not fancy, but they are hearty breeds and good layers. Be sure they are selling sexed chicks, so you don't end up with a bunch of cockerels — that is, young roosters. Young hens are called pullets.

If you want a fancy breed of chicken, or if you want to buy an adult chicken, an individual breeder or small farm is your best bet. Finding these nice people might take some time. Your first recourse is asking other urbanites with fancy chickens where they got theirs. Next, search the web pages related to the breeds you are interested in. Just like the world of show dogs, there are chicken breeders, chicken shows and breed clubs. Go to state fairs and livestock shows. Write to a club and ask if they have any members in your area. Buying from a breeder who is dedicated to improving the breed and is the best way to find high quality stock. The cost of these chickens will vary widely, depending on the rarity of the breed, the age of the bird, and the breeder.

When you research chicken breeds online, you will find hatchery websites, McMurray's being the best known. These are huge operations that specialize in selling eggs and newborn fowl of all sorts. They are a great source of pictures and breed information, but not ideal for the urban homesteader because they sell in bulk.

Large hatcheries are accustomed to selling to folks with much larger operations than yours, so a minimum order of 25 is common. This is not out of cantankerousness as much as it seems that packing the little chicks together improves their chances of surviving shipping. Yes, shipping. As amazing as it sounds, they put newly-hatched chicks in boxes and send them to you by U.S. mail. It seems that chicks come out of the shell fortified by their yolk, so can survive for a day or two without food or water.

With the growing popularity of backyard chickens, there are now a few places willing to cater to people who only want a handful of chickens. These places are like boutique hatcheries, and are willing to sell chicks or pullets in small numbers for slightly higher prices than the mammoth hatcheries. One such company is My Pet Chicken. We've not ordered from them ourselves, but they have a minimum order of three chicks, and a fair selection of breeds.

A word of advice about ordering from a hatchery. Chicks are sold "straight run" or "sexed." "Straight run," which means the chicks are sold in mixed gender groups. "Sexed" means that sorting experts have sorted out the newborn pullets from the cockerels. You'll want to look for the term "sexed pullets." It's actually quite an art to sex a chicken, and the accuracy rate is about 95%. If you want to be 100% sure of the gender of your chicks, your only option, apart from buying adults, is to buy Sex Link chicks: hybrids with coloration linked to sex.

You also might find a chicken by chance. Look around your neighborhood for people who raise chickens. Once you start looking, you will spot them. They might have spares. Try online listings like Craigslist, or try the animal shelter if you want to do a good deed, but be prepared to pay steep adoption fees.

No matter where you end up getting your birds, or how old they are, look for chickens that are brimming with health. They should be active, alert and bright-eyed. Their plumage should be clean. Look at their rear ends in particular—if their butts aren't clean and fluffy there's a problem. Don't adopt sickly chickens out of pity. Sickly chickens don't have a lot of disease resistance, and they could endanger the rest of your birds.

Also look at the whole operation. Are the chickens well housed? Are they clean? Does their food and water look clean and fresh? Does the place stink?

You just don't want to take chances on bringing home a chicken with diseases or parasites. If the place is dirty, just walk out.

I talked about keeping chickens long before I had them. Finally, one of my garden students was moving and had to find a home for her own two hens, and into my lap they fell, coop and all. Convenient, yes? How could my husband Nick say no? This was about 12 years ago. I was immediately hooked.

I have a list of virtuous reasons for loving our hens:
- Delicious eggs with golden orange yolks.
- The cycle of the chickens in the garden — feeding them kitchen and garden scraps, their manure cooking our generous compost heap into a rich dark (and fast) pile of garden soil.
- The bad bugs they eat (Nick brings them the grasshoppers, snails and slugs he collects in the garden).
- The urban farm-girl that our daughter Lily has become; learning the garden cycle while collecting eggs daily and delivering fruit-rinds and greens to the girls.

But the things I flat-out enjoy the most are not about virtue or use — they are about having them. Naming them, feeding them, talking to them (which is stupid I know, and I don't care) and just plain watching them. There is a chicken culture, a pecking order, a collective grooming, relationships, even personalities, and that is what keeps me maintaining a flock. They populate the garden, they are of the garden and yet alien creatures. I don't speak their language except when I bring food. I am not their friend but their provider, willing to wash feet and delouse when necessary.

Really, an urban chicken is a pet that provides. I love the providing of our daily eggs and the cycle of glorious decay and growth from it that they provide for the garden, but I must admit, that I am as much a collector of these creatures, and it is their presence here that I enjoy the most, their lovely movement through the garden.

Laura Cooper, Los Angeles, CA

How Many Chickens Should I Get? What About Roosters?

Chickens are social creatures. It is cruel to keep only one. How many you decide to keep will ultimately depend on how much space you have, and how many eggs you want. Three to six hens is a pretty reasonable city flock.

On your urban homestead, you should only keep hens. Roosters are illegal in most cities, and nothing will get you served with a complaint faster than a crowing rooster. That said, roosters are undeniably handsome, full of personality, and valiant guardians of their hens. If you live in the rare neighborhood where you can get away with it, by all means get yourself a rooster.

What Kind Of Chicken Should I Get?

The world of chicken breeds is astonishing. A short jaunt on the Internet will open your eyes to the possibilities. Search for poultry breed clubs and fan sites.

The catalogs and websites of hatcheries — commercial suppliers of chickens and other fowl — are good places to find pictures and a quick rundown on the different varieties.

If you're interested in helping to preserve rare heritage breeds in your home flock, look up The Society for the Preservation of Poultry Antiquities (see resources). This is a great way to help preserve genetic diversity—and get to keep some mighty fine chickens at the same time.

There is considerable difference in temperament between breeds. No matter what the breed, though, temperament does vary by individual, and it is also affected by how the chicken is raised.

The only breed we would stay away from the Cornish Cross, the most common meat chicken in the world. These big white birds are bred to put on massive amounts of weight quickly, often overtaxing their skeletal system. They are meant to be slaughtered young, and have neither the common sense nor the immune system to make a good backyard chicken. There are more sturdy, savvy meat chickens to be had, if that's what you want.

Note that chickens come in two size categories: standard and bantam. Standard chickens are in the six- to ten-pound range, while bantams weigh in at only two to four pounds. Yes, that's where we get the name of the boxing class, *bantamweight*. Bantams are a great choice for folks with limited space. Three bantam eggs = two standard eggs. Not bad for such little guys.

If you do not wish to consider your chickens pets, the best thing to do is to keep a flock that is all one breed, and try not to name them. It is much easier to keep a business-like attitude regarding your hens if you don't see them as individuals.

Raising Chicks

Tiny baby chicks need lots of attention. They have to be kept constantly warm and safe. They need to be housed in a brooder, and need special chick food. They are undeniably cute, and always entertaining, so playing chicken nanny for a few weeks is kind of fun if you've got the time. It also makes them more comfortable with you in turn, which is good, because that means they'll be easier to handle as adults.

Adult Hens

The adult hen is the plug-and-play poultry option. They will not need special tending. From the start they can live outside, in their coop, where they won't take up too much of your time. Best of all, they will lay for you immediately (or at least as soon as they relax and settle in to their new home). If you get chicks, you will have to wait until they are six months old before you will get your first eggs. If you get an adult hen, you will be guaranteed against getting a rooster by accident. Purchasing adult hens takes the trouble and guess-work out of acquiring chickens. You will just have to put in more research on the front end to find yourself a small farm or breeder who is willing to sell you a few hens.

We've heard lifespan estimates for a pet chicken varying from three to 15 years, depending on the source of the information. There seems to be no agreement on the matter. A hen rarely dies of old age — disease or predation generally take them first. But even five years is a long life compared to the fate of the majority of chickens. In factory situations, broilers are slaughtered at seven weeks, laying hens just after they pass their peak production season: 18 months.

What Kind Of Setup Do I Need To Keep Chickens?

Hens need a little house to sleep in at night, and a place to lay their eggs. This is called a henhouse. The henhouse should have a fenced exercise yard attached to it, so they can come outside, but still be contained. That's called the run. The henhouse and the run in combination are called the coop.

Our coop measures 4' x 12'. The walls of the run are made of ½" hardware cloth affixed to pressure-treated lumber. The house is made of corrugated aluminum roofing material and plywood. All of the doors lock. We put a small door on the exterior wall of the house that leads to the nesting box. This modest-sized coop is big enough for our four hens because they are let out most days to free-range.

Your henhouse can be hand-built, appropriated, or purchased readymade.

It can be a trashy-looking thing made out of scrap wood or an elegant petite chateau d' poulet. People re-purpose doghouses and tool sheds for chickens.

They could even live in an old trailer or van.

In the simplest terms a henhouse is a box with a dirt, wood or concrete floor, a bar for roosting and a nesting box or two for laying. They like to share nesting boxes, so you don't need one for every hen. One box for four hens is sufficient.

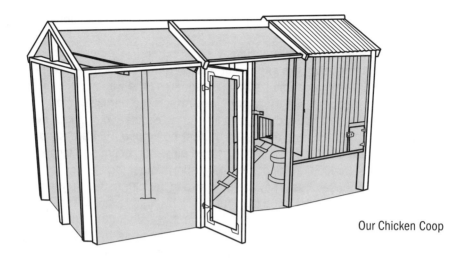

Our Chicken Coop

Size-wise, think doghouse for three hens and suburban garden shed for six to eight. If you let your chickens out of the house and into their run, or out to free-range during the day — and we are hoping you will — the henhouse proper is just a place for the chickens to sleep at night and lay their eggs, so you need only allow about four square feet per hen. However, if they are going to spend a lot of time inside, then you should allow at least 10 square feet per hen.

Whatever you build or buy or improvise, it's important that the whole thing should open up for easy cleaning, for your sake as well as the neighbors'. If it is a pain in the ass to clean, you won't clean it often enough. It's best if you can stand up in your coop.

The house needs to be built tight so that the chickens aren't drafty in the winter, but it must have good cross-ventilation for the summer. Chickens, especially the big fat breeds, do very well in the cold, but unless you live in southern climes, do insulate their henhouse, and give them lots of thick deep bedding in the winter. A south-facing window on the house really helps raise the daytime temperatures inside, and on the coldest nights, you might want to consider running a heat lamp.

More than anything else, your henhouse must be built to keep out predators.

Raccoons, dogs, cats, opossums, coyotes, snakes, skunks and hawks are all more than happy to eat your chickens or eggs if given a chance. The raccoon is the craftiest chicken predator of all. As a result the henhouse should lock down like a high-security prison at night. Think about this: raccoons can eat chickens right through one-inch chicken wire. Yep, that's right, they just pull the chickens through one bite at a time. The problem with raccoons is that they have hands.

Therefore "chicken wire" is obviously a misnomer. The largest wire you can get away with using anywhere in your coop is ½" hardware cloth — not a cloth, really, but wire mesh made up of sturdy ½" squares. The wire must be stapled tight, because raccoons will try to pry it up. Attach the hardware cloth to the wood with the kind of heavy-duty galvanized staples that you nail in, not the kind that shoot out of a staple gun. The safest henhouse will have solid walls and ½" hardware cloth over the windows and air vents, because raccoons are expert climbers. In addition, all doors and windows must lock — not just latch. Raccoons can open latches. They are also strong enough to bend plywood and pry open doors. Protect the coop from tunneling by sinking wire or metal sheeting beneath the ground, or building a solid floor. If you doubt that these precautions are necessary, take a spin through any chicken message board and you will find enough bloody tales of predator ingenuity to scare your pants off.

The chicken run is the yard attached to the henhouse. You don't have to have one, but it allows them to be outdoors, yet still safe and contained. The run should be four times the square footage of the henhouse, at minimum. It is usually made of wire mesh stapled over a frame. It should be roofed, or partially roofed, to keep out hawks and allow the chickens to escape the sun and the rain. Aviary netting is an inexpensive way to keep hawks out and keep chickens in.

The most ideal run would be situated to catch morning sunshine (sunshine kills bacteria) and some shade from the hot afternoon sun. But if you don't have these exact conditions, don't let it stop you from getting chickens, because they are adaptable creatures.

What Do They Eat?

We give our hens constant access to an organic feed formulated for layers so we know they're getting their vitamins and minerals. On top of that they get handfuls of whole grain from our kitchen, or their much-loved scratch, scattered in their playpen and/or run to keep them busy. Chicken scratch is a cheap blend of cracked corn and other grains that they just go nuts over — it's a high-carb treat for them.

Chickens adore greens, so to keep them happy, and to coax their egg yolks to that deep orange color, we give them greens every day — weeds, thinnings from our garden beds, vegetable prep scraps from the kitchen, whatever is on hand, as long as it is fresh. They eat fruit too. Ours love to chase after grapes, making grape races our favorite sport here at the homestead.

And of course, they always have a sharp eye out for bugs.

A Galvanized Water Fountain
for Chickens

So that's how we do it, for what it's worth. We think variety and a lot of fresh food is key. Other people feed them nothing but commercial feed. Others go the opposite route, study chicken nutrition tables and concoct custom feed blends for their girls. Still others feed them a base diet of scratch, and then let them forage the rest.

Chickens need grit, which is fine gravel, to help them digest their food. If they eat nothing but commercial feed, you don't have to worry about it, because it has grit in it. And if they are free-ranging in a yard with access to dirt, they'll find grit on their own, but if they are confined, and eating anything besides commercial food, then they'll need supplemental grit. You can buy this at feed stores and just put a tray of it out for them, or sprinkle it over their food.

Another supplement they'll need when they're laying is calcium. You can clean and pulverize their own eggshells to make a calcium supplement, or buy a bag of ground oyster shells at the feed store. If you go the eggshell route, never throw recognizable eggshells to them, or they might develop a taste for their own eggs.

Chickens need plenty of fresh water. You'll need to get yourself a poultry fountain. This ingenious device cannot be perched on, pooped in or knocked over, and delivers constant fresh water. Best of all, you don't have to fill it very often.

There are plastic or galvanized steel models—we prefer the latter. They are an example of beautiful industrial design.

Caring for chickens takes a bit of time, but the real work is all on the front end, raising them from chicks, and setting up the coop and containment systems.

Once you've got that stuff sorted out, they're not really much more trouble than a house cat, or more precisely, a bunch of cats. They need daily care, and a watchful eye. You have to monitor their food and water, collect their eggs and keep their coop clean.

Besides these basics, if you let them loose in your yard, you have to monitor their comings and goings, and close them up in their house at sundown for their own protection. In the morning they depend on you getting out of bed and letting them out again. Chickens are morning people. If you have the schedule of a vampire, you might not be a chicken person.

Coop cleaning isn't a huge chore if you only have a few hens. Unless they are confined in the henhouse, they won't stay in it past dawn, except for laying.

So all they really do in the henhouse is sleep up on their roost, and their droppings end up in a neat line beneath the roosting bar. We just sweep them out into a big dustpan every other day and drop them in the compost pile. In the run, where they do their wandering and scratching, we use something called the deep bedding technique.

Chickens are diggers. In a confined space, they will turn ordinary ground into a moonscape within days, so we provide them with a thick layer of bedding to dig in. We only do this in their run, because they do nothing in their house but sleep, but if your hens will spend a lot of awake time indoors, you'd want deep bedding on the floor of the house too. The bedding is whatever we have on hand, usually a mix of fallen leaves, aged wood shavings and straw, laid down a foot deep. This mulch layer gives them something to scratch in, and it also catches their droppings. As they scratch, they work their poop into the mulch. In essence, the floor of their run becomes a compost pile. It's not stinky, it makes them happy, and best of all, you don't have to change it out very often. How often will vary by the size of your flock and the depth of your mulch, but we're talking months here. And when you do change it for fresh, the stuff you take out is ready for mulching.

Will The Chickens Get Along With My Dog? My Cat?

Maybe, maybe not. Many people find that dogs and chickens ignore each other entirely. Chickens-as-pets type books are very rosy about the whole thing and imply that your yard can be like a peaceable kingdom, but we've heard enough gruesome stories to make this a dubious claim.

It makes sense to err on the side of caution, and never leave your dog alone with your chickens. Be aware, too, that many dog attacks don't come from the household dog, but from neighbor dogs who break into the yard, so secure your gates and fences, and remember that dogs can dig under fences.

As far as cats go, it is doubtful that a cat will try to take down an eight-pound hen, but a pullet or a bantam hen, being close in size to pigeons, are within cat capabilities. Chicks (fluffy, squeaky, tasty) are the most perfect cat toy ever invented and must be defended vigilantly from all kitties.

What About The Noise?

A rooster's crow is a joyous, life-affirming assertion of his fine-feathered masculinity.

We live within earshot of two roosters, and while it is pleasant to hear them from the distance, we wouldn't want to live next door to them — they crow all the time. They might crow at dawn, sure, but the fact is that they crow whenever they damn well feel like it.

Hens make noise too, but at a much lower order of magnitude. Mostly they have throaty clucks and coos that are pleasing to hear, but once in a while they do cackle. Cackling is that classic *"cluck-cluck-cluck-cluKA!"* noise that you will recognize from the background soundtracks from films and TV shows set in the country, and it can be quite loud. Hens cackle before, during, and just after laying an egg. Some lay quietly, others make a big production about it, and frankly, we don't blame them.

In our neighborhood, chickens are part of the soundscape, quieter than the barking dogs, the squawking of crows and feral parrots, the band practicing up the street, the roar of helicopters and lawnmowers, and the broken soundtrack of an omnipresent roving ice cream truck. Your neighborhood may be different. Generally speaking, the more affluent and tidy the neighborhood, the higher your risk of complaints about the noise.

A good thing to know is that chickens wake up to sunlight, and sleep when it is dark. So if you keep them in their house at night, and their house is lightproof, then they should stay quiet until you get up in the morning and let them out.

What About Avian Flu?

This particular concern happens to be low on our list of worries. But yes, theoretically it is possible that your birds could catch avian flu, so we're going to give you the official line on the subject.

First, keep wild birds from interacting with your chickens by keeping them in a covered enclosure. Keep wild birds from pooping near your chickens, or sharing their food and water. The second and more important line of defense is simply keeping other people who own chickens away from your flock. Likewise, if you visit another flock, change your shoes and clothes before walking into your own coop. That is how contamination is most likely to happen in the urban environment — by a person transferring the disease from one flock of chickens to another.

If you want a realistic peek into the chicken world, try visiting one of the online chicken forums listed in the resources section of this book to get a sense of the challenges of chicken raising, but remember that people tend to post when they have problems, not when everything is going swimmingly.

Inspecting Their Asses

A good indicator of chicken health is a fluffy, clean butt. When things go wrong, the ass is often the first indicator of trouble. You might find poop gathering up there ("pasting up"), or even more appealing, crawling lice. Most homesteaders are DIY when it comes to chicken medicine: dusting them for lice and mites, or oiling their legs for leg mites, hitting them with some antibiotics if they develop a respiratory infection, or de-pasting their asses. The best medicine is prevention. If you keep your hens clean and dry, feed them right, let them have lots of sunshine and fresh air, you will go a long way toward preventing trouble.

Keeping Them From Killing One Another

Chickens live to peck. Sometimes they start pecking one another, out of boredom, or to figure out their place in the hierarchy of the flock. This is where the phrase *pecking order* comes from. If they draw blood, they'll peck all the more enthusiastically, and if one chicken starts this, the others will join in, sometimes pecking one of their hapless coop mates to death. Cannibalism of this type is common in situations where the birds are confined, overcrowded and bored. This is why all factory chickens are de-beaked. Cannibalism is thankfully uncommon among spoiled home flocks, but once in a while a bad seed turns up — a hen who just can't stop pecking her neighbors. There are several ways to discourage this behavior, beginning with introducing toys in the coop and ending with a stock pot and a *bouquet di garni*.

Out-and-out cannibalism should not be confused with pecking-order squabbles, though they can be interrelated. You can expect that the chicken on the lowest rung of the coop's social hierarchy will receive her share of pecking, but the damage should be more along the lines of lost feathers, not open wounds.

The Smell

Chickens coops smell if you don't commit to keeping them clean. The job of sweeping out the henhouse is really not hard, but must be done regularly. And you should also know that chicken poop also attracts flies.

Culling

Even if you never intend to eat your chickens, you still may have to do the dark deed. You might acquire a rooster by accident and be unable to fob it off on anyone. You might have a cannibal chicken that you cannot reform. You might have a sick chicken that is suffering. To our way of thinking, it is inevitable that the path of keeping chickens will, at some point, converge with the path of killing chickens. Welcome to the cycle of life and death.

Possible Trouble With The Neighbors Or The Law

Regulations regarding the keeping of backyard livestock are usually found within your city's municipal code, which you can find online off your city's homepage. It may be listed under land use regulations, public health regulations or animal control regulations. What you will find are guidelines as to how far your livestock must be kept from your neighbors and/or how many animals you can keep, if any, and/or whether or not you must apply for a permit.

Some cities effectively forbid homesteaders from keeping chickens by mandating that the chicken coop must be kept at great distances (100 feet, for instance) from all neighbors. More reasonable cities stipulate distances in the range of 30 feet or so. But even 30 feet may be prohibitive on a small urban lot. This is one reason that would keep many a homesteader from registering his stock with the city.

The truth is that many people who keep chickens or other backyard livestock ignore, or remain studiously unaware of, city code — just as many dog owners do. As long as they can keep in good standing with their neighbors, there is, after all, no need for the city to ever know about their pet chickens.

If your city forbids livestock keeping, we encourage you to change the law. In 2004, a group of poultry fanciers calling themselves "Mad City Chickens" in Madison, Wisconsin did just that. Under organized pressure, the city changed its poultry laws from disallowing any poultry-keeping at all to allowing four laying hens per backyard.

Neighbors, not the city, are the real x-factor in whether or not you will be able to keep your backyard flock. The city you live in probably doesn't have time to search out chicken code violators, but they will enforce the law if neighbors complain.

Some people have negative associations with chickens. You need to educate them on the vast difference between a overcrowded poultry factory and your tiny, pampered flock. Other people will be generally ignorant of basic things, like the fact that hens do not crow. Your most recalcitrant types will understand all of this, but still fear that the mere presence of chickens will send their property values plummeting.

Take stock of your situation before you bring home your chickens. If you can maintain a flock within the letter of the law, you have less to worry about.

If you are going to try to stretch the law a bit to keep chickens, then you must be able to negotiate with your neighbors, and appease them any way you can.

This will vary by situation. If they can see into your yard, for instance, you might want to build an attractive coop, show them how clean and well considered your setup is. Bribing them with eggs is an excellent strategy, too. If your neighbors are of the type that never step outside, they might never even know you have chickens. In that case, discretion is your watchword.

The following pages cover other livestock options for the urban homesteader, critters you might want to keep instead of chickens, or better yet, in addition to chickens.

HOW TO SET UP A BROODER FOR YOUR NEW CHICKS

A brooder is just a warm box, and is not to be confused with an incubator, which is a much more sophisticated piece of equipment designed for hatching eggs. The purpose of the brooder is to replicate the body temperature environment that the chicks would have under their mother's body. They need heat assistance, though progressively less of it, for their first five weeks.

When chicks are newly hatched they are extremely sensitive to temperature fluctuations and drafts, so it is your job to keep them as warm as possible. Ideally, you will have your brooder all set up and ready to go when your chicks come home.

Most people keep their chicks in the house for four to six weeks, both to keep them warm and to keep a close eye on them. (The truth is you'll find it hard to take your eyes off the chicks.) But if that is not possible, you may keep the brooder out in the henhouse or in the garage, as long as you can manage to keep them warm and safe, but be warned—they do require a good deal of attention at first, so it is actually easier to have them close at hand.

To set up a brooder you'll need:
- A cardboard box, size varies by chick quantity
- A desk lamp with an adjustable neck
- A 60-watt bulb for the lamp. Red preferred, but white is OK.
- A piece of screen or an old kitchen towel
- Dry litter (see below for options)
- A chick feeder and waterer
- A long, skinny stick

Start With A Box

A brooder is nothing but a box full of litter with a lamp warming it. A cardboard box with tall sides works well for this purpose. An aquarium would work too, but not a bird cage, because that's too drafty. The size of the box depends on how many chicks you have, but to begin it does not have to be large at first. As they grow, you can move them into progressively larger boxes. You'll get a feel for when they need more room just by watching them go about their business.

Then You Need A Lamp

The chicks must be kept at 90°–95° for their first week of life (which is not necessarily the first week you have them—ask their age when you buy them). After their first week, you can lower the temperature by five degrees per week for five weeks. At five weeks of age they have all of their feathers, and should be able to live without extra heat, unless the weather is very cold.

If you are keeping them indoors, all you need to do to keep their box warm is put a 60-watt bulb (a red bulb is nice) in a gooseneck lamp and aim it at the floor of your brooder. If you put a thermometer on the floor beneath the lamp it should read in the 90°–95° for new chicks. Move the lamp neck up and down to adjust the temperature. You may have to cut a slit at the top edge of the box to allow the neck of the lamp to lean low. Of course the far corners of the box will be cooler, and that is a good thing, because it gives the chicks options.

The chicks will tell you if you've got the temperature right, so much so that you don't really need the thermometer. If the area under the lamp is too warm, they will avoid it, and sleep in remote corners. If the whole box is way too hot, they'll stand around with their beaks hanging open, panting. If they are cold, they will huddle in a pile right under the lamp and peep in a loud, shrill, complaining manner. That's bad. What you want to see relaxed chicks moving at will all around the box, cheeping occasionally, exploring all the corners. They will usually sleep beneath the lamp, but they won't be in a miserable huddle.

If you want to keep the chicks out in the henhouse or in the garage, and the outdoor temperatures are low, you will need to use a proper heat lamp to ward off the cold. You can buy these at a feed store. If the temperatures are mild, a regular light bulb of higher wattage might provide enough heat. Just be sure to make frequent trips out to the henhouse to monitor the chicks' behavior, and back up your observations with a thermometer.

And Some Litter

Lining the floor of the box with sheets of newspaper alone is a bad idea because it is a slippery surface which will make the little guys' legs splay—permanently. Chicks need a surface that they can grip. We used some plastic screen material that we had on hand, with newspaper beneath it for absorbency. You can also use an old kitchen towel or piece of burlap instead of screen. For their first day in the box this is all they should get in the way of bedding. They need to learn where the food is kept. Once they know that, then you can add some litter. If you introduce them to a new food source and new litter at the same time, they might end up confused and start to eat the litter. Chicks do need some protection from themselves.

On day two, you can add litter to the box. You don't have to: you can just keep changing towels. In big operations chicks are raised on elevated wire because it is cleaner, but it is fun for them to scratch in litter. Scratching and pecking is *what they do*. The first moment you offer them dirt or litter, they will start scratching instinctively— joyously.

For litter you can use anything dry and clean, with the exception of cedar shavings and fresh pine shavings because both give off fumes that can overwhelm chicks. You can use soil from your garden, or dry peat moss, or straw, or sand, or shredded paper, or aged wood shavings. Whatever you use, you must change their litter frequently—like every other day—because poor hygiene leads straight to sick chicks.

Chicks cannot be allowed to live in wet or dirty conditions, because they are susceptible to a deadly disease called coccidiosis, which is caused by an intestinal parasite called coccidian that is naturally present in the chicks' guts and thrives in dirty brooders.

And Don't Forget A Lid

For the first week you will want to cover the top of the box to help keep the heat in. This never works gracefully, because the lamp is in the way. But you can balance a piece of cardboard or drape a towel over the top of the box. Be sure to leave some space open so they get enough air, be sure the lamp doesn't burn the cardboard or cloth, and be sure the lid does not make it too hot in the box. It seems to work out somehow, but to us, scalding hot lamp + flammable litter + fluffy chicks = high disaster potential.

Another good reason for a lid is to keep the chicks in the box. It seems that just when they don't need the extreme warmth any longer and you could do without the lid, they start to flap and jump like maniacs. An old window screen over the top of the box will gently deflect

Chick Feeder

those high jumps (we swear they'd brain themselves on something hard). Aviary netting also works, the kind you buy in garden centers to keep birds off your plantings.

Put In A Feeder And Waterer

Special chick feeders and waterers are available at feed stores and online. Of course chicks have survived for eons without any equipment at all. The idea behind specialty feeders and waterers is that they keep the food and water clean, and the litter in the brooder dry. Chicks must have a constant supply of fresh water, and they definitely know if it is fresh or not. Store-bought waterers are designed to magically refill themselves as the chicks drink, and to prevent the chicks from soiling and/or accidentally drowning in water dishes. Being cheap, we didn't want to buy equipment we'd only use for a few weeks, so we improvised a waterer with a tuna can, and made a feeding trough out of a toothpaste box. We made it through, but next time, we'll fork out the cash for the store-bought, impervious models. Chicks are great at making messes.

NOTE: When you first bring your chicks home, it is important that you show them where they can find a drink. Do this when you first put them in the brooder, by gently dipping each of their beaks in the water.

And, Finally, The Stick

Poke a long, thin stick, somewhere between pencil and finger width, all the way through your box, about two inches off the ground, to provide them with a perch. It takes them a while to figure out how to perch, but they love trying.

Ducks

Ducks are an alternative or complement to chickens. Obtaining and raising ducks is similar to chicken keeping: e.g. you can buy them from hatcheries or feed stores, ducklings are raised in brooder boxes just like chicks, and like chickens, ducks need a safe place to sleep at night, and should be fenced off from your crops.

Many people prefer ducks to chickens, describing their temperaments as sweet and goofy. They are definitely cuter. Ducks lack the sharp claws and beaks of chickens, so they are not as hard on your landscaping, and not as scary to folks who are a little freaked out by fierce chickens. As with chickens, there are many breeds of ducks, but Khaki Campbells and Indian Runners come recommended by other homesteaders as good urban ducks, because they lay well, are not too large, or too noisy, and don't mind having nothing but a baby pool for a pond, and being a little confined. Other breeds need more wander room to be happy.

Ducks are social creatures, so you should keep at least a pair, and yes, chickens and ducks can intermingle peaceably. As with chickens, you only need a male duck, a drake, if you want fertile eggs. Drakes don't crow—that's the good news. The bad news is that a drake can be aggressive toward you as well as the other poultry, so much so that one of our duck-keeping contributors wrote to us, saying, "be sure to tell them, *no boys!*"

Ducks lay eggs. Their laying powers are not quite those of chickens, but some breeds, like the esteemed Khaki Campbells, do produce eggs at chicken-like rates. Duck eggs are a little larger than chicken eggs, and they are richer, with a higher fat content, that happen to make very good pastry. But they do not keep quite as long as chicken eggs because their shells are more porous.

Like chickens, ducks are also good at eating bugs—even flying bugs—and are particularly valuable for keeping slugs and snails under control. But ducks also love to eat greens, so you need to keep them out of your vegetable beds. They'll gobble up any tender plant. They'll also go after your berries with a vengeance.

Duck Ponds

A swimming pond is not absolutely necessary, but kind to the ducks. It keeps them cleaner and more comfortable. On an urban homestead a baby pool will have to serve as duck pond. If you happen to have a pond or a water feature of some sort on your property, you will want to fence it off because the ducks will make short work of it.

Baby pools are handy because they are portable, so you can move them around to lessen the mud factor. A more permanent solution to mud is to dig

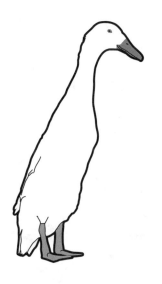

Indian Runner

a shallow pit a little broader than the pool and fill it with a few inches of gravel. Keep the pool on this gravel bed. Mud puddles are not only a mess, but bad for the ducks to stand around in, and even worse for them to drink.

Ducks also need ample drinking water, and the water has to be deep enough for them to submerge their heads, because that is how they clean their eyes and nostrils. So instead of the sipping fountains that chickens use, ducks drink out of big buckets of water. It is best if these watering stations are also kept over gravel for the above mentioned mud reasons.

Both their drinking water and their swimming ponds must be kept clean. Dirty water leads straight to disease. The drinking water must be changed every day, and more than likely the baby pool too.

Duck Houses

At night you want to keep them in secure quarters, because they need protection from nocturnal predators, most especially the persistent raccoon, but also the other standard culprits: opossums, skunks, coyotes, dogs, cats and foxes. This means the house must be built solid and have a bottom, otherwise some marauding critter will dig under the walls. All openings must lock down securely in ways that will foil busy little raccoon fingers. The inside of the house should always be clean and dry, and lined with fresh bedding, like straw or dried leaves.

A good duck house will allow two to six square feet for each duck, depending on the size of your breed. Ducks don't roost like chickens, so the house will really just be an open space, a duck garage, if you will, with a laying box or two inside. It need not be tall either—three feet tall is enough. A dog house with a secure door would do the trick for a couple of ducks. Preferably, though, you will be able to get into your duck house with a minimum of trouble to clean it out. Give them lots of ventilation, because ducks are more likely to suffer from stuffiness than from cold. Ducks are quite cold-hardy, but not so heat-tolerant. After all, they do wear down coats year round. Just make to cover all ventilation windows or holes with sturdy hardware cloth for safety's sake.

In addition to the house, they need a fenced run to hold them if they're not free-ranging. See the chicken section for more discussion on runs. If they spend all their time in this run, then this is where their swimming pond has to stay, too, so size it accordingly.

We just found out why the salad bed looks like ducks have been foraging in it — It's because ducks **HAVE** been foraging in it! They found a way to squeeze through the pea trellis into the garden and have their way with the chard and the lettuces. Everything else was left alone — collard, romanesco, broccoli, kale, onion, mustard, tatsoi, arugula, mizuna, cilantro, cabbage, sugar snap pea.... What a quacking commenced when they realized they'd been found out! It clearly translated to "It wasn't me! I swear!" They were then put back to work on the outside of the drift fence surrounding the bed to gobble up sow bugs, earwigs, slugs and snails.

With the exception of this incursion we have thoroughly enjoyed our backyard ducks. Khaki Campbells seem to be a perfect size for the urban homestead. They are happy with a tub of fresh water to bathe in, a pan of chicken mash and scratch with crushed oyster shell to nibble on and free range of the entire backyard. They put themselves to bed at night in an old doghouse outfitted with nest boxes and dry hay for bedding. We lock the doghouse door each night for their safety. They are a whole lot less work than the chickens who have to be confined (bunch of teenagers that they are) because they'll trash the place otherwise.

Suzanne Mackey, Petaluma, CA

In addition to the house and the run, ducks appreciate a grassy garden to wander in a few hours each day. A cramped duck is an unhappy duck.

Duck Food
Ducks love bugs: slugs, snails, grasshoppers, flies, mosquito larvae. They graze grass, pull weeds, pull up your seedlings, and will eat tender green trimmings from your kitchen. In addition to all these things they should also get quality commercial duck feed (a.k.a. waterfowl feed) for their adult stage of life.

Rabbits

Rabbits are quiet, fluffy, and decidedly more huggable than chickens. They will nibble on your green waste, and out of it they will make the best organic fertilizer available anywhere. So if you already have pet rabbits, or want to acquire rabbits, they definitely have their place on the homestead.

Wonder Pellets

Rabbit poop has more nitrogen in it than any other kind of manure, and it is odorless (once the urine has dried off of it). For this reason rabbit manure is highly prized by organic gardeners, so much so that you can sell it. It will definitely heat up your compost pile. You can also let it dry for a month, then use it directly on your plants. One caveat: If your bunnies have been free-ranging and eating weeds, those weed seeds will be in their poop, and so will sprout wherever you lay that poop.

The best thing to do with rabbit droppings is feed them to your worms. If you have a worm bin the worms will adore you for giving them rabbit poop, and they will swiftly transform that rabbit poop into amazing, high-quality worm castings, the ultimate in fertilizer. The pairing of rabbits and worms is so potent, so valuable, that folks with rabbits scheme to streamline this process — designing their hutches so that the droppings fall straight down into the worm bins.

At one time, urbanites kept rabbits for their meat and fur. They are ideal urban livestock because they are clean and quiet and can be kept just about anywhere without disturbing anyone. Their legendary reproductive rates mean that a breeding trio of rabbits can feed a family on their own.

We've spoken with older people whose parents kept food on the table through the Depression by raising rabbits in the backyard. One woman we spoke to told us how much she hated slaughtering day, because the rabbits screamed. We asked her if that put her off dinner, and she answered, "Of course not. When you're hungry, you eat the rabbit."

Angora rabbits sit in an interesting middle place between farm animal and pet, because you can harvest their hair without killing them. Angoras molt every three months, at which time you can comb loose hair off of them. This hair can be spun into yarn at home with a simple drop spindle. (Your local yarn store can point you in the direction of a basic spinning class.)

Pure angora is far too warm to be used to knit an entire garment, but is used instead for trim, or blended with wool fiber. You can sell it, though Angora fanciers will tell you that the price you get for your Angora hair is not going to compensate you for your time, care and feeding of the rabbits. Angora raising has to be done out of love for the breed. Still, it is intriguing from a home-steading point of view. Any knitter has to be a little tempted by the possibility of raising their own yarn.

Pigeons: A Modest Proposal

If you have ever eaten squab you've eaten pigeon, young pigeon. Our city pigeons, more properly known as feral rock pigeons, are descendants of birds that we domesticated for food. Evidence of the historical popularity of doves and pigeons as domestic stock remains in the form of dovecotes, or pigeon houses, which are often beautiful architectural follies on the grounds of historical homes. And though Americans have clearly lost their taste for pigeon, this is by no means universal. A friend of ours tells us that his family in Egypt keeps a pigeon house, and assures us that the meat is excellent. From a practical standpoint, raising pigeons for food makes perfect sense for the urbanite. They don't take much room or feed, breed fast—six times a year—and lord only knows they are not hard to find. Odds are one is groaning outside your window this very moment.

Cities spend tons of money on pigeon abatement programs, trying to rid our public spaces of sky rats. If we were to propose a permacultural solution to this problem, it would be to make the pigeon a domestic animal again. The pigeons would get off junk food, and out from under bus wheels. We'd eat more lean, homegrown meat. Instead of soiling statuary, their poop would feed compost piles. Is anybody up for Roasted Squab with Bartlett Pears and Porcini Mushrooms? Or what about squab kabob?

Quail

Coturnix Quail

Coturnix japonica, commonly known as Coturnix Quail, is the smallest of all domesticated birds, and reputedly the easiest of all to raise. They are so small, and so quiet, and thrive in so little space that even apartment dwellers can raise them in quantity in indoor aviaries. Unlike pigeons, it is easy to find all sorts of advice and resources regarding the raising of Coturnix quail for meat and eggs. The eggs are prized in Asian restaurants and markets, so much so that you might be able to make a little side income selling your fresh eggs to your local sushi shop.

They are amazingly prolific little birds. They lay a single, mottled egg almost every day, and the hatchlings mature in six weeks. At that rate of reproduction, you almost have to eat them, or at least the eggs, to keep from being up to your elbows in quail. Admittedly, living with a cage full of quail that you intend to eat might be a little like setting up a lobster tank next to your sofa. For that reason when there is a choice, they are often kept outdoors, or in out-buildings. They can fly, so if you let them loose in the backyard, they will probably take off. A nice compromise might be keeping them in a greenhouse, where they will run around and eat bugs, but won't molest your plants, because they don't eat greens.

Bees

Bees are livestock that make a lot of sense in the city. They are silent, odorless, and take up so little space that they can be kept on an apartment balcony. Yet they are an ancient symbol of productivity for good reason—one hive can produce 50 pounds of honey or more per year. That's enough to not only provide honey for your table—and your friends' tables—but also to make a nice batch of homemade mead. In addition to honey, your industrious bees will also give you beeswax and propolis. And of course, their pollination services are invaluable to all of us.

Beekeeping requires some specialized equipment and the easiest way to get started is to purchase a basic kit. Kits, which range in cost from around $100 to $200, contain a hive, frames, assorted tools such as a smoker and hive tool, an instructional book and protective equipment including a veil and gloves.

There are two ways to obtain bees. You can order them by mail—and receive a box containing several thousand bees and a queen. Or you can capture a wild swarm, or transfer a wild hive into your hive boxes. We follow a school of organic beekeeping called "Backwards Beekeeping," which advocates working with feral bees and intervening with them minimally. Our bees were once a wild hive that had taken up residence in an abandoned shop vac. They've settled into domesticated life nicely.

It's up to you how you want to keep bees. What's most important is that you find yourself a good beekeeping mentor or beekeeping group. Yes, you can learn beekeeping by reading books and watching YouTube videos, but nothing beats having someone with experience by your side as you learn the ropes.

You might want to start your search for a mentor by going to Meetup.com and searching "beekeeping" for groups in your area. To find out more about Backwards Beekeeping, just Google that term.

Locating The Hive

In most cities in the U.S. it's illegal to keep bees, though, as with chicken laws, these ordinances are being challenged nationwide. Meanwhile, an urban beekeeper must combine stealth with neighborhood diplomacy. A beehive is not particularly noticeable if you're not looking for it, but many people are irrationally afraid of bees, so it's best to be very circumspect about your beekeeping.

Bees enter and leave their hive in an orderly "bee line," like planes departing a busy airport. This is to our advantage. Hives can be situated so their flight path does not cross where people and pets travel. Placing the hive in the back of your yard near a fence or wall forces them to exit and soar upwards, out of harm's way. Rooftops are another good place to keep a hive. This positioning keeps their flight path elevated and nearly invisible. John Howe, an urban beekeeper in

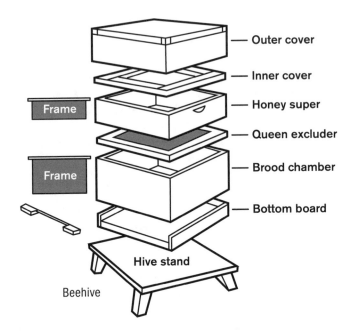

Outer cover

Inner cover

Honey super

Queen excluder

Brood chamber

Bottom board

Frame

Frame

Hive stand

Beehive

Brooklyn, New York, keeps his hives on the roof of his building. From there they collect their pollen from the flowers of local parks and flower shops.

Worker bees prefer to fan out over a three-mile radius during the course of their day, so have no fear that your yard (or your neighbor's yard's) will be overpopulated with bees.

Swarming

When bees leave their hive en masse and hang out in scary bunches on tree branches and picnic tables and the like, it means they had to leave their hive for some reason. Sometimes this is because of external stresses, like an ant invasion. In other cases, the problem is that the hive is overpopulated and is splitting in half. It creates a new queen and the old queen subsequently flies off with over half of the workers. These types of swarms occur in the spring.

A knowledgeable beekeeper can observe early warning signs that a colony is about to swarm and take preventative measures. It's also possible to round up the swarm and transfer it to a new hive. An interesting fact: swarms are exceedingly mellow. If you see one, there's no need to panic. Bees attack to protect their honey and their young. When they're in swarm mode, they've left that all behind, and so are quite gentle. Experienced beekeepers often capture swarms barehanded.

Africanized Bees

Honeybees native to Africa were accidentally released in Brazil in 1957. Ever since that fateful year they have been making their way north, bringing with them an overwrought fear of bees and a few bad disaster movies. Each bee colony has its own personality, and even some European honeybee colonies, the kind you'd order from a supplier, can be ill-tempered. There are certain conditions that make any honeybee cranky. But one of the defining characteristics of African bees is that they are more defensive and more easily offended than their more docile European relatives.

Africanized bees will often enter a European hive and take it over, interbreeding with them or killing the European queen and establishing an Africanized queen and colony. Despite their reputation, it is possible to work with Africanized bees. In Brazil, African bees are now the favored species of bee

Keeping Bees In Brooklyn

I have three beehives on my roof and I've been doing it for about six years now. I first realized I could do it when a honeybee landed on my plate when I was eating at an outdoor restaurant. I thought about doing it in the country when I retired but it never occurred to me that I could do it in the city. So I just went on the internet and Googled around and found that it was feasible, that there was a club in Long Island that I could join, and that everything I needed to order was available online. So I got books and spent the whole winter researching the project and I decided to go ahead and start the beehives, and I've been getting honey ever since.

It's illegal in all New York City to keep bees. You have to keep the neighbors on your side. You have to be very diplomatic about it. I give honey to everyone. It's a delicate thing because bees swarm. My neighbors freaked out when they saw this huge basketball-sized bee cluster hanging from a tree and they thought it was a wasps' nest and they had them exterminated and I had to pay for it too. Another time they swarmed a street lamp and everybody on the block was fascinated by it and the police came and although some people knew it was my hive, they didn't say so and I didn't get in trouble.

People always wonder where they get their nectar in the city. There's a small park near me called Fort Greene Park and I've seen them on the clover and I know they're my bees because there are no other hives in the neighborhood.

John Howe

for beekeeping due to their hardiness and increased productivity. Africanized bees are already established in the southwestern and southeastern corners of the U.S. They don't do as well in colder northern climates, but there is disagreement on exactly how far north their territory will eventually extend.

Here in Los Angeles, any wild hive you find is likely to be hybridized with African bees. The bees in our own hive are likely hybrids, but we don't have any trouble with them. Don't let the fear of "killer bees" keep you from beekeeping. Remember, every hive is a unique entity, whatever its origins.

Colony Collapse Disorder

Colony Collapse Disorder should not put you off beekeeping, either. In fact, it should encourage you to help our bee friends and keep pollinators in business. In brief, no one really knows yet what causes these sudden bee die-offs, but it is not a new phenomenon, and it does not, as some media hype would indicate, foretell the end of the world. It most likely has to do with a combination of pesticides, mites and industrial beekeeping practices. Few organic beekeepers have reported losses, we've heard, perhaps because their bees are under less stress and have stronger immune systems.

Chapter Five
Revolutionary
Home Economics

Revolutionary Home Economics

> The callings and disciplines I have spoken of as the domestic arts are as instructive and as pleasing as the so-called fine arts. To learn them, to practice them, to honor and reward them is, I believe, our profoundest calling. Our reward is that they will enrich our lives and make us glad.
> —Wendell Berry, *In Distrust of Movements*

We've lost our knowledge of farming and animal husbandry, and more recently, we've lost most of our practical knowledge regarding housekeeping. Housekeeping is no longer considered an art. If we have the money, we outsource it. We earn money so we can buy prepared food and pay someone else to clean our home. The home is little more than crash a pad where we watch TV and a storage unit where we keep the things we buy when we are not working.

The home used to be a place where we made things. We made the things we used, and the things we ate, and we made them with pride. With generations of experience guiding their hands, homesteaders transformed the harvest into usable goods. They could make almost everything they needed. There is power in that, power that we've exchanged for convenience.

This exchange is often celebrated as a liberation from drudgery, but art is never drudgery, even if it is hard work. The practice of art is profoundly satisfying, precisely because it is challenging, and when it comes off well, you know you've created something of real value. Drudgery is not about hard work, rather, it is a condition of skilless work. One of the big lies of the last century was that the home arts were drudgery that needed to be abandoned in favor of commerce. We gave them up, just as we ceded farming to factories.

Now the tide is turning. Just as there is growing interest in growing food and raising livestock among people who were not raised up with these skills, there is also a resurgence of interest in the indoor arts. If we take the kitchen back from the microwave, we discover a whole new world of flavor, a world of living, healthy, nutritionally complex foods. The kitchen becomes an arena where you, the domestic artist, learn to harness the forces of life. It is time to resurrect the lost domestic arts before they are lost for good.

Preserving The Harvest

Whether your harvest comes from a dumpster dive, your neighbor's apple tree, or your own garden, you will often find yourself suddenly in possession of more food than you know what to do with. This is the nature of harvest. Sooner or later, you will find yourself uttering the age-old question of any farmer or forager: how do I keep all this stuff from going bad?

You can freeze some of your haul, but more than likely you don't have enough room in your freezer for all of it. Our ancestors came up with all sorts of ways of preserving food without the help of electricity. Some methods, such as lactofermentation, were once universal and are now nearly forgotten. Others, like drying, are still familiar. All of them are well worth learning to do yourself.

Nature Gives In Cycles, It's Your Job To Adapt Accordingly.

We're accustomed to eating whatever we want whenever we want. This is amazing evidence of how far we have evolved as a species. Yet some of that accessibility comes at a price. When we eat fresh fruits and vegetables that are out of season, the odds are we are eating food which has been shipped to us from across the globe, necessitating a enormous expenditure of fossil fuels for an act as simple, as primal, as eating. But even if we had all the fuel in the world to spare for shipping grapes from Chile to Minnesota, there is still a cost in terms of the nutrients lost in the long wait between harvest and the table, and the loss of flavor that is also part and parcel with foods that are shipped long distance. These foods are bred to be travel-tough and to look good when they reach their destination, not to taste good. We think taste and nutrition should be our first priorities when it comes to choosing what we eat. Life is too short to eat crap.

So we enjoy food as it comes out of our garden, or as it comes into the local farmers' markets. In doing so, we've learned to associate food with seasons. Nature gives in waves, and we've learned to surf these waves. Trees fill with apples and apricots, vines go heavy with cucumbers and grapes, tomatoes start coming in faster than you can eat them. Rather than waste this food, we've figured out how to preserve it so we can enjoy these flavors throughout the year.

Growing up, most of the food we ate came out of a package, a can or the freezer. How the food got into the package, can or freezer tray was one of those things we didn't think about much, but we came to accept the idea that food storage could be dangerous if not left in the hands of professionals. Neither of us had a grandma who canned, or an uncle who made beer, or a cousin who made sauerkraut, so when we started figuring how to pickle, brew, ferment, can and otherwise preserve, we were scared to death we'd die of botulism. That said, but with a few simple precautions, anyone can preserve food.

Not All Bacteria Are Bad; In Fact, Some Are Delicious

Microorganisms surround us and inhabit us. We eat them, drink them, sleep with them. Friendly bacteria form complex ecologies in our gut, help us digest food and train us to fight disease. Our modern world has become so sterile that we are actually missing out on some of the benefits these little beasties bring us. Something called the hygiene hypothesis has been gaining support in the scientific community for a few years now. This hypothesis states that lack of exposure to bacteria, particularly early in life when our immune systems are developing, results in off-kilter, overreactive immune systems. It may just be that our overly clean environments are actually the cause of the increasing incidence of all sorts of conditions with immune responses at their core, conditions like allergies and asthma, rheumatoid arthritis, and inflammatory bowel disease.

Of course this involves a whole range of environmental factors, including the overuse of antibiotics and anti-bacterial soaps, but it also applies to our food. Pasteurization, canning, freezing and irradiation are processes that certainly do protect us from bad bugs, but they kill all the good bugs too, bugs we need to support digestion and a healthy immune response. Probiotic adherents believe that we can increase our exposure to beneficial bacteria by changing the way we eat, by including a host of cultured and fermented foods in our regular diet, foods that used to be part of a standard human diet, but which have been replaced with dead food over the last few decades.

Preservation Is Transformation
Culturing, drying and most of all fermenting foods opens up whole worlds of flavor and texture that just do not come about any other way. Fermentation is a living, active, constantly changing process. If you leave food out, it might spoil, or it might transform into something wonderful. Our ancestors figured out how to harness this process, particularly the versatile bacteria species *Lactobacillus*, to make some of the most essential and elemental of human foods, like cheese, sourdough bread, pickles and of course, booze.

When you are fermenting or culturing you are not exactly preserving a food, since the word "preserve" seems to imply that the food remains unchanged. This is really only true for canning, the most modern of the preservation processes we are going to talk about. The other forms we're going to discuss **transform** food into something new, something that lasts longer than its fresh counterpart, something eminently useful, beneficial and flavorful in its own way. A cucumber is one thing, full of its own flavor and benefits. A dill pickle made via fermentation with *Lactobacilli* is something else entirely, with a different flavor and set of benefits.

Nowadays we extend the shelf life of milk by ultra-pasteurizing it, which turns milk into tasteless lactose water that keeps for ridiculous amounts of time. Far better to keep milk around by culturing it and transforming it into yogurt, *crème fraiche*, or cheese. A grape is preserved by transforming it into wine, or drying it into a raisin. You can harness these powerful transformative forces in your own kitchen. You don't even need special equipment—just lots of jars.

When you grow your own food, you never want to see any of it go to waste. If we have an overabundance, we preserve it somehow. As a result, our cupboard is never bare anymore. It is loaded with bottles and jars, each one holding a memory, how we grew the food, or found it, how we processed it, what we learned. It is an intensely personal relationship to food, which brings new meaning to sitting down to the table.

What's more, this stock of food serves as a safety net. If for any reason we can't go to the store, or the stores are empty, we have food on hand. That, combined with whatever is growing in the garden and the staples we keep on hand, gives us a cushion of protection from random disaster and disruption.

There are two books on the subject of food preservation that we cannot recommend enough. Both blew our minds and changed our attitude toward food permanently. The first we read was *Preserving Food Without Freezing or Canning*, by the gardeners and farmers of Terre Vivant. This is a French book, published in English by Chelsea Green Publishing, full of all sorts of Old World methods.

What pushed us over the edge is the wonderful, radical *Wild Fermentation* by Sandor Ellix Katz. *Wild Fermentation* is as much a manifesto against lifeless food as it is a cookbook. It as well as *Keeping Foods Fresh* make you understand that our sterile, packaged food is dead food, and will make you want to change the way you eat for good.

First Things First: When To Sterilze And When Not To

For perfect safety you will want to sterilize all jars and lids that will hold things that are not going to be canned (that is, heat processed), like jars for yogurt, or flavored vinegars, or lacto-fermented pickles.

To sterilize, either use your jars straight out of the dishwasher, or boil them for 10 minutes, covered with water, in a lidded pot. Put a rack or folded dishtowel at the bottom of the pot to protect the jars. You'll need tongs for lifting them out. Fill your jars while still hot.

If you are planning on canning, whether or not you have to sterilize the jars depends on the size of the jars you are using. Quart-sized jars used for actual canning don't have to be sterilized, They just need to be clean and hot when you fill them. The canning process sterilizes both the jar and the food in one go. Pint and half-pint jars have to be sterilized though, because their processing times are so short that sterilization isn't assured.

Canning lids should not be boiled if you are going to use them for canning. Just wash them in warm soapy water and use a new one each time you can something. Don't run canning lids through the dishwasher before you use them in canning. The sealing stuff around the rim is heat-activated and meant for one use. For this reason you should never reuse lids for canning. But do boil your lids or put them through the dishwasher if they are intended for non-canning projects.

It's also worth knowing that you can buy handy plastic lids that fit Mason jars. They're not for sealing the jar, but for using after you've opened the jar and broken the seal instead of the persnickety ring and disk lids. These can be ordered from any outfit that sells canning supplies.

Note on bottles and jars: You can find canning jars or "Mason" jars at restaurant supply stores, some hardware stores, the rare grocery store, and of course online. A case of 12 will cost around $12–$15. They come in wide and narrow-mouth versions. Generally speaking, the wide-mouthed ones are more convenient. If you buy a case, they come with lids, but you can purchase extra lids separately.

How To Can

NOTE: The USDA changed their canning guidelines in 1989. For this reason, we recommend that you search for books on the subject published after that date. Generally we are all for referencing ancient housekeeping guides and collecting '70s treasures at garage sales, but this is one case in which we can't recommend that.

Canning is the one form of preservation that we recommend which is not transformative. It does pasteurize food, and lower nutritional values somewhat. However, it's the best way to keep jams and the like, so is worth knowing if only for that. It might sound like a big, scary production, but it really isn't that complex, and all it takes is some basic, inexpensive equipment. Canning high-acid foods like sugary jams, pickles and fruit is safe and simple because these things don't harbor bacteria easily. With high-acid foods all you have to do is boil your packed canning jars for a specific period of time, the length depending on what you are canning and the size of your jars. The heat kills all bacteria, yeast and mold in the food and seals the jars, thus creating a hermetic environment that allows the food to keep for at least a year. It only goes bad if the seal is not properly made, or if the heating was insufficient. Each kind of food requires boiling for a specific length of time. Guidelines for processing times are available in all canning books and also available online.

Canning meat and low-acid fruits and vegetables is more complicated, and more dangerous if you screw up, because of the serious risk of botulism inherent in the low-acid environment. Moreover, to process low-acid food you have to use a special device called a pressure canner — hot water baths on the stovetop are just not enough.

The Water Bath Process

We're going to give you an overview of the hot water bath canning process here so you can see that it actually is pretty straightforward, but we recommend that you don't can on the basis of our instructions alone.

There are plenty of resources out there, including free ones. The USDA wants to protect you from botulism, so they have extensive canning guidelines on the web, and the good people at Ball, makers of canning jars, have an excellent website as well. Consult these resources first, paying close attention to the specifications for the particular food you are trying to can, before you begin.

Always follow a recipe when canning to make sure that whatever you are canning is sufficiently acidic to can without a pressure canner.

- Proper canning jars, also called Mason jars: Ball or Kerr brands. This is no time to be recycling your old salsa jars.
- Proper canning lids, the kind that come in two parts: a ring and a disk. The rings are reusable, but you have to use fresh disks every time you can, because they are coated with a sealing substance that is only good for one shot.
- A big deep pot for a water bath — it has to be tall enough to submerge your jars completely with at least one inch of water covering the lids. There are special canning pots "canners" which are made to hold many jars at once and fitted with a special rack to keep the jars from touching the bottom of the pot. You can improvise a canner with a big stock pot with a folded kitchen towel in the bottom.
- A pair of canning tongs to lift hot jars in and out of the water bath.
- A bendy spatula, or a chopstick, or a long slender wooden spoon.
- And optionally, something called a canning funnel. This is a wide-mouthed funnel that makes filling jars a lot easier.

This kind of equipment is easier to find in some areas than others. It used to be stocked in all grocery stores, but this is no longer true. Most stores will stock the lids in the baking aisle, and sometimes the jars. Family-run hardware stores often stock canning jars, perhaps more for their use around the wood shop than for the kitchen.

When in doubt, order online. Search "canning kit." You can get a complete canning kit, which includes a canner and rack, funnel, tongs and a set of jars and an instruction book for under 50 bucks.

Getting Your Canning Supplies Ready

Start by making sure your jars are very clean by running them through the dishwasher or by cleaning them with hot soapy water. They don't have to be sterilized if your processing time is longer than 10 minutes — they just have to be clean and hot. Heat the jars by simmering them in your canner just below a boil (around 180°) and keep them hot until ready to use. Be sure never to out-and-out boil the disk part of your lids, or run them through the dishwasher, because that will prematurely activate the sealing substance around their edges. For that same reason you should never use the lid twice, though you can use the rings and jars over and over. Simply clean the lids with warm soapy water. Again, canning will sterilize them.

Your countertop, hands, and all of your other utensils, need to be scrupulously clean too, of course.

Preparing To Pack Your Jars

If you don't already have a simmering bath going to heat your jars, fill your canner or stock pot with water and bring that to simmer.

The key to canning is heat. You want the jars you pack hot, and ideally you want what you're canning to be hot too. For instance, you'd be pouring your newly made batch of jelly hot out of the pan into the hot jars. You never want to make something, put it in the fridge for a few days, then decide you're going to can it. The hot part of this process is important, as is the fresh part.

Packing It Up

Take your first jar out of the hot bath, hot oven or hot dishwasher, drain it and fill it up with whatever you are canning, leaving just a ¼" of space at the top. Tap the jar on the counter and run a bendy plastic spatula, or a chopstick, around the sides of the jar to make sure there are no air pockets in the jar. Those will make your canning go bad.

Don't work in assembly-line fashion, however tempting that might be. You want to fill and seal each jar one at a time.

Clean off the rim of the jar with a clean cloth or paper towel. Put the lid on — not super-tight, just as tight as you make it using your fingers only. In other words, don't use your full arm strength to crank the lids down. They need to be able to vent just the tiniest bit. Put the jar aside and fill your next one.

When all your jars are ready, use your tongs to lower them into your simmering water bath. The jars should be completely submerged. Add water from a tea kettle if you have to top it off. Put the lid on the pot and turn the heat up to bring the water to a full boil again. Set the timer when it comes to a full boil.

The amount of time you cook the jars varies by the types of food being canned, altitude and the size of the jar. Charts with times can be found easily online or in a canning manual. The typical time range is 10 to 50 minutes.

When the processing time is up, spread a dishtowel on the counter. Rescue the jars from the water bath using your tongs and line them up on the towel to cool and dry. Don't fuss with the lids or move them around while they are cooling. The canning magic is still happening. You should hear a "ping" sound shortly after you remove the jars from the water bath as the lids click down to form a seal.

After 24 hours check to make sure the lids are a little sunken in the middle. Press the center gently. It should not pop up and down. Nor should the jar rims be wiggly. If any of this is so, the jar is not properly sealed and you need to use it right away — or replace the lid, and process it again.

Remember, most cases of botulism in the U.S. (less than 200 a year) are associated with bad home canning. If there is any doubt about something you've canned, just cook it before you eat it. Cooking at high heat for 10 minutes kills *C. botulinum*.

Keep your canned goods in the dark. They will taste best if you eat them within a year.

Pickling via Lacto-Fermentation

Back before the advent of canning, much less freezing, folks preserved their vegetable harvest via lacto-fermentation. This process, once commonplace, survives today mostly in the form of sauerkraut and kimchi. Old-fashioned dill pickles are also made this way, though you are probably more familiar with the kind made in vinegar. Lacto-fermentation uses no vinegar at all.

In lacto-fermentation salt is added to vegetables, either by covering them in salty water, or by mixing them with salt to draw out their own juices. Either way, the vegetable ends up soaking in salty liquid. Lactic microbial organisms (the same beasties that spoil milk) take hold in this environment and make it so acidic that the bacteria that causes food to spoil cannot live there. The result is a pickled food that will keep without canning or refrigeration, although canning and refrigeration do extend the shelf life.

Just about any firm, sturdy vegetable can be lacto-fermented. Radishes, cucumbers, cabbage, baby onions, green beans, carrots, garlic cloves all would work. All you have to do is pack a canning jar or crock with your veggies and cover them with a brine solution and leave it somewhere dark and cool. A recipe follows. After four to seven days, try your pickles. If you like them, start eating, or put them away to ferment a little longer. Fermenting time varies by taste, vegetable, weather and your patience level.

A Pickle's Variable Lifespan
Lacto-fermented veggies generally last a few weeks. It depends on their storage temperature. If you transfer them to the fridge, they'll last a long time. If they stay out on the counter, their lifespan will be much shorter, especially in

the summer. Remember, lacto-fermentation is a living process that does not stop evolving unless you heat-process and can the pickles. They'll be changing in flavor and texture as you work your way through the jar.

If you make a big crock of something, a crock too big for the fridge, it is best to keep it in the coolest room in your house, whether that be the basement, or the garage, or the mudroom. The big crocks will form scum on the surface as they sit. Just skim that off whenever you see it.

Wherever you keep them, pickles become stronger tasting over time. You'll know that they're starting to go south when they go soft, or when the flavor isn't what it once was. If they go slimy, you know they're done for. The best way to become comfortable with the process and timing is to start by making small, quart-sized batches of pickled foods and studying their ways. Make two identical jars, and keep one in the fridge and one in the cabinet and watch how they each progress.

If you want to keep your fermented foods for a long time, can them. Canned foods keep for at least a year, but the heat-processing does kill off the living, beneficial bacteria in your ferments. In addition, canning may also soften pickled foods. There is a balancing act between longevity and quality. We never can our pickles, because we eat pickles and krauts for their bacterial benefits, in the same way we eat yogurt, so killing the bacteria seems beside the point. Nonetheless, the USDA and FDA recommend that you can and heat-process all fermented and pickled foods as a matter of course to prevent botulism. Please consider yourself officially warned.

PROJECT

DAIKON RADISH PICKLES

This is the first lacto-fermented pickle we ever made, and it's still our favorite. It makes firm, salty, garlic-flavored pickles that are pretty addictive. Best of all, it takes just a few minutes to make. This basic technique can be applied to other firm veggies equally well. For instance, think about doing this with tiny cucumbers, flavored with dill and garlic, or parboiled pearl onions, or sliced turnips, or even green nasturtium seed pods.

Ingredients:
- Daikon radish — enough to fill a quart jar — one big one is usually enough. Scrubbed, peeled and cut into rounds, quarters, or matchsticks, about ¼"–⅓" thick. The only shape you should not use is long spears, because the idea is to keep the pickles under liquid. We've figured out that as the jar

empties, tall spears end up with their "heads" above the brine level, which hastens their spoiling.

- One peeled garlic clove, and a few peppercorns. The garlic odor/flavor is assertive, so skip the garlic if you're not a fan.
- Two tablespoons (or more) of sea salt or any salt that is *not iodized.* Iodized salt will kill lactobacillus bacteria and interfere with the fermentation process.
- One quart of water. Bottled or filtered is best, but we've used tap successfully.

Fill a very clean quart-sized canning jar with your sliced daikon, and a clove of garlic if you like. Mix your salt and water together in a separate container and pour it into the jar over the daikon slices, leaving a little breathing space at the top, say one quarter of an inch. Close the jar tight, and put it in a cool, dark cabinet. The flavor changes over time, so try opening different jars at different times to see what stage of fermentation you prefer. The earliest you should try would be three or four days after bottling; we usually wait a week or so.

When you open it there might be some fizzing, which is normal. The pickles should be crunchy (but not raw, definitely transformed) and pleasantly garlic-flavored. If they are a little salty for your taste you can rinse off the brine before you eat them. Keep the opened or unopened jars in the fridge to extend the life of your pickles.

PROJECT

L'HAMD MARKAD or PRESERVED SALTED LEMONS

This is a much-loved Moroccan application of lacto-fermentation. Should you ever find yourself in possession of a large quantity of lemons you could make lemonade, or you could make *l'hamd markad.*

Preserved lemons are used extensively in Moroccan cuisine, on fish and in salads especially, either straight out of the jar or cooked. We like to chop up these salty/sour lemon rinds and use them the same way we'd use olives or anchovies to add a flavor punch to whatever we are cooking. Just recently, a homesteading friend told us that she's found that the addition of the preserved lemon pulp and rind to her homemade hummus yields fabulous results.

Ingredients
- Organically grown lemons, unblemished, scrubbed. Thin-skinned Meyers are the preferred sort, but all work. Gather enough to fill at least a one-quart jar.
- Sea salt. Tons of it.
- Fresh lemon juice. Which means just a few more lemons. Don't use bottled juice.
- Spices, optional. You could put a cinnamon stick in each jar, two or three cloves or a few peppercorns, or all three.
- A clean, sterilized quart jar with a lid.

Warning: if you have hangnails, prepare to suffer.

Pat lemons dry. Cut them into quarters and coat each slice generously with salt. If your lemons are small, you can leave them whole, slit them open with four vertical slices and stuff them to the gills with salt. Put the lemon quarters or whole lemons in the jar, pressing them as you go to release their juice. Sprinkle even more salt between layers. If you want to add spices, pack those in as you go. When you get to the top add more lemon juice if necessary to cover the lemons completely. They must always be submerged in juice.

Let the lemons sit in a dark cupboard for four to six weeks before using. Turn the jars upside down once in a while to encourage the salt to dissolve and the spices to mingle. When they are done, the rinds will be soft, and the salt and lemon juice liquid they've been stewing in will have turned a little viscous. You eat the rinds. You can choose to use the pulp also, or just scrape the rinds clean. Rinse the rinds if you want them to taste a little less salty. Once opened, store in refrigerator where they will keep up to six months.

EUELL GIBBONS' CROCK

Euell Gibbons, author of *Stalking the Wild Asparagus* and other classics, liked to keep big crocks of vegetables, both domestic and wild, pickling in brine and herbs. The bigger the crock, the better, he advised, saying he often kept a 10-gallon crock going through the summer.

Like our recipes for daikon radish pickles and preserved lemons, Gibbons' crock is another way to employ lacto-fermentation in the kitchen.

A dill crock is a wonderful means of corralling random vegetables from your garden, those thinnings and extras that you don't know what to do with, such as that handful of beans, the little green tomatoes left on the vine come frost, or a bumper crop of baby eggplants.

There is no set recipe for this. Experiment with different vegetables and seasonings. Allow each crock to be a unique creation.

What you need:

- A large glass jar or ceramic crock
- Sea salt for a making a brine solution (see below)
- Lots of fresh dill
- A few peppercorns
- A fresh grape leaf or two to keep your veggies crisp (optional)
- Almost any kind of firm, flawless vegetable. Baby vegetables are great. Cut up big ones into bite-sized pieces.
- Possibilities include: carrots, radishes, hard green tomatoes (not red ones; they'll go mushy), baby eggplants, peeled Jerusalem artichokes, tiny onions or big onions cut into wedges, cauliflower broken into florets, hot peppers, tiny summer squash, chopped cabbage, green nasturtium seeds, blanched green beans (only beans need to be blanched), and chopped leeks. Cukes are a natural too, but pick them small and leave them whole.

Start with a very clean crock or jar. Layer the bottom with fistfuls of dill, your grape leaves and a few peppercorns. If you like garlic, put some peeled cloves in, but be aware that even a few will make the whole batch of pickles garlic-flavored.

Next start to add your veggies in layers. You don't have to fill up the whole crock at once. You can add to it over the course of a week or so, throwing in veggies as they come to you.

When your initial layers of veggies are in, cover them with a brine solution.

Brine solution

Dissolve sea salt (never iodized salt) with water at this ratio:
¾ measure of salt to 10 measures of water

Fermentation

It's important to keep the pickles beneath the surface of the brine to prevent spoilage, so weigh them down. If you're using a big crock, sink them under a plate weighted with a clean rock or a jar of water. If you're using a large jar, try slipping a smaller jar filled with water into the mouth of the big jar. Another good option is to use a ziplock bag filled with brine solution. Brine instead of plain water, just in case it leaks.

Cover your setup with cheesecloth or a light kitchen towel, securing the edges with string or a rubber band to keep flies out. You don't want to put a lid on it because the fermentation process needs air.

Leave the crock out at room temperature to ferment. Fermentation times vary according to both your taste and ambient temperatures. Minimum time is three days, maximum maybe two weeks. Start sampling your crock after three days. When it tastes done to you, it's done. The flavors will become stronger as time passes, and the character of the vegetables will change.

During the fermentation period, check daily for mold forming on the surface. This is not such a bad thing. Just skim it off if you see any.

When you're ready, transfer it to the fridge to slow the fermentation. It will keep for a couple of months. It's okay at this point to take out the weight, change containers, and to use a lid (to prevent your entire fridge from smelling like pickles), but keep the veggies in their own brine.

If you make lots of pickles and want to keep them for a long time, can them in their own brine, following canning instructions for dill pickles, which can be found easily online or in any canning book.

Dehydration: Why Save It For Hangovers?

Dehydration, probably the most ancient food preservation method, works best with high-acid foods like fruit, and it's a great way to deal with bumper crops from your garden. Drying works by removing the moisture from foods, which foils moisture-loving bacteria. There are many ways to dry food—we prefer using a solar dehydrator, but you can also purchase a commercial electric dehydrator. Drying in a conventional oven is possible, but it's hard to get the temperature low enough and you'll use a lot of energy.

Your goal with dehydrating is to remove at least 80% of the water content of fruits and 90% from vegetables. The scientifically-minded can estimate the moisture removed by weighing the food before and after drying and doing the math. But really, after getting the hang of dehydrating you'll get a sense just by touch if you have either dried too much or too little. If any wetness oozes out when you squeeze it it's not dry enough. It should be leathery. The temperature range we recommend for dehydrating is between 100° and 140°. Anything more than 180° and you'll begin cooking, any less than 100° and you risk contamination.

Preparation For Drying

Wash fruit and inspect for insects as you slice it for dehydrating. The thinner the slices, the faster the process. Some commercially-dried fruit, especially apples, apricots, nectarines and pears, is treated with sulfite to prevent browning and to deter spoilage. The safety of sulfating foods is controversial and we've never done it ourselves. Browning and spoilage can be more easily and safely deterred by soaking your fruit in a solution made from two teaspoons of powdered vitamin C (ascorbic acid) in one quart of water. Add another teaspoon of ascorbic acid for every third batch you soak.

When you are done drying, make sure to store dried food in airtight containers with tight-fitting lids. We once had an entire summer's worth of sun-dried tomatoes turn into a jar full of seething larvae that would make David Cronenberg gag, all because a pantry moth got into the jar. This scenario can also be prevented by pasteurization, that is, freezing the food for several days after drying, but we like to avoid pasteurization because it destroys some of the flavor and nutrients. We reserve freezing for foods that seem to be particularly larvae-prone, like figs.

Three Methods For Drying Food

Sun-Drying

If you live in a place where the temperatures are scorching hot and the humidity low—the desert, essentially—it's possible to dry fruits and vegetables in the sun. Otherwise please skip to the next method, the solar dehydrator.

If you are a desert person, all you will need to do to dry your food in the summer is make some racks out of wood or an old frame with a piece of plastic or stainless steel screen material stretched across them to hold the fruit. Do not use hardware cloth because the metal it's made out of can contaminate food. Cover the trays with cheesecloth or muslin to prevent insect damage. Put the trays in full sun and turn the fruit two or three times during the day to ensure even drying. As sun-drying can sometimes take several days, make sure to bring in the food at night, since evening moisture will cause it to rehydrate and get moldy. The key factor with sun-drying is low humidity—sun drying will not work with even moderate humidity no matter how hot it is outside, so this method is limited to folks who live in desert regions.

Air-Drying Herbs

Herbs are easy to air-dry and don't need the extremely low humidity required to safely sun-dry fruits and vegetables. Just bundle up herbs that you have picked early in the morning and tie them in bunches by the stems. Hang them upside down indoors out of direct sunlight, and they should be dry in a few days. You know they are dry when the leaves crumble at your touch. Strip the leaves from their stems and store them in jars in a dark cupboard. Exposure to light will degrade them.

Sun-Drying Meat

While indigenous peoples around the world dry fish and meat outdoors, our sensitive modernized stomachs may not be able to deal with the risk of contamination. Meat and fish should be dried in a store-bought electric dehydrator to ensure food safety.

The Appalachian Solar Food Dryer

We've used a homemade solar dehydrator with great success at our urban homestead for the past few years and it's our favored method of drying. While sun-drying only works in a few hot, dry places, solar dehydrators will work just about everywhere.

Our solar dehydrator is called an Appalachian dryer. It's composed of two parts. The first part is the collection box: a long, shallow glass- or plastic-covered box lined with black material that collects the heat of the sun. A vent at the bottom of the collection box pulls in air which is heated and flows up into the second part of the dehydrator. The second part is a cabinet where the food sits on racks, basking in the flow of hot air from the collector.

Our dryer sits in our front yard, positioned to catch the best of the morning sun, looking like an odd, homemade pinball machine. We painted it the same color as our house, but somehow that makes it even more ridiculous-looking. Nonetheless, we love it, and wouldn't give it up for the world. The scent of drying tomatoes coming out of it is one of the best scents of summer. To give you an idea of its efficiency, it takes about a day and a half to dry tomatoes in it.

We made ours from plans found in the issue 57 of *Home Power Magazine* (February/March 1997). *Home Power* sells a PDF download of these plans for $5 online at homepower.com. Issue 69 (February/March 1999) contains further refinements to the design for increased efficiency.

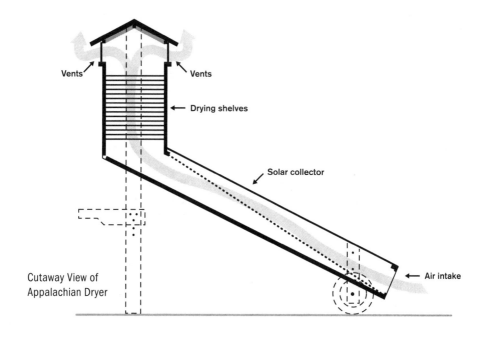

Vents

Vents

← Drying shelves

Solar collector

Cutaway View of Appalachian Dryer

← Air intake

A half-size version of the Appalachian dryer can also be found in the book *The Solar Food Dryer: How to Make Your Own Low Cost, High-Performance, Sun-Powered Food Dehydrator* by Eben Fodor. Fodor also offers detailed plans for building another kind of simple solar dehydrator that occupies a single box.

You can make a quick and cheap solar dehydrator in a similar design out of nothing but cardboard boxes. It's not a permanent solution, but it would be good for at least one summer's worth of drying. Plans for this and every imaginable solar cooking contraption can be found in the resource section in the back of the book.

Commercial Dehydrators

If you can't quite muster the ambition to build a solar dehydrator, you can buy a commercial electric model—just make sure to get one with a thermostat and fan. Store-bought dehydrators are the safest way to make fish and meat jerky, since you can control the temperature and minimize the drying time.

Electric dehydrators come in two basic designs, one with the fan and air flow oriented horizontally, the other vertically. Each has its advantages and disadvantages. A horizontal model keeps food flavors from migrating between trays if you're drying more than one kind of food at a time. Vertical models have the advantage of being more efficient, because heat rises. In a vertical model, a top-mounted fan will prevent drippings from gunking up the fan blades and motor.

So whether you hang bundles of mint in your kitchen, or you build yourself a big honking Appalachian eyesore like ours, we hope that you will give dehydrating a try, because there is no easier, or more direct way of saving the flavors of the summer over the winter.

Preserving With Vinegar

Herb-Infused Vinegar

Infusing vinegar with herbs is an easy way to preserve your herbs for the winter. We are all familiar with those decorative condiment bottles tied with raffia and packed with lord knows what, like some country kitchen cabinet of curiosity. One has probably been sitting in your mother's kitchen window since 1997. These are not those. These are the real thing. They will not have herb bits in them when they're done. They will live in the fridge, not the windowsill.

Choose glass bottles with screwtop lids or corks. Bottles for vinegar should not have metallic caps, because those will corrode. Sterilize your bottles. Your herbs should be cleaned, picked free of any rot or bruising, and the leaves dry from washing. The best time to pick your herbs, incidentally, is in the morning, just after the dew dries. They are at their strongest then.

1 Choose your herbs. Good candidates are dill, parsley, rosemary, thyme, tarragon and sage. Mixes can be great, but often single-herb vinegars work best. You can use fresh or dried herbs, but never use ancient, flavorless herbs. Also think about spices like peppercorns, or make a fruit-infused vinegar with berries.

2 Choose your vinegar. Plain white vinegar is good for delicate herbs. Apple cider vinegar is good for fruit vinegars. Wine vinegar is good with the stronger herbs.

3 Pack your clean herbs into your bottle or jar. The amount does not have to be precise. In recipes you'll often see a ratio of about one part herb to four parts vinegar. You do not have to chop or bruise them, but you may if you wish. If you do, they might infuse a little faster.

4 Heat your vinegar on the stove until it is very hot—just about to boil. Use a funnel to pour it over your herbs while it is still hot, and seal the bottle.

5 Let the infusion steep in a dark cabinet for three or four weeks. Take it out and strain the vinegar through cheese cloth or a coffee filter into a freshly sterilized bottle. This will keep for six to eight months in your refrigerator, or three months in your cabinet.

Pickling With Vinegar

Most pickle recipes you find will use vinegar instead of salt water. The lacto-fermentaion process described above is much older, and has been largely supplanted by vinegar pickling.

If you want to try pickling in vinegar, all you have to do is bring white or apple cider vinegar up to a boil along with any spices you like—garlic cloves, peppercorns, red pepper, cloves, and dill being common; add some sugar if you like sweeter pickles, and pour the hot, flavored vinegar over any firm vegetable packed into a sterile jar. Good pickling candidates are cucumbers, green tomatoes, green beans, carrot sticks and baby onions.

Don't be afraid to experiment. This is pretty much impossible to screw up. But if this much freedom of choice makes you nervous, vinegar pickle recipes abound in books and on the internet.

If you are pickling tougher veggies, like green beans, you should parboil them first (parboiling means just dunking them in boiling water long enough to turn them bright green). After packing the jars, put them in the fridge and let it sit a day or so, then you can eat them. They'll keep in the fridge like this for at least three weeks.

If you wish to can them so you can keep them longer, pack them into hot jars, and consult a canning guide to find out the appropriate processing time for that vegetable and the size jar you are using. Canning instructions follow which will explain this all a little more.

Preserving Fruit In Alcohol:
Le Cherry Bounce (*Cerises à l'eau-de-vie*)

Our friend Jean-Paul contributed this ancestral recipe from the Monsché homestead in Alsace. It requires sour cherries (also called tart or pie cherries—like the Morello or the Montmorency varieties). These are emphatically not the table cherries you buy in stores. You might get them at a farmers' market, or out in the country, or maybe off your own tree.

In the States this kind of thing is called a cherry bounce, though the high-class addition of cherry *eau-de-vie* makes it particularly French. We encourage you to also try stewing whatever fruit takes your fancy in brandy and sugar, and see what happens.

1 Put two lbs. of sour cherries (clean, but not stemmed or pitted) into a big glass jar, or divide them between two jars.
2 Add ¾ lb. granulated sugar, and then cover with cherry *eau-de-vie* (also called *kirschwasser*, or kirch). For reasons of economy, you may substitute regular brandy for up to ⅔ of the volume of *kirschwasser*/ cherry *eau-de-vie*.
3 Close the jar hermetically (otherwise the spirits will evaporate). Gently swirl the jar around to distribute the sugar. It will dissolve more over time.
4 Wait two months before opening.
5 Sip the liquor, nibble the cherries.
6 Happy maceration!

Preserving Root Vegetables

Root vegetables can be convinced to keep through the entire winter without canning or freezing. Folks used to depend on this fact to feed themselves during snowbound months, but we seem to have forgotten these old-fashioned, but highly effective, storage methods.

One note: if you live in the southern latitudes where the winters are mild, these techniques will not work, because they depend on cold ambient temperatures. But you are compensated for this loss because unlike your snowbound friends, you can grow food all winter long.

Keep It In The Ground

The first thing to do is to extend your harvest as long as possible. The first frosts of the season are deadly to tomatoes, but they don't harm root vegetables. And some greens, like kale and broccoli, are actually improved by the cold. Seriously, you can dig kale out of the snow and it will be perfectly good, and you can harvest like this until the ground freezes solid.

To stave off freezing, mulch super-heavily over your root vegetables. Put down a full foot of straw over your vegetable beds, or even pile all your fallen leaves there, marking where your plants are as you go, so you can find them again.

You can also make a temporary greenhouse out of plastic sheeting to protect your plants from frost and extend your harvest. With the proper setup—deep mulching, tents, cold frames, etc.,—you can contrive to keep a few crops growing most of the winter. This is one of those cases where it will really help you if you can tap into the local databank of knowledge and experience.

Take It Inside

All root vegetables keep best where it is cold, but not freezing—somewhere between 32 and 40 degrees is ideal. The warmer it is, the faster the vegetables will rot, but even a 50- or 60-degree environment is better than your warm kitchen. If you have an unfinished, unheated basement or cellar, especially one with a dirt floor, your are in luck. That is the best thing you can have. A cold garage will also work. If you have a finished, heated basement, you can build a cold storage room in it, one that encloses a window or a vent to the outside. If this room is heavily insulated, and the cold winter air is allowed in, it makes an ideal storage space. It is ambitious, yes, but it could be very deluxe, what with all the racks and shelves you could build to hold your boxes of food.

Storage Conditions

Now, some vegetables require wet conditions, and others like it dry. Garlic and onions like it dry. They are best kept in airy bags or boxes. Potatoes are the same way. They need a combination of air and darkness and coolness. They can go in burlap bags, ventilated boxes or even a laundry basket. Just sort through all of your potatoes first and make sure all of them are in perfect condition. A little rot in one will spread to all the others.

All the rest of your root vegetables: carrots, beets, radishes, parsnips, celeriac and similar need moisture to keep from withering while in storage. If they are kept moist and cold they will last all winter long. But cold is the operative word. 32°–40° is the ideal temperature. If they are kept moist and warm they will turn into compost. You keep them moist by layering them in damp sawdust, peat moss or sand.

As with all stored food, first sort them out and keep only perfect specimens. The imperfect ones can be eaten immediately, used to make stock,
offered to your animals or sent to the compost pile. Layer the veggies and
damp sawdust (or whatever you're using) in plastic buckets or bins so that the
veggies don't touch each other, only sawdust. The sawdust should be moist,
not sopping wet. Top off the bucket with one last layer of sawdust that covers
everything, and keep these boxes or buckets *uncovered* in the coolest place
you can find.

Or Take Them Outside Again

The most intriguing storage ideas involve digging holes in the ground. If you
don't have a basement or a garage, but you have open ground, you can make
yourself a little storage pit. There are a lot of ways to do this, and our resource
guides will lead you some different sources and illustrations which will make
this easier to understand.

One basic technique is sink a vessel of some sort into the ground and
make a mini-cellar of it; something like an old cooler or fridge would work
well. It needs to be rust- and rodent-resistant. Then you pack it with straw and
vegetables, or wet sand and vegetables, as described above. The top foot or
so should be packed with dry insulation, like straw or leaves. Top it off with a
sturdy lid to keep out the critters.

If critters are not a worry, you can store your vegetables above ground
in mounds. You make these by spreading a thick, circular layer of soil on
the ground (somewhere high and well-drained so rain won't pool around your
cache). Pile your veggies there pyramid-style. Pack about 12 inches of straw
around the pyramid, and then pack it all down with a three-inch layer of earth,
forming a dome shape. Take a handful of straw and let it stick up vertically
through the dirt at the top. This "chimney" will allow moisture to escape the
dome. Since you have to destroy the mound to get into it, they are one-use
affairs, so it is best to make a few smaller ones rather than one large one.

Transforming Excess

The following projects are not preservation techniques that keep food around
for a long time, but they transform food that might otherwise be wasted into
more useful forms.

How To Culture Milk

One way to deal with excess milk is to transform it. Yogurt, cheese, sour
cream, cultured buttermilk are all ancient methods of dealing with abundance.

Milk spoils quickly at room temperature, but if certain bacteria colonize it, it becomes something new and useful. Over time, people learned how to encourage the bacterial colonization in different directions, so that a humble pail of milk could yield yogurt or sour cream or farm cheese.

But why should you, as a city dweller with a nice fridge, learn to culture milk? First of all, it's good for you. When milk is cultured it becomes much more digestible, because the live cultures break down lactose. Cultured products, most famously yogurt, also colonize with good bacteria, repairing damage done by courses of antibiotics and a bad diet, and helping to control yeast populations. What would we do without sour cream, yogurt smoothies and buttermilk for pancakes? Being able to make your own allows you to control quantity and quality, avoid trips to the store and excess packaging.

Making Yogurt

Yogurt is a fermented milk product made tasty by a culture of *Lactobacillus bulgaricus* (or *L. acidophilus*) and *Streptococcus thermophilus* and its health benefits are widely acknowledged if it has active cultures. To make yogurt you need to gather:

- One quart of milk. (Whole milk makes the creamiest yogurt, but you can use whatever you want.)
- One tablespoon of live yogurt as a starter. For this first batch you need living yogurt, either from a friend, or from store-bought yogurt. If you buy it, be sure the container reads "contains live cultures." Some yogurt is pasteurized, which kills the cultures, but you can usually find live yogurt even in an ordinary supermarket. You can also order exotic yogurt cultures online if you are a real yogurt connoisseur.
- Quart jar
- Small, insulated cooler
- Thermometer

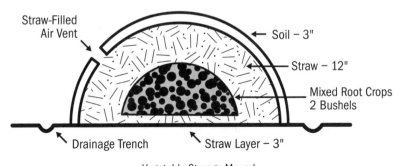

Vegetable Storage Mound

To begin you should sterilize everything that will come into contact with the final product. Keep your hands and work surfaces clean.

Pour the milk in a pot with a thick bottom or use a double boiler to prevent burning. Heat the milk up to 180°. Stir frequently to prevent burning. Don't bring it to a full boil. Then remove it from the heat and let it cool to 110°. While you wait for it to cool, heat up your quart jar and your cooler by pouring hot water into them.

When the milk is down to 110° (this is a touchable temperature, like a hot bath) stir in just one tablespoon of live yogurt to inoculate the milk. More is not necessarily better. Use just the one tablespoon.

Pour the cultured milk into the hot jar, cap it, and put the hot jar in the hot cooler. Fill the rest of the cooler with 110° water and maybe also jars full of 110° water (literally hot water bottles!). Let it sit for 8–12 hours, checking the temperature of the water periodically, adding fresh hot water if necessary.

Check on it after some time has passed. The yogurt should be thick and have a tangy flavor. If not, it needs a boost. Add one more spoonful of starter, and heat up the cooler again by filling it with hot water. Keep this water around 110°. The *Lactobacillus* needs a hot place to breed. Let it sit again for several hours, and with luck it should firm up. If it doesn't, maybe your culture is no good.

Your yogurt will keep for a long time in the fridge, though it will get more and more sour as it gets older. Use some of your last batch of yogurt to make your next batch. As long as it isn't covered in mold, you know the cultures are still there.

Making *Labaneh*, Or Yogurt Cheese

If you drain the water from yogurt, you end up with a tangy, spreadable cheese along the lines of cream cheese. This cheese is made anywhere people eat yogurt, and goes by many names, but we call it by its Lebanese name, *labaneh*.

Take a big piece of cheesecloth and use it to line a strainer or colander of some sort. Pour in your yogurt. It shrinks down, so if you want one cup of cheese, use two cups of yogurt. Tie up the ends of the cheesecloth to make a bundle. Set the strainer with the bundle in it over a bowl that will catch the liquid that drains off. Put it in the fridge, and let it drain overnight, or all day while you're at work.

When the cheese is drained, it will be a little tangier than cream cheese, but similar in texture. Fattier yogurt makes creamier cheese. You can flavor this cheese with herbs or fruit to make an excellent bagel spread. Or you can make a classic *labaneh* sandwich by spreading it on bread or pita, studding it with olives, spicing it up with thyme and/or mint, and garnishing with tomato slices.

By the Whey – That liquid that drains off is called whey, and it is rich in protein. You can add it to smoothies, or use it in the place of water in just about any recipe. It will keep in the fridge about as long as milk will keep.

Fil, Piima And Viila

All three of these are dairy cultures well known in Scandinavia, but not here. Each has a slightly different character, but they are similar enough that what we're going to say about the *fil* culture, which is the one we keep here on the homestead, applies to all three. All three transform milk and cream into delicious yogurt and sour cream-like substances with minimal effort on your part.

Our introduction to *Fil* and *Lactococcus* came through the gift of a baby food jar filled with *filmjölk*. The original culture came from Sweden — a bottle of it was smuggled back from a trip, and then nurtured. You can purchase *fil* and many other cultures through the mail from G.E.M. Cultures. We got ours by visiting an inspiring group of people called, naturally enough, the Culture Club. They all know each other because they are part of the same food co-op, and now they get together in a café once a month to swap cultures and plot revolution.

To keep *fil* alive you just have to keep making more *fil*. Unlike sourdough starter, it doesn't need much care. All you have to remember is to transfer a little of your last batch of *fil* to some fresh milk or cream every week or so, and you've always got some on hand.

Being lazy, we really like the *fil* lifestyle. *Fil* needs no heating at all. It's like magic. If we want to make the *filmjölk* all we do is put a couple of spoonfuls of the last *fil* batch into a jar of milk or cream. Then we leave it sitting on the counter, or maybe on the back of stove where it's a little warmer, for about 24 hours. No temperature gauge, no special equipment needed. The Nordic people are geniuses!

All there is to making *fil* is waiting for it to thicken to the consistency we want. Then we put in the fridge. How many times during your childhood did your mom yell at you to put the milk back in the fridge? It is not at all comfortable at first to leave dairy products sitting around. Certainly not overnight. The first time we did it, we were highly dubious of the result. But it smelled fine, and it tasted even better. *Fil* is mild and clean-tasting, and its sourness has a pleasing lemon quality.

Put it in milk (whole or not). Put two teaspoons of anything cultured with *fil* into a quart of milk and leave it sitting out overnight and you will get *filmjölk*, something sort of between buttermilk and yogurt in terms of texture. We bake with it, because we like quick breads which require buttermilk, and love not having to run to the store to buy a quart of buttermilk whenever we want to bake, half of which always goes bad because we don't like to drink cultured buttermilk. This *fil* stuff we like to drink. If you salt it and put mint and cucumbers in it, it is very like a salty *lassi*, or *ayran* or *doogh*—any of that family of cooling yogurt drinks from hot places. If you blend it with fruit, you've got a fruit smoothie. Or you can eat it out of a bowl with muesli or fruit like the Swedes do.

Put it in cream (or half and half) and watch a miracle happen. It resembles *crème fraiche*, or clotted cream, or something similar. Cream infused with the *fil* culture turns silken and ever so slightly tangy, good enough to eat straight off the spoon. It works as both sour cream and whipped cream, so it ends up smeared on scones, wrapped in burritos, tossed with pasta—or best of all—in a bowl with strawberries. Just add one teaspoon of anything cultured with *fil* to a pint of cream and let it sit out overnight.

Cheesemaking

...cheese, milk's leap toward immortality.
— Clifton Fadiman

Cheesemaking is a fascinating process. All of the great cheeses that you know by name—Brie, Comte, Stilton—have their origins in particular cultures. You can order these cultures, and all of the equipment you need, from cheesemaking suppliers. Read *Home Cheese Making* by Ricki Carroll for a clear overview of cheesemaking processes, terms and equipment. In the meantime, we're going to show you how to make ricotta with a few things you're likely to have on hand.

Whole Milk Ricotta
Genuine ricotta is made out of the whey (a protein-rich liquid) which is a byproduct of cheesemaking. You can make your own quick and dirty ricotta using whole milk. It's a good way to use up extra milk that might go bad.

- **½ gallon organic whole milk.** Pasteurized milk is fine, ultra-pasteurized (UP) is not.
- **¼ cup lemon juice**
- **½ teaspoon sea salt**, or more to taste

1 In a large pot mix together the milk, salt and lemon juice.

2 Heat the milk to 185°, while stirring to prevent burning.

3 As the temperature rises you will start to see the curds separate from the liquid. When the milk gets to 185° turn off the heat and let it set for 10 minutes.

4 Take a colander and line it with muslin. Ladle the curds carefully into the muslin, tie up the corners and let it drain for 30 minutes.

5 You can eat the cheese immediately or store for up to two weeks in the refrigerator.

Variations:

1 Use more lemon juice for a lemon-flavored cheese.

2 Use ¼ cup apple cider vinegar instead of lemon juice for a queso blanco. Let the cheese drain in the muslin bag for a couple of hours for a firmer texture.

3 Flavor this cheese with olive oil and herbs to make a savory filling, or add honey and spices to make a sweet filling.

Ambitious cheesemakers can move on to making hard cheeses, which begin their life as a soft cheese just as above, but continue on to being pressed, air-dried and aged in a cool (55°–65°) environment. There are also more advanced forms of soft cheeses made by introducing molds that will produce blue cheeses. For these you can use mold harvested from store-bought cheese or order mold cultures.

Making Butter

Butter, particularly if salted, lasts a good long time, so it is another classic method of transforming excess milk into something that keeps. It may not seem worthwhile at first glance, but it actually is not all that hard, and makes a much more rich, fluffy, fresh tasting butter than store-bought. It's definitely one of those things worth doing for company, or if you have a pint of cream near its expiration date.

Start by acquiring a pint of cream. It can be any kind of heavy cream, as long as it is not marked "UP" or "ultra-pasteurized." UP products are processed with extremely high heat, allowing for more lax sanitation standards in the factories, and also making the product more shelf-stable than regular pasteurized products. This means they can be shipped great distances from factory farms, and it means they can hang around the store for weeks without going bad. But UP is a peculiarly lifeless substance, one that can't be used to make homemade yogurt, cheese or butter. So look for cream without the UP label, organic preferably.

Put your pint of cream into a clean quart-sized jar. This leaves lots of sloshing room, and that is important. The more sloshing, the better. Leave the cream out to ripen at room temperature (72°) for about eight hours — say you put it out in the morning and make the butter that evening for dinner. (This, by the way, is why dumpster cream is okay — you'd be souring it anyway.) If you forget to make the butter that night, you can put the soured cream in the fridge to arrest the ripening process, and continue the next day. Just be sure that you let the cream come back to room temperature, or close to room temperature (50°—70°) before you start the next step.

The next step is best done through teamwork, or perhaps delegated to the more hyperactive members of your household. Screw down that lid tight and shake that jar in the air like you just don't care. You have to shake hard! Some people put a marble in the jar to speed up the process.

If all that shaking and hopping around is not your style, you can also use a food processor fitted with a plastic blade, a standing mixer fitted with a paddle or even a regular old blender. Perversely, we only make butter by the shake method, and want everyone else to as well, because it is such a simple miracle. But if you must use a machine, this is how you do it. Start with the cream at room temperature. It's not necessary to let the cream sit out all day, but the flavor will be better if you do. Set your machine to mix at a low setting, if possible.

However you go about churning, you will eventually see the butter "break"—globules will appear in the liquid. It will look like cottage cheese. Keep shaking, cranking, blending, or whatever a little while longer until it seems like no more globules are coming. The break will happen within a minute or two with an electrical device, and between five and ten minutes if you're shaking the jar.

The solid globs are butter. The liquid is true buttermilk. True buttermilk bears no relationship to the substance sold in markets as "buttermilk." That stuff is a thick cultured milk product, more closely related to yogurt than butter. It was developed to replace real buttermilk, not in taste, but rather its function in baking. Buttermilk (real or cultured) is used in biscuits, pancakes, etc., because it gives the bread a tender, springy quality, and it helps the dough rise. The difference between them is that real buttermilk is sweet and thin and mild. Try it! It is a pleasure to drink, a forgotten treat.

Back to the buttermaking. Drain the buttermilk off the butter lumps and set it aside for drinking or cooking. The newborn butter will have the consistency of whipped butter, but will be richer-tasting on the tongue. Don't worry that it is so soft, it will stiffen up when you chill it. The final steps are to "wash" the butter, and then to salt it—otherwise it will quickly go rancid.

Butter Washing

Put the butter in a bowl. Add a splash of ice-cold water to the bowl and press the butter with the back of a big wooden spoon to squeeze out the buttermilk. Any hidden buttermilk in the butter fat will turn the butter bad within a couple of days. Pour off the cloudy liquid and repeat several times until the water runs clear. That means the buttermilk is all out. Another method is to keep the butter in the jar (if you used the shaking method), and keep adding water and shaking and draining until the water runs clear.

Salting

The last step is to add salt to preserve the butter even more. This is purely optional. Let your taste buds be your guide. Just massage it in thoroughly so you don't end up with extra salty chunks. Press the butter into a little dish with a cover and refrigerate. The butter will become more solid when it chills. If you decide to make butter churning a habit, you might want to get a butter mold so you can form your butter into appealing shapes.

Troubleshooting

If the butter tastes cheesy, you left the cream sitting out too long in the ripening stage. The warmer the ambient temperature, the less time the cream should sit. If the butter will not form, check to make sure it is not UP cream after all. If not, well...keep churning.

How To Make Fruit Butter

A Process Of Reduction

Fruit has an annoying way of all coming in at once. When you find yourself up to your earlobes in whatever kind of fruit you grow or pilfer from around the neighborhood, it is time to make fruit butter. Fruit butter is simply a cooked-down puree of any substantial fruit, apple butter being the best known, but you can also make peach butter, apricot butter, plum butter, etc. Any meaty fruit will work, but not fruits high in water content like citrus or melons.

Fruit butters are really tasty, easier to make than jams and jellies, and getting hard to find in stores. They do not contain any butter, but are called butter because of their creamy thickness. Because of this density, and because they are often not as sweet as jelly, they pair well with meats. They also find employment as dipping sauce, tart filling and pancake topping.

Fruit butter, like stock, is simple, endlessly forgiving, easy to improvise on, and hard to screw up. We offer you an apple butter recipe here. You use the same technique to make any other kind of fruit butter. As you read these instructions, don't be put off by the long process. Apple butter doesn't mind at all if you have to go away and do something midway through the making of it. Just put it in the fridge until you have time to come back and finish.

Apple Butter

There are three basic steps to making apple butter. First, the apples are cooked in liquid just long enough to soften them. Next, the apple stew is removed from the heat and pulverized into applesauce. Then the applesauce is cooked down until it thickens into a spread.

The variables include the liquid you use to cook the apples, quantity of sugar used, type of spices employed, how the apples are pulverized and cooked. It is the kind of recipe that can be made to suit whatever kind of supplies and equipment you have on hand.

There are no amounts here because precision really isn't necessary. All you should know is that it really, really cooks down, so you have to start with a fair amount of apples for it to be worthwhile. Two pounds of apples results in about one cup of apple butter.

If you are making apple butter with the intention of canning it, this is not the recipe for you. Please read the note below before you begin.

Apples, any type, peeled, cored and cut into rough chunks
Apple cider or water
Sugar or honey
Cinnamon
Ground cloves
Lemon juice
NOTE: if you use a food mill or sieve instead of a blender, you don't have to peel or seed the apples before boiling, as the mill or sieve will filter out peel and seeds. You know that, of course. This is just for the enlightenment of others.

Put the apples in a big, non-reactive pot—stainless steel, copper or enamel—and add just enough cider or water or both to cover them. You want to use a deep pot, because this stuff bubbles and splatters. A heavy bottom helps prevent burning. Cook over medium high heat, simmering until the apples are fork tender, about 20 minutes.

When the apples are tender remove them from the heat and pulverize them. You can do this in the pot with a hand-held blender, in a countertop blender, in a food mill, or by pushing the apple mass through a sieve. If you use a countertop blender only fill it halfway, otherwise you'll have a hot apple puree explosion. You do not have to use all the liquid in the pot. You are making applesauce, basically. Aim for that texture. More liquid means a longer cooking time. If you think there's too much liquid, pour some off before you start blending.

Return your applesauce to the pot and simmer it a long time over medium heat to reduce the volume of the liquid. It will behave like burping lava. Stir frequently so the stuff at the bottom doesn't burn. This is a good project for when you are doing something else in the kitchen, like baking, so you can keep half an eye on it.

Taste the apple puree as it cooks down, and stir in sugar, spices and lemon to taste. If you use sweet apples, or cider instead of water, you may not wish to add any sugar at all. Remember, the natural sugars of the apples are being concentrated. Whatever you do, add the sugar sparingly, a spoonful at a time. You can keep sweetening it until the end, but you can't take the sugar out. Add the spices and lemon juice just as carefully.

Keep cooking, and stirring, stirring lots at the end as it dries out, thickening and darkening. It will transform from hot applesauce into something very thick and rich. You can feel the difference in your mouth when it becomes true apple butter. It should not be at all liquid. Test by putting a spoonful of sauce on a cold plate. It should glom on to the plate, nice and firm. If it is runny, you have to cook it more.

The apple butter will keep for a couple of weeks in your fridge. It's so good that we've never had to resort to preservation. It's never lasted more than a few days. If you have more than you can eat within two or three weeks, the simplest thing to do is freeze the excess, or can it.

Important note on canning the apple butter: If you want to can your apple butter, you need to be aware of a couple of things. Apple butter made as described may not be acidic enough to can safely using the water bath method. If you have a pressure canner, you have no worries—those were made for canning low-acid foods. But if you don't, then you have to use a different recipe for apple butter than the one offered here.

The difference will be that you will have to add vinegar to the recipe stated above to acidify it, at the ratio of ¼ cup vinegar (white or apple cider) for every pound of apples, then it is necessary to adjust sugar ratios to balance out the sweetness. The Center for Food Preservation Safety offers a recipe on its website: uga.edu/nchfp/how/can_02/apple_butter.html

Jams And Jellies

Jams and jellies are another great way to deal with a bumper crop and/or imperfect fruit. Jam is easier to make and more forgiving. Jelly by definition is clear — it is made with fruit juice, so it requires the extra step of cooking the fruit and then pressing the juice out.

Jams and jellies gel through the combination of sugar and a substance called pectin. Jelly is not hard to make, but you need to find a good recipe and follow that recipe exactly to insure that the jelly will set correctly.

Pectin is present naturally in some kinds of fruits such as the citrus, plums and cranberries and is especially concentrated in apples. With low-pectin fruits such as nectarines, strawberries, peaches, pears and figs you'll need to add pectin to your jam or jelly, either by mixing in apples or by buying pectin, which can be found in the baking isle of your supermarket. The pectin box comes with instructions for each different kind of fruit, so if you buy the pectin, the secret to success is to follow the instructions it provides to the letter, especially for jelly. Three good recipe sources are any early edition of *The Joy of Cooking*, *The Jamlady Cookbook*, or for more sophisticated recipes, *Mes Confitures: The Jams and Jellies of Christine Ferber*.

Making Stock

Soup stock is frugal in the best of ways, and solid homesteading. It takes all the scraps you would otherwise throw out and makes them into something completely delicious and useful.

Stock is not just the basis for soup, though it does make great soup. You can sauté vegetables in stock instead of fat. You can drink it straight. You can cook rice, risotto, beans or polenta with stock—it makes simple things like that taste heavenly. Hell, you can boil your boxed mac 'n' cheese with it. Try it once and you'll be an addict. Use it whenever a recipe tells you to add water. You'll get a boost in both flavor and nutrition. It is not for nothing that the French call stock *fond de cuisine*: "foundation of the kitchen."

Stock doesn't keep more than a week, so make a big batch and freeze it. Freeze some in ice cube trays so you can access small quantities. You can make a stock concentrate by letting your stock simmer down by half.

There are a million ways to make stock. The best thing is that you can't screw it up. Throw scraps in pot and boil is the gist of it. It's caveman cooking, and yet, as any chef will tell you, it is the basis of fine cuisine.

Any good recipe book will show you how to make meat or fish stock, and we highly recommend you try it. But for now, we're just going to explain how to make vegetable stock, since once you start farming you'll find you have vegetables in abundance, and the desire to make good use of them.

Vegetable Stock

The only rule with vegetable stock is that you should not use cabbage in it, or cabbage's cruciferous friends like broccoli and cauliflower because they will overpower the stock with their special, slightly stinky scent. Tomatoes make good stock, but too many make tomato soup, so add sparingly. Otherwise, you can make stock of any vegetable matter that is clean and not too far gone. This is where you put all your peelings and trimmings and odds and ends—potato peels, mushrooms, artichoke leaves, everything. Even that half bag of slightly dried baby carrots from the back of the fridge.

The simplest way to make veg stock is to just throw all your vegetable scraps in a big pot along with a quartered onion, some salt, a few pepper-corns, a bay leaf and maybe some parsley, or thyme. Cover with about an equal amount of water. Simmer for up to an hour, strain the liquid off and throw the stewed veggies in the compost heap.

A richer stock comes from sautéing a little chopped onion and herbs of your choice in some butter or olive oil at the start, then adding the veggies to that base as above.

Five Ways to Preserve a Tomato

At the height of summer, the abundance of even a small garden can be over-whelming. You eat as much as you can, give a lot away, and then what? You preserve. We are going to put the lessons of this section to work here, and show you five ways to preserve your homegrown tomatoes. We could have chosen any vegetable to illustrate this section, but we chose tomatoes because they are most people's favorite homegrown food, and their season is all too short. It is possible to keep some of that flavor all year long, so you won't have to resort to buying tasteless tomatoes and tomato sauce. Each time you enjoy your pre-served tomatoes during the long winter, you will remember the warm summer air, the bushes heavy with fruit, and the green scent of tomato foliage.

1. Extend the harvest

Tomatoes don't do well in the cold—it ruins their texture. But if you still have unripe tomatoes on the vine when you get your first frost warning of the year, you can save them. Bring them inside and they will ripen slowly. They won't be as good as they would have been had they spent more time in the sun, but they'll still be better than store tomatoes.

There are two schools of thought on bringing tomatoes inside. One says to pick all of the tomatoes, wrap each of them individually in newspaper and stack them in a box, putting the ripest on top, the greenest on the bottom. They will ripen up over the next couple of weeks, faster or slower depending on the temperature. The other method is to just pull up the plant, shake the dirt off the roots, and hang the whole thing upside down. The fruit will ripen on the vine. Whether on the vine or in a box, store them out of the freezing cold, but keep them somewhere relatively cool if you can.

If you don't have space for storage, have a green tomato party. You can make lots of things out of green tomatoes, like fried green tomatoes, green tomato jam and green tomato chutney. We use green tomatoes as a vegetable in their own right. Just slice or chop them, squeeze some lemon juice over them (this is important—it brings out their flavor) and then treat them sort of like bell peppers: sauté them, put them on skewers, over pasta, that sort of thing.

2. Dried tomatoes
Homemade dried tomatoes are amazing. Drying heightens their sweetness turning them into a kind of tomato candy. They are so good, especially those made with cherry tomatoes, that we are hard-pressed not to eat them all up as they come off the dryer. This is another food where once you have the real stuff, it is very hard to go back to the store-bought version.

The best tomatoes for drying are cherry and Roma-type tomatoes, also called plum or paste tomatoes. Paste tomatoes have more meat and fewer seeds than the big juicy slicing kind. Cherry tomatoes are good for drying because they have an intense flavor that only deepens with drying, so you don't really care if they are a little seedy, or if they dry up to the size of a dime.

See the section titled "Dehydration: Why Save It For Hangovers?" to learn more about your options.

3. Candied tomatoes for the freezer
We figure if you're going to take up freezer space with tomatoes, it ought to be with something spectacular. These fit the bill. They'll keep for about three months in the freezer, just long enough to help you ease through the dreaded tomato withdrawal at the end of the summer.

These are tomatoes baked in oil. They are truly wonderful, rich, succulent and fragrant. They can be used in any sun-dried tomato application, or just tossed over pasta. This recipe is adapted from *The Italian Country Table* by Lynne Rossetto Kasper who explains that in Italy these are traditionally made in cooling bread ovens, thus the slow decline in heat while cooking.

Oven Candied Summer Tomatoes

2 to 2 ½ pounds of ripe, delicious summer tomatoes. Not plum
   tomatoes, unless they are extremely flavorful
1 cup robust extra-virgin olive oil
Salt

1 Preheat the oven to 400° F. Core the tomatoes and halve vertically,
   but do not seed them. Leave small tomatoes in halves; cut slightly
   larger tomatoes into wedges.

2 In a half-sheet pan, or two 2 ½ quart shallow metal baking pans (not
   glass or enamel), arrange the tomato wedges cut side down and ½ to
   1 inch apart. Coat the tomatoes with the olive oil. Sprinkle with salt.

3 Bake 30 minutes, then lower heat to 350°F and bake another 30
   minutes. Turn the heat down to 300°F and bake 30 more minutes, or
   until the edges are slightly darkened. If the edges are not yet colored,
   turn the heat down to 250°F and bake another 10 to 15 minutes.

4 Remove the tomatoes from the oven. Cool 20 minutes.

5 Layer the tomatoes in a storage container, cover them with their own
   oil, and refrigerate. Or freeze them in sealed plastic containers up to
   three months.

4. Home-canned tomatoes

You need:
2 ½–3 ½ pounds of tomatoes for each quart canned, plus extra for
   juice. These should be ripe, flavorful and unblemished. Remember,
   canning doesn't make them any better. The truth is rather the
   opposite, so start with good stuff.
Bottled lemon juice, because of its predictable acid levels
Salt
A big pot for cooking the tomatoes
Pint- or quart-sized glass canning jars with rings and brand new lids
   (meaning the disk parts)
**A canner with a rack, or a big, tall stock pot with an improvised rack
   at the bottom, or a folded dish towel at the bottom of the pot**
Tongs for lifting the hot jars out of the water

A ladle
A chopstick or long wooden kitchen implement of some type
Paper towels or clean kitchen towels

Prepare your jars and lids for canning as described in the canning section.

In the meanwhile, prepare your tomatoes. Dip them into boiling water for one minute, then dip them into cold water. After that, you should be able to peel them easily. After you peel them, cut out their core, and either leave them whole, or chop them into halves or quarters. They just have to be small enough to fit through the mouth of the jar.

Establish a base of juice at the bottom of a large pot by cutting up and squishing some of your less perfect tomato specimens. Add the peeled and cored tomatoes to this juice and bring it all up to a boil. You are not cooking them, just heating them to a boil. As soon as they are hot, you can start to pack your jars.

Use your jars hot. Pull the first one out of the water bath, or dishwasher, or oven, and keep the rest in.

Before packing, add 2 tablespoons of lemon juice to your quart jars, 1 tablespoon of lemon juice to each pint jar. This is necessary to acidify the tomatoes, which makes them safe for water bath processing. You can add a little salt too, if you want.

Use your ladle to scoop hot tomatoes into hot jars, pressing down as you do to squeeze out their juices. You want them surrounded by their juice, and the juice to come up within a ½ inch of the top of the jar.

Remove any air pockets from the jar by running the handle end of a wooden spoon or a chopstick around the inner wall of the jar.

Wipe the mouth of the jar clean with a towel, and put on a lid. Finger-tighten the band over the lid—meaning tighten only as tight as you are able using finger strength only.

Start your next jar. Do all the jars one by one until you are done. Don't do them all at once, assembly-line-style. You don't want the contents, or the jars, cooling while they wait for you to get to them.

Then put the jars in the hot water bath in a rack or on a folded towel. The water should cover the jars by 2 inches. Bring the water back to a rolling boil and start timing. The quart jars need to spend 45 minutes in the bath, the pint jars 40.

When they are done, take them out carefully with the tongs and put them on a cloth on the counter to cool overnight. Don't move them around or fiddle with them while they cool. After 24 hours take a look at the lid to make sure you have a good seal. If you press the lid it should not pop up and down. If it does, it is not sealed. Either process it again, or put that jar in the fridge and eat it first.

Keep your jars in a dark, cool place and they should be good for a year.

5. Canned tomato sauce

More useful than whole tomatoes might be jars of simple tomato sauce ready for eating or a little doctoring. This is a recipe that eats up a lot of tomatoes, because it is a reduction sauce. But it is very easy to make, and you'll learn to love having it on hand through the winter. It is tasty and thick and versatile enough to go on pizza or over pasta, to dress up meat or polenta.

Note: consider putting your sauce up in pint jars instead of quart jars unless you have a big family.

Fundamental Tomato Sauce

Ingredients:

All of the **tomatoes** you have on hand, any kind, the more the better.
  They should be cored, but peeling is optional.
Garlic cloves, coarsely chopped—about 5 for every 3 pounds of tomatoes
Salt and pepper
Bottled lemon juice or citric acid

Cover the bottom of a big stock pot with olive oil and sauté the garlic over medium heat just until it's soft; don't let it brown. Add all your tomatoes. Either chop them first, or squish and tear them with your bare hands as they go into the pot. Bring it to a lively bubble and then let it burble at moderate heat until the volume reduces by half. Stir frequently. This reduction really condenses the flavors. Salt and pepper it to taste.

Once it is reduced, take it off the heat and let it cool a little, then smooth it into a nice puree using whatever device you have on hand: a mixing wand, a countertop blender, or a food mill.

You could freeze this sauce instead of canning it. Try freezing it in ice cube trays, then transferring the cubes to a freezer bag. That way you can grab as many cubes as you need at a time. Or can it for long-term storage. Please consult any canning source for precise directions, but the process is very similar to canning whole tomatoes, as described previously.

Any canning recipe you find will instruct you to acidify the sauce by adding lemon juice or citric acid to the jars. This is unfortunate from a culinary standpoint, but necessary for food safety since tomatoes are on the borderline in terms of the level of acidity required for canning without a pressure canner. If the sauce tastes a little off as a result, counterbalance the lemon by adding a bit of sugar.

The ancient art of fermenting grains and fruits into alcohol is another iteration of the concept of preservation through transformation. But this transformation is the most profound of all, because it leads to the creation of intoxicating, even sacred, spirits.

Beer

Most beer is made in soulless factories, the remainder is in the hands of microbrewers. God bless the microbrewers for doing what they do, but somehow they also make beer-making look really hard. We need to return beer making to its rightful place — the kitchen — as part and parcel of the homestead economy, along with bread making, pickling and other fermentation processes. To do so would be a quiet revolution, and the reinvigoration one of the ancient housekeeping arts.

Beer making is not such a serious affair as the authorities might have us believe. Never be put off by technicalities, or intimidated by the process — and this applies to all home brewing, not just beer making. As herbalist Stephen Harrod Buhner, author of *Sacred Herbal Healing Beers*, says, "There is a lot of talk about the necessity for the use of chemicals to keep everything sterile, the need for other chemicals to make the beer work well, the crucial necessity for Teutonic authoritarian temperature controls, and the importance of complex understandings of minuscule differences in grains, malts, hops, and yeasts. Generally, this frightens off a lot of people and takes all the fun out of brewing."

So don't let the Man get you down — get brewing! Begin with a basic brewing text, or a class at your local homebrew supply shop. We took one evening class, but John Palmer's book *How to Brew*, while overly technical, does have some simple step-by-step instructions that will get you started. Most beginners start brewing with what is called malt extract, a thick molasses-like syrup plus a few grains added for flavor. Advanced homebrewers graduate to all-grain brewing where you extract fermentable sugars with special equipment that you can make yourself. We advise skipping beer kits and just asking for a reliable recipe using a malt extract at your local homebrew shop.

One of the most compelling reasons to brew beer is to experiment with sacred, medicinal and even psychotropic additives that used to be a part of traditional beer making. For these sorts of recipes seek out Buhner's *Sacred and Herbal Healing Beers*, an astonishing read complete with a set of recipes that will further your understanding of the significance beer has played in indigenous cultures for thousands of years. Your herb garden can complement beer making nicely by providing additives not found in over-the-counter brews.

Country Wines

Our definition of wine extends beyond grapes, which is slightly heretical. There are those who will argue that if it is not made with grapes, it simply is not wine. For the sake of this discussion we're going to agree to disagree. Whether you are making your ferment with grapes or dandelions, the process is similar enough to be considered under one name: wine.

"Country wines" are fermentations made with virtually anything except grains (in that case they would be beer). Everything from apricots to stinging nettles can be encouraged to become an alcoholic beverage. Most country wine recipes involve soaking your harvest, again anything from fruits to flowers to weeds, in boiling water, adding sugar and then straining the liquid into what is called a "carboy," a large glass bottle with a narrow top such as a five-gallon glass water jug or a one-gallon glass cider bottle. You throw in some wine yeast, which can be found at homebrew shops. (Regular bread yeast will ferment wines but will lead to nasty flavors.) Your carboy is then fitted with a fermentation lock, an inexpensive glass or plastic device that allows carbon dioxide gas, a byproduct of fermentation, to escape but prevent contaminants from entering which can spoil your fermentation and create vinegar.

After the initial fermentation slows, you'll "rack" the wine, which means siphoning the liquid into another carboy and leaving the solids behind. After the fermentation has completed you bottle your creation for aging, with corks, old bottles and a special corking tool. Some country wines are left to age in the bottle, others are enjoyed young.

Mead

Even if you don't tend a hive, mead — fermented honey — is one of the most straightforward fermentations to pursue on the urban homestead. The mead maker mixes together honey and water, perhaps some herbs or fruit, adds wine yeast and allows the mixture to ferment for a period of weeks, months, or years depending on the desired results. The process and tools are basically the same as with country wine. Bottle it up and enjoy the oldest of humankind's fermented beverages, the mead of inspiration.

Vinegar

Traditional vinegar making involves the introduction of a "mother" culture, acetobacter bacteria, to wine, beer, cider and countless other fermented beverages. You can purchase a mother of vinegar culture, use already-made vinegar, or wait for wild spores floating in the air to start the vinegar process. You can also make it by accident, and in fact will when some of your fermentation experiments fail. Quality vinegar, however, is made purposefully, another reason to give it a try.

Sake

Sake is made by first cultivating a specific kind of mold called *Aspergillus oryzae* contained in inoculated rice grains called *koji* which you can get at Japanese markets and some health food stores. You cook up a batch of rice and add *koji* to get the special mold growing. There are a few different ways of proceeding, but all involve adding yeast and fermenting the moldy rice you've just created. You end up with what the Japanese called *doburoku,* a difficult-to-translate word that basically means something like "sake moonshine." You can also use *koji* to make a sweet non-alcoholic rice beverage called *amazake*.

Distillation

Distillation is an advanced, and in most places illegal, practice which involves heating fermented fruit or grain in a still in order to concentrate and collect a beverage containing a high level of alcohol. In the civilized nation of France, you take your fermented fruit to a farmer who is licensed to run a still, and he'll make up a small batch of your own house brand of *eau de vie* for you. Lacking the assistance of a genial French farmer, you'll have build your own still if you want to make your own "water of life," or any other hard spirit.

Begin your distillation research with a copy of Matthew B. Rowley's book *Moonshine!*, which contains instructions for building a still, recipes and an amusing history of the craft. Additional resources for detailed plans for stills are in the resource section at the end of this book.

Baking On The Homestead

Baking With Sourdough

A sourdough starter is the traditional way of leavening bread, a process wherein wild yeasts are cultured in a container you keep on your countertop. It's more accurate to call breads made with such a culture "wild yeast" or "naturally leavened." Bread made with a wild yeast starter was, of course, the only way to make bread for thousands of years before the advent of commercial yeasts, and we happen to think it is still the best way. It creates a sturdy loaf with a tangy, chewy crust. The crumb—the inside of the loaf—is both springy and tender to the tooth. A hot slice of crusty sourdough smeared with fresh butter is about as close to heaven as we can get on earth. What's more, sourdough is better for you than regular bread. In *Good Bread is Back*, which details the revival of sourdough bread making in France, Laurence Kaplan points out that sourdough "is richer in certain vitamins and enzymes that are by-products of lactic fermentation, and it contains less phytic acid, which blocks mineral absorption." And he also points out what we know from experience: sourdough keeps longer than bread made with commercial yeast.

Now, the idea of making real, crusty artisanal loaves of sourdough in your own kitchen might sound impossible, but it is in fact entirely within your grasp. And once you get into the groove of baking with your own starter you'll never want to go back to the stale and lifeless loaves from your local supermarket. The science behind sourdough is complex, but the process of actually making and maintaining a starter is simple.

But first a brief mention of the science. When water meets flour a miraculous biological process begins. As the mixture ferments wild yeasts, which in most cases probably originate in the flour itself, form a symbiotic relationship with lacto bacteria. The lacto bacteria feed on metabolic products produced by the yeast, while simultaneously producing lactic acid which serves to prevent unwanted organisms from infecting your starter and gives wild yeast bread its distinctive flavor.

But you don't need to know the science to make a sourdough. All you need is a starter, or what some people call a "mother," and that is nothing but flour and water.

Starting The Starter

1 Get yourself a glass or ceramic container with a lid. It should be able to hold at least three to four cups of liquid. A quart-sized Mason jar works well. Don't use a metal container. It's okay to use metal utensils to stir your starter, since they are only in contact with it for a few moments—not enough time to cause any damage.

2 We've created starters from rye, whole wheat and white flour. You use different starters to make different types of bread, but more on that later. We recommend beginning with a white flour starter. Later you can convert the white starter to a whole wheat or rye starter. The reason to begin with white flour is that both whole wheat and rye flours have a tendency to rot before the beneficial symbiotic culture of lactobacillus and wild yeast have an opportunity to develop.

3 To begin your white flour starter, mix one cup of white flour with one cup of lukewarm water in your glass or ceramic container and stir until smooth. Put it in a warm place. In the winter we keep it on top of our stove, so it is warmed by the pilot light. Optimal temperatures are in the 70°–80° range, so in the summer we keep the starter on the countertop.

4 Every day, pour off one cup of your starter and add a half cup of flour and a half cup of lukewarm water back in to feed what remains. The biggest mistake most people make, and probably the most common cause of a starter failure, is neglecting to feed it every single day. Unfed starters will begin to mold very quickly, and in any case will not create a successful loaf. We can't repeat this enough—if you want sourdough bread you need to feed the starter every day without fail.

5 Your starter should begin to get bubbly in a few days. A layer of liquid, known in sourdough circles as "hooch," will form on top. Don't be concerned, this is natural and simply stir it in every morning when you add the additional flour and water.

6 After two weeks, you should have an active culture of wild yeasts that you can bake bread with. You can now throw out all those little packages of commercial yeast in your cupboard. Their day is over.

7 After a week or so has passed, instead of throwing out that cup of starter in the morning, use it to try to make a loaf of bread. The starter will get stronger as it gets older, but give it a try at about a week, certainly by two weeks. You can also use it to make a batch of the best sourdough pancakes you've ever eaten.

8 If you aren't going to bake for a few days put the starter in the fridge, and feed it once a week. To revive it, take it out of the fridge and give it two or three days of feedings before you use it.

9 To create a whole wheat or rye starter first begin with a living white flour starter at least two weeks old. Instead of feeding it the half-cup of white flour and half-cup of water, instead feed it a half-cup of whole wheat or rye and a half-cup of water. In a few days you will have "converted" your white flour starter to a whole wheat or rye starter. With both whole wheat and rye it is especially important to feed every day, as these flours have a tendency to develop molds much more quickly than white flour starters.

Sourdough Mythologies

Unfortunately the internet and bread cookbooks contain a great deal of misinformation about sourdough. Here are some myths that we've debunked from personal experience:

You should add grapes/potatoes/rice to the flour and water mixture to hasten the development of wild yeasts. Sorry folks, the wild yeasts are in the flour and you don't need anything except flour and water to get your starter going. The wild yeasts on the skin of grapes are a different beast and not the kind that make bread rise.

You should add some commercial yeast to get it going. Wrong. Commercial yeast is another type of beast entirely. More, it does not survive in the acidic bacterial stew that makes up a healthy starter culture, so adding it is a waste of time.

You should mail-order a sourdough starter to replicate a regional flavor. In all likelihood the wild yeasts in the flour you use will eventually dominate any mail-order cultures you purchase. Your starter will become local to wherever you live. Just make your own starter. It will be ready to use about the same time it would take to mail-order a starter. Wild yeasts, like love, should be free.

You have to use bottled water. We've made starters with plain old chlorinated Los Angeles tap water with no problems. If your water is heavily chlorinated and you're having problems with your starter you can de-chlorinate your water by letting the water stand without a lid for 24 hours.

Wild yeasts are in the air and you have to "catch" them. Yes, there are yeasts in the air, but there are many millions more in the flour which, in all likelihood, is the origin of the beasts that will make your starter bubble.

So now you have no excuses — get into your kitchen and get your starter on.

Baking A Sourdough Loaf

Our sourdough bread making method results in an artisanal, old-world loaf with a hard crust and complex flavor. Every time we make it, we can't believe we made something so good. The thrill just doesn't wear off.

The miracle of this bread is its accessibility. You don't need a wood-fired oven, or a culinary degree. All you need is persistence. The first few loaves you try might be successful, or they might be complete disasters. If they are disasters, you simply must persevere. We promise you will get a feel for it. Once you get the hang of it, your loaves will not only be better than execrable supermarket bread, but will even be better than high-end bakery breads. Yes, that good.

All you really need to make bread is flour, water, salt and your own two hands. However, there are a few tools that will make the job a lot easier.

Heavy-Duty Mixer

If you've got the time, by all means knead by hand, but what we like about heavy-duty mixers such as the highly dependable KitchenAid mixer is that you can throw the ingredients in the bowl and eat breakfast while it kneads your bread with its dough-hook attachment. When you're finished with your coffee, your dough is ready to start rising. Heavy-duty mixers ain't cheap, but they will pay for themselves eventually if you take up bread making as a routine part of your domestic life. Keep an eye out for a used one. A heavy-duty KitchenAid goes for about $200 new, but a friend of ours just found one for $25 at a garage sale, in what must be the garage sale coup of the year.

Baking Stone

Baking stones help more evenly distribute the heat of your oven and assist in producing a good hard crust. Get an inexpensive square one and don't ever clean it with soap. You don't really need to wash it at all, just sweep it off. Ours just lives in the oven all the time.

Scale

One of the keys to bread making is being able to repeat the process reliably. And due to the vagaries of humidity it's difficult to get accurate measurement of flour with just volumetric means, i.e. measuring in cups. Measuring your ingredients in ounces will help ensure consistency from loaf to loaf. You don't need a fancy scale — a simple cheap one will do.

Bread Forms

Bread forms, which come in wooden and plastic models, give your bread an attractive shape, and leave a nice flour pattern on the crust. Sometimes known as *bannetons*, they are available at high-end kitchen shops in oval, oblong and round shapes and cost around $30. We use a small round one. You don't need one, however. You can just shape the loaf in a bowl lined with a heavily floured towel.

Sourdough Recipe

This recipe, inspired by Nancy Silverton's techniques in *Breads from the LaBrea Bakery*, will yield a gourmet loaf with a hard crust and scrumptious sourdough flavor. Though the instructions are long, this is an easy recipe with a reasonable chance of success, assuming that you have been good about feeding your starter every day and keeping it in a warm place.

Though far less complicated than manufacturing methamphetamine (not that we know anything about that), sourdough also benefits from precision in measurements, so the use of a scale is the only way to guarantee success. That is why the measurements are given in ounces, not cups.

You're aiming for dough that is somewhat sticky. In general it's better to have dough that's too moist than a dry and stiff dough. Moist dough helps in the formation of carbon dioxide bubbles that give a good dough a light and open texture, though an extremely wet dough will be too sticky and hard to handle when it comes time to remove it from the proofing basket later. Repeat this recipe enough times and you'll learn to tell if your dough is the right consistency.

Some health circles hold any use of white flour as heretical. This loaf can be made with both a white flour-based starter or a whole wheat starter. We like to use a mixture of whole wheat and white flours for our dough, since the white flour helps to lighten the texture of the bread. You can adjust the proportions to your own taste. Many store-bought "wheat" breads are not actually "whole wheat" and many have preservatives, sugar and long lists of unnecessary ingredients. This naturally leavened bread is close to bread at its most elemental — flour, water and salt.

Ingredients
8 oz. sourdough starter
13 oz. unbleached white bread flour
3 oz. whole wheat flour
2 tablespoons wheat bran
8 oz. cool water
1 ½ teaspoons sea salt

1 Mix the starter, flours, wheat bran and water into a dough. If you are doing this by hand, stir the ingredients together and then knead the loaf vigorously for five minutes. If you have a standing mixer, put all the ingredients in the mixing bowl, fit the machine with the dough hook attachment, and just let it stir for five minutes. It will mix the dough, and then knead it for you.

2 Cover the dough with a cloth and let it rest under a cloth for 20 minutes.

3 Mix in the salt and knead by hand or machine for another six minutes. If you've used a mixer you should do a small amount of hand kneading to make sure that the salt has been thoroughly integrated into the dough.

4 Put the dough in an oiled bowl and cover with plastic wrap or lid. Let it ferment in a warm place for three to four hours. We use our stovetop, which is always warm from its pilot light.

5 Shape the dough into a *boule*, which is a pretentious way of saying a flattened ball, and place in a floured proofing basket. We recommend using a wooden proofing basket, called a *banneton*. The alternative to a *banneton* is to line an ordinary basket, or even a bowl, with a floured cloth, called a proofing cloth. Your proofing cloth should be

made out of a piece of linen or canvas which you rub with flour, quite heavily, so the weave is saturated. Never wash either the *banneton* or the proofing cloth. Just shake off the excess flour and let them dry before storing so they don't go moldy. They get better with age, becoming less "sticky" and developing native yeast populations which will help your bread proof.

6   Cover your basket or bowl with a plate or plastic wrap and put it in the refrigerator for eight to 24 hours. This long rest gives the loaf time to develop complex flavors.

7   Take the *boule* out of the refrigerator and put it in a warm place to ferment for another three to four hours.

8   Preheat the oven to 500°. Take the *boule* out of the proofing basket by turning it upside down onto a stiff piece of cardboard that is covered with flour or cornmeal. You'll use this to slide the loaf into the oven. Professional bakers and pizza makers use a flat, shovel-like tool called a peel to do this, but a piece of cardboard will work just as well. Shake the loaf around on the cardboard a little to make sure that it will slide off smoothly into the oven without sticking.

9   Using the cardboard, slide the loaf into the oven on top of your baking stone. (If you don't have a baking stone, you can bake your loaf on a floured cookie sheet which has been preheating in the oven, but the crust will not be as good as it would be if you have a stone.) Immediately turn the oven down to 450°. Get some steam going either by giving the oven walls several quick squirts with a spray bottle, or by tossing a shot glass full of water against the wall. Either way, do it quickly and close the door so you don't lose heat. This simulates the fancy steam injection systems that commercial bakeries have. Steam will give your loaf a hard crust. **The revolution will not be soft-crusted.**

10   Over the next five minutes open the oven two or three more times and spray more water in. We've also just tossed in a little water from a glass if we don't have a sprayer on hand.

11   After the five-minute steam injection period is over, continue to bake for another 20 minutes, and don't open the oven door.

12   After 20 minutes open the oven and rotate the loaf. Bake for another 15 to 20 minutes for a total of 40 to 45 minutes until the crust turns a dark brown.

13 Remove the loaf from the oven, but resist the urge to break into it. It's still cooking, and you could get a stomach ache from the still-active wild yeasts. Let it cool down before slicing.

After reading this you might think this is too much work, but it really isn't as bad as it looks. Once you get into the groove, there's really not much labor involved with making this bread especially if you've got a mixer, but it does require some scheduling.

Sourdough Pancakes

These are our favorite kind of pancakes, and a great use for excess starter. This recipe requires two cups of starter. This is one more cup than you will have to spare daily if you are following our starter-feeding instructions, which generate one cup of extra starter a day. You can make a half-batch with one cup, which will make four large pancakes—enough to feed two people if they're willing to be reasonable about calorie intake. But if you plan ahead you can either double your feeding of the starter the day before, or stockpile starter for a couple of days.

This recipe is also adapted from Nancy Silverton's *Breads from the La Brea Bakery*, which should be on your bookshelf if you start baking in earnest.

2 cups sourdough starter
2 tablespoons maple syrup
3 tablespoons light oil
2 eggs
½ teaspoon salt
½ teaspoon baking soda
1 teaspoon baking powder

In a large mixing bowl whisk together the liquid ingredients: the starter, eggs, syrup and oil. Then add the rest of the ingredients, making sure they're well incorporated. Preheat a griddle or skillet and then oil it. It's hot enough to cook when you flick a drop of water on the surface and it skitters around and burns off quickly. Pour 1/4 to 1/3 cup of the batter on the pan and cook over medium-high heat until bubbles cover the surface of the pancake. Flip it and cook for about one more minute more. You'll see that this batter makes thin, tender, elastic pancakes riddled with little holes. Keep the finished pancakes warming in the oven while you cook the rest.

Soda Bread

As much as we love our sourdough bread, we still make soda bread. Soda breads and yeast breads are entirely different beasts. Soda breads are more related to cake than anything else. They lack the chewy, elastic quality of yeast or sourdough bread. Soda breads are heavier and more crumbly, and are best eaten by the slice, smeared with butter, or dipped in soup. They need the leavening agents of buttermilk and baking soda to come alive, unlike the marvelously elemental sourdough loaf which is nothing but flour and water. But soda breads have their place in the urban homestead kitchen. They have their own comforting qualities, they are easy to make, forgiving and endlessly adaptable. And best of all, they are there for you whenever you need to round out a meal. You can have a hot loaf of soda bread on the table one hour after you get the notion to make it.

Brown Soda Bread

This makes a hearty, nutty, ever so slightly sweet loaf bread that comes together quickly. Like all soda bread, it isn't very springy, so doesn't stand up too well to sandwich duty (though it can be made to work), but is excellent with cheese, or soup, or just toasted and buttered.

This recipe and the classic soda bread that follows are adapted from recipes in the May 1996 issue of *Bon Appétit*. You know a recipe works when you use it for more than 10 years

1 ¾ cup all-purpose flour
1 ¾ cup whole wheat flour
3 tablespoons toasted wheat bran
3 tablespoons toasted wheat germ
2 tablespoons old-fashioned oats
2 tablespoons packed brown sugar
1 teaspoon baking powder
½ teaspoon salt
2 teaspoons chilled unsalted butter cut into pieces
2 cups or so of buttermilk, or any soured milk

Note: The oats, bran and wheat germ are optional. They add texture and fiber to the loaf. Omit them or change them up as you please.

Preheat oven to 425°F. Butter a 9-inch loaf pan.

Put everything except the butter and buttermilk into a large bowl and mix thoroughly. Add the butter and rub it into the flour with your fingers until you can't find any chunks of butter anymore. You can opt to cut the butter into the flour using a food processor, but then you have to wash the food processor.

Sheer laziness keeps us using our fingers. Stir in the buttermilk until a soft dough forms and you can scrape up most of the dry bits from the bottom of the bowl. You might want to use your hands bring the dough together, but don't overwork it. This will be a fairly wet dough.

Put it in a greased loaf pan and bake about 40–45 minutes. Do the toothpick test in the center to make sure it is done. The toothpick should come out clean. Turn it out of the pan, and let it cool on a rack.

Classic Soda Bread

Classic soda bread is a white loaf. We often make this recipe with a kind of King Arthur flour called "white whole wheat," a very mild whole wheat, which gives the loaf a little more nutritional integrity. This loaf is even quicker and easier to make than the brown loaf above. It is made all in one bowl, and doesn't even need a baking pan. It comes together in seconds.

3 ½ cups flour
2 tablespoons caraway seeds (optional)
1 teaspoon baking soda
¾ teaspoon salt
1 ½ cups buttermilk, yogurt, or other soured milk

Preheat oven to 425°F. Flour a cookie sheet and set it aside.

Mix all the dry ingredients in a large bowl. Stir in the buttermilk a bit at a time, just until the dough turns into clumps. Put down your spoon and use your hands to gather the dough together into a ball, adding a little more buttermilk to make all the dry bits come together if necessary. Don't knead it too much. Unlike yeast breads, soda breads, biscuits and all their kin don't like to be handled. Just shape the dough into a ball as quickly as possible. Drop this ball onto the cookie sheet and flatten it slightly so that it is 2 or 3 inches thick. Take a sharp knife and cut a deep X across the top of it. Bake until it browns, about 35–40 minutes. Test to see if it is done by tapping the bottom—it should sound hollow. You can also do the toothpick test into the center of the top. The toothpick should come out clean.

Variations:

Sometimes we make this white loaf into a sweet loaf, something reminiscent of scones. There is no set recipe for this, just a little improvised tricking up. It starts by adding a little bit of sugar, white or brown. Since the goal is not to make it super-sweet, just slightly sweet, that means adding about ¼ cup of sugar. Then you can up the fat content to make the loaf a little richer and longer-lived by working some butter into the flour. Take ¼ to ½ stick of chilled butter, cut it into chunks and use your fingertips to rub it into the flour until it disappears. This only takes a couple of minutes, but you can also do it with a food processor. Then throw in some dried fruit, like raisins, currants or chopped dried apricots. Leave the caraway seeds in, or take them out. We like the way their flavor blends with raisins.

Add the buttermilk and form the loaf and continue as described in the original recipe. You can brush the top of the loaf with milk to make it a little more attractive. The cooking time will lengthen a little because of the fruit and butter. Do the toothpick test after 40 minutes to make sure that there isn't any wet dough in the center.

Cleaning The Urban Homestead

Anything they have to advertise is something you don't need.

We didn't make up that little bit of brilliance above, we paraphrased it from Jerry Mander, author of *Four Arguments for the Elimination of Television*, a worthwhile read if there ever was one.

We're starting off our section on cleaning talking about advertising, because advertising is really at the heart what we think of as our national cleaning problem. Cleaning is a simple task, requiring nothing more than soap, water, and a rag. Advertising is what convinces us that we have to buy new, improved, and extra-strength whizbangs, different products for every task and for every room in the house. All this false specialization would just be another relatively harmless iteration of the marketplace if the ads weren't peddling poisons.

There is no dust bunny, window smudge or grease stain that warrants chemical warfare, yet a lifetime of watching commercials has convinced us that unless we're cleaning our homes with an arsenal of the strongest chemical compounds available, we're just not cleaning. Peruse the labels of the things you are cleaning with right now. Do you see the words POISON, WARNING or DANGER anywhere? Most likely you do. When you clean, you are distributing these dangerous chemicals all over your house, cleaning your dishes with them, washing your clothes with them, letting them taint the air you breathe. How can a home full of toxins ever be called "clean"?

Is toxin too strong a word for our standard store-bought cleaning products? No, it is not. You might (reasonably) think that nothing all that harmful would ever be allowed to be sold in stores for home use, but you would be wrong. Cleaning products do not have to be independently tested to confirm their safety before they go to market. Companies are legally free to sell just about anything they want, and don't need anybody's okay to bring it to market. They don't even have to disclose all the ingredients in their products on the labels.

The individual chemicals that make up commercial cleaning products are not particularly well regulated either. Thanks to the Toxic Substances Control Act, an Orwellian name if there ever was one, chemical manufactures are not required to prove a new chemical is safe. Instead, the burden falls on the EPA to demonstrate that the substance poses a significant risk to the public. Over 2000 new chemicals go to the agency for approval each year, leaving little time for a thorough vetting. Most applicants are approved in just three weeks.

So most of the chemical compounds in our cleaning products are of recent invention and for the most part, ill-tested, especially for long-term health and environmental effects. Serious scientists, not just New Age paranoiacs, are beginning to associate these common household cleaners (or perhaps the chemical cocktail they create in mixed use) with cancer, asthma, allergies, immune system disorders and reproductive disorders. And that is just in us humans. They are also tainting the water, and affecting the entire ecosystem.

Are We Too Clean?

If you watch advertisements, or cruise the supermarket shelves, you can't fail to notice that everything is anti-bacterial now, as if common household bacteria have suddenly become as exotic and deadly as Ebola.

It's a great marketing coup, but potentially a dangerous one. In our enthusiasm for all things anti-bacterial we are, thanks to the law of natural selection, breeding even more deadly forms of bacteria that laugh at our anti-bacterial handsoap. Just as with the overuse of pesticides and antibiotics, the overuse of anti-bacterial products assures that only the fittest bacteria survive, thereby selecting out ever more virulent strains with each new generation.

For this reason, in 2000, the American Medical Association recommended that the practice of adding common antimicrobials to household products be discontinued. Of course, no one listened to them.

And in our quest for antiseptic environments we lose the low-key exposures to both friendly and not-so-friendly bacteria that keep our immune systems in good working order. This is not to say we should wallow in filth, but it may well be healthier to wallow in a mud hole than in a vat of antiseptic gel. Soap and water are quite enough for any cleaning you have to do, and more than enough to keep your hands clean.

DIY Cleaning Products

Here at our homestead the majority of our cleaning is done with homemade solutions, though we resort to the commercial eco-products for a few things, which we'll mention later on. We choose to make our own for health reasons, to save money, and to reduce packaging waste. The contents of our kitchen cabinet have changed a lot since switching over. If you look there now, you'll see a gallon of vinegar, a big box of baking soda, a bottle of castile soap, and three or four recycled spray bottles filled with different homemade solutions.

You may have tried homemade cleaning products in the past, or heard that they don't really work. Give them another try. The trick of it is to use the right substance for the task at hand.

One common thing we hear is "I tried cleaning (fill in the blank) with vinegar and it didn't work." A weird cult has risen around vinegar, so if you're surfing the internet seeking information on cleaning with vinegar, you'll find a lot of dubious claims. Vinegar is very useful, but for specific applications. We'll talk more about that later.

If you can't quite give up the alluring convenience of packaging, there are eco-friendly cleaning products to be found at health food stores and fancy supermarkets, and we recommend you use those. But be sure they are the real deal. Beware of "greenwashing"—products claiming to be natural or environmentally friendly when they are no better than regular products. The words "green" or "natural" in the name don't mean anything at all. Those terms are not regulated. Warnings like "Avoid contact with skin" and "Use in a well ventilated area" are hints that these products are not the gentle daisy juice their labels might lead you to believe.

Our Three Principles Of Clean

1 Everything we clean with should be nontoxic and easy on the skin. You shouldn't have to clean with gloves on.

2 Everything we clean with should be cheap.

3 Everything we use for cleaning should serve multiple purposes — we want as few items beneath our sink as possible, both to save our sanity, and to save on packaging. For example, baking soda has uses in cooking and cleaning, in the bath and in the laundry.

Our Cleaning Cupboard

The Big Three, All You Really Need

Baking Soda
Baking soda is a scrubber and deodorizer. It replaces scouring powder and is gentle enough to use on porcelain. It can be dissolved in water and used for all-purpose cleaning, but we don't do that because it can leave behind a

I make my own cleaning products because it's cheaper, time-effective, and "eco-friendly," as we say these days.

I find it much cheaper and more time-effective to mix vinegar and water for example, instead of having to go to the store, find the equivalent product, buy the product, come back home, and finally realize that I don't like the feel or smell of it. Even if it's a product I have used many times and am satisfied with, I will get tired of the scent, so I prefer to make my own, mix in the essential oils I want, and switch whenever I feel like it by not making too big quantities.

The other main reason for me to do this process is because at least I am sure of what I put in my products. I don't particularly enjoy finding out that the products I buy in a general store don't biodegrade, pollute our water sources and/or are simply bad and sometimes dangerous to breathe or be in contact with!

Severine Baron, Montreal

white residue that has to be rinsed—there are more convenient all-purpose cleaners, which we'll talk about later. But baking soda is great for scrubbing out sinks, tubs and toilets. It is also a laundry additive: it improves the performance of your soap by softening the water. You're going to be using it by the cupful, so buy it in quantity at restaurant supply stores or big-box outlets.

Distilled White Vinegar

Vinegar is a mild acid, a disinfectant, a deodorizer, and a fabric softener. It is great for wiping down tabletops, appliances, mopping the floor and cleaning toilet seats, because it is a mild disinfectant, and it leaves nothing behind except a slight shine. But we've found it doesn't do much to cut grease or heavy soap scum. It prefers to leave the heavy lifting to soap and baking soda. The smell is not a problem because it vanishes as soon as it dries, and takes any other unpleasant odors with it. It is easy to find white vinegar in gallon containers at any grocery store.

Liquid Castile Soap

Castile soap is used in place of all liquid detergents and soaps as a general cleaner for home and body because it is simple and safe. Castile soap is soap made with 100% vegetable-based oils, and nothing else. Other liquid soaps and detergents are often made with petroleum byproducts. They clean very well and rinse easily, but when they go down the drain, they throw off the chemistry of our natural waters.

The best-known brand of castile soap is Dr. Bronner's which is widely available in health food stores and some mainstream markets and drugstores. Remember to follow the advice on the bottle: "Dilute! Dilute! Dilute!" If you don't like Dr. Bronner's, remember that all castile soaps are not the same. They vary in character and price depending on what types of oils they contain. Take a look online and you'll find a lot of options.

Other Cleaning Aids You Might Want to Keep Around

Essential Oils
Use these to tart up your cleaning preparations. Citrus, lavender, eucalyptus and rosemary are commonly used to evoke "clean" associations. But hey, if you want your toilet bowl to smell like patchouli, we're behind you 100%. Look for them in health food stores, or order them online for better prices.

Tea Tree Oil
Lots of folks like to add tea tree oil to their cleaning products for its antibacterial properties. Tea tree oil is also found at health food stores.

Hydrogen Peroxide is a non-toxic disinfectant and a bleach. Use the 3% solution, the drugstore kind.

Olive Oil or lighter oils like safflower can be used with vinegar to polish furniture.

Beeswax makes a really high-quality furniture polish for the über-homemaker. You can buy beeswax from beekeepers/honey suppliers, and anywhere you buy candle-making supplies, but if you only need a limited quantity it might be easiest just to buy a small beeswax candle.

Lemon juice is another acid, like vinegar, and is often used for bleaching. Scrub your cutting boards with salt and lemon to disinfect them.

"Green" Cleaners We Are Not Really Down With, But Others Use:

Borax (usually found in the laundry section of the supermarket as "20 Mule Team Borax") is a naturally occurring mineral salt, often used in the alternative cleaning circles as an all-purpose cleaner, scrub powder and laundry booster.

While it is certainly better for the environment than most of the cleaning products you find on the supermarket shelves, borax does not make our cleaning cut for two reasons. The first is that it is irritating to skin and eyes, so you have to be careful when you use it, and the second is that it is toxic if swallowed.

Baking soda duplicates borax's functions: scrubber, cleaner, laundry additive, but baking soda is actually good for your skin (you can bathe in it, use it as an exfoliator, or use it to soothe insect bites) and while you should not ingest lots of it, you can take it as an antacid. Why would anyone bother keeping borax around when baking soda is the safer alternative? Probably because borax is a little stronger. But that's not enough of a reason for us.

Ammonia is a naturally occurring substance, and it often finds it way into green cleaning lists. Its functions are similar to vinegar, but it is stronger. However, it is also caustic, and irritating to the lungs and eyes, so it is just too much trouble to use. Stronger is not always better. Vinegar is the common-sense alternative.

Non-Toxic Cleaning Formulas For The Homesteader
We've spoken to a lot of urban homesteaders about how they mix up their cleaning products. It turns out that none of us do it exactly the same way twice. We're all mixologists and mad scientists on cleaning day. So consider the recipes that follow as starting points for your own experiments.

All-Purpose Spray Cleaners

Formula 1 for kitchens:
Fill a regular-sized spray bottle ⅓ of the way with vinegar, fill the rest with water. Add a tablespoon of castile soap. Shake before each use.

If you have a clear bottle, you'll see that when you first add the soap to the vinegar water, a reaction happens which separates the fats out of the soap. This will disperse after a few minutes, but a tiny bit of fat ends up floating at the top of the bottle. Since you're drawing water from the bottom of the bottle, this is not going to be a problem.

This formula mixes the shining and deodorizing qualities of vinegar with just a little soap to cut grease, making it a great all-around cleaner. We use it primarily in the kitchen on things like the grimy fridge door or the greasy stove. It's also good for wiping down counters. The vinegar smell disperses as it dries, and deodorizes the whole room.

Vinegar-Free Variation: If the fat dispersal or the vinegar smell bothers you, a simple solution of ⅛–¼ cup of castile soap in a quart-sized spray bottle full of water also works very well for kitchen clean-up.

Formula 2 for bathrooms, and anything that shines:

50% water plus 50% white vinegar in a spray bottle.

We find this blend good for general wipe-down purposes, as long as what you're wiping isn't greasy. Vinegar and water is particularly good for bathroom cleaning, since vinegar is a mild disinfectant and a deodorizer, and is good for shiny surfaces, tile, toilet tanks, even mirrors. It doesn't require rinsing. The little bit of soap found in Formula #1 makes it not as ideal for leaving a shine.

We keep a bottle of this mix in the bathroom, and use it to clean everything in there except the tub and toilet bowl. The soap scum on the bottom of the tub requires a scrub, and the bowl gets a dose of straight vinegar. More on that later.

NOTE: Vinegar should never be used on stone surfaces. If you have granite countertops, marble floors, or the like, you might be stuck using the manufacturer's recommended cleaners. We have no experience with stone and don't want to be accountable for the ruination of your $30,000 countertops. That said, washing them with water infused with a couple of drops of castile soap seems safe enough (acids like lemon juice and vinegar are your big concern), but the soap might leave a film. For what it is worth, we know one intrepid natural cleaner who wipes down his granite countertops with a very dilute (5% or less) solution of rubbing alcohol in water, but the safety and effectiveness of this will surely vary by how your stone surface is sealed.

All-Purpose Scouring Powder

Get a sugar shaker from a restaurant supply store — or be trashy like us and punch some holes in the lid of a jar — and fill it with baking soda. If you want scented scrub, add a few drops of essential oil to the baking soda in the can, cover the holes, and shake well. The scent will last a long time, and can be refreshed as necessary.

Baking soda is a gentle and effective scrubber, safe for porcelain sinks and tubs, tile and grout, pots and pans, and strong enough for stovetop grime. It is also good for getting stains out of mugs.

For tough, baked-on crud in pots and pans, make a paste with a little water and soda and let it sit for a good while, then come back and scrub with a scouring pad. If the soda is not enough try scrubbing with regular salt. Salt is much more abrasive, though, so don't use it on delicate surfaces.

Sink Bleaching

If after you scrub your sink clean it still looks a little yellow, try doing a second scrub with the rind of a lemon. Leave the juice and pulp sitting for a little while, then rinse. Put the used rind down the disposal to make it smell better.

Floor Cleaner

Vinyl, linoleum and tile floors can be mopped with ¼–½ cup of vinegar in a bucket of water. A wood floor can carefully damp-mopped with the same mixture, just make sure your mop is only damp, barely even damp, in fact, and certainly not wet.

Use hot water to increase your cleaning power, and for fun add just a few drops of an essential oil of your choice. Rosemary and eucalyptus oil clear the sinuses as you mop. Keep a little of the soft scrub (see below), or your baking soda shaker, to attack really gunky spots.

NEVER use vinegar on marble, and to be safe, any stone floor.

Dish Liquid & Automatic Dishwasher Detergent

Here we confess to resorting to store-bought. Castile soap leaves a slight film on dishes. Some people use borax for hand-washing dishes, but as we've said, we're not huge borax fans. So we look for a plant-based, phosphate-free, biodegradable dish liquid made with the fewest ingredients possible. The longer the ingredients list, we find, the more likely there is to be trouble.

Similarly, we don't know of any effective homemade substitute for dishwasher detergent, and so have to rely on an eco-product for this as well. If you are disappointed with the first alternative dishwasher detergent you try, keep looking. All eco-products are not all alike, and you'll find one that works for you.

Disinfecting Sprays

Here at the Urban Homestead we sigh rather heavily at the thought of a disinfectant spray (see our rant above), but our friends with babies swear they need disinfectant. So if you don't trust soap and water to do the job it was born to do, and need to specialize, these are our recommendations:

Regular Old Hydrogen Peroxide (3% Solution): Keep it in the opaque bottle it comes in because it is light-sensitive. Just screw a spray bottle nozzle on the original bottle, spritz and wipe. Remember, peroxide is a bleach, as any truck stop blonde can tell you, so don't spray it on fabric. Straight vinegar is also a fair disinfectant, by the way.

The Nuclear Option: If you want the true nuclear option for disinfecting, we've got a neat trick for you. Spray your suspect surface with straight hydrogen peroxide and follow it immediately with a spritz of straight vinegar. Actually you can spritz in either order, but keep the two liquids in their own bottles. If you mix them together in one bottle they create a new substance called peracetic acid which is dangerous. But used separately, one right on top of the other, they pack a devastating one-two punch for the bacterial kingdom and remain perfectly safe for you.

This technique was developed by Susan Sumner, a food scientist at Virginia Polytechnic Institute and State University, and tested in their labs. They tried this technique on heavily contaminated surfaces and found that it eliminated virtually all salmonella, shigella and E. coli bacteria.

She actually developed this as a food treatment, as a way to disinfect meat and produce. It is non-toxic, and after rinsed off under running water, is said to leave no flavor behind. We're sure Susan is right about this, but we'll stick with rinsing our food with water.

What About Tea Tree Oil?: Many people we talk to regularly add a few drops of tea tree oil to their homemade cleaning products hoping for a boost in anti-bacterial powers. Straight tea tree oil is a powerful natural antibacterial and antifungal agent. The problem is that we don't know how well it works diluted, and have not found any research on the subject. A solution of one tablespoon of tea tree oil to one cup of water is effective at removing musty, mildewy smells from things that have been in storage, that we know. Does that mean that concentration will kill other bugs? That we don't know. *Caveat emptor.*

Fruit And Vegetable Wash

There is no need to buy or make special fruit washes. Rinsing your produce under running water, and perhaps scrubbing with a brush, is perfectly adequate and recommended by the FDA. The exception to this might be if your soil is carrying heavy amounts of lead. Under ordinary conditions, just rinsing with water and maybe scrubbing does a good job of removing bacteria and surface pesticide residue. Tests have shown that commercial washes are no more effective than plain water. Homemade preparations involving soap, vinegar or bleach are also not recommended because they may leave a residue on the food that will, at the very least, affect flavor.

If you are worried about pesticides, buy organic because pesticides are not only on the skin, but also absorbed into the produce. Or better yet, grow your own food.

If you are worried about E. coli and other bacteria, wash your hands before handling food. You are probably the biggest food contamination risk in your kitchen. Then cut off or discard any wilted or bruised sections of your produce before putting it away — these spots are where bacteria breed. And, at the risk of sounding redundant, grow your own food.

Loving The Rags

You can spray disinfectant all you want, and clean every minute of the day, but if your sponge is full of bacteria, you'll just be spreading a fresh layer of bacteria around every time you wipe down a surface or wash a dish. We recommend you switch away from using cellulose sponges in the kitchen and use cotton dishcloths instead, changing out to a fresh one every couple of days. They don't add too much to the laundry burden, and they're a lot more sanitary than sponges. When they become stained and worn, they can be downgraded to cleaning rags. Best yet, if they are all-cotton, you can compost them at the end of their lives.

Toilet Cleaner

The 50/50 vinegar and water spray works very well for the toilet seat and bowl. It cleans, deodorizes and leaves no residue behind. To clean the inside of the toilet, lower the level of the water in the bowl by bucket flushing (dumping a bucket of water in the toilet). Then pour straight vinegar around the sides of the bowl and scrub with a toilet brush. This basic vinegar approach is more than sufficient cleaning for any toilet. The idea that stronger, more toxic cleaners are necessary is ridiculous, because no matter how sterile the bowl is after cleaning, that state lasts only until the next time the toilet is used.

If the state of the bowl is dire, after bucket flushing escalate to scrubbing with straight baking soda with your toilet brush. If you mix baking soda with vinegar it will foam like crazy. This foaming is harmless (unlike the dreaded bleach and ammonia reaction).

Magic Soft Scrub For Soap Scum On The Bottom Of The Tub And Other Things

Put a half-cup or so of baking soda in a little bowl. Mix this with a little castile soap. Keep adding soap until the mix resembles frosting. Add a few drops of essential oils if you wish. This stuff is really good for scrubbing bathtub rings and gunky sinks. It excels at removing soap scum. It is so pleasant to use (especially if it smells like peppermint, like ours does), you might end up wandering around looking for more things to scrub. You do have to rinse after scrubbing, or it will leave a powdery residue behind.

If we're in a rush, we clean our tub scum by spritzing first with our spray bottle of soapy water, then sprinkle on some baking soda and scrub with a nylon poof. The combo of soap and soda dissolves soap scum very well, no matter what form it comes in.

Mold And Mildew
Spray vinyl shower curtains with straight vinegar and then scrub to remove mildew spots. If there's lots of soap scum and mildew on the curtains, it's easier to take the curtains down and put them in the washing machine on the cold cycle.

Freshen stuff like camping gear which has taken on a mildew odor in storage by misting it with your 50/50 vinegar and water blend, or if it's really bad, straight vinegar or, if you have it around, a solution of one tablespoon of tea tree oil in one cup of water.

Mineral Deposits
Vinegar is great at removing mineral deposits. That is why manufacturers recommend running vinegar through their coffee makers now and then. If you have mineral build-up at the bottom of a teakettle, boil a little vinegar in the kettle and it will come right off with no scrubbing. Vinegar will also dissolve lime deposits around faucets or in a toilet bowl — just soak paper towels or rags with vinegar (hot vinegar works faster) and lay them directly on the mineral build-up for a while, then scrub off the softened lime with a scouring pad and/or some baking soda.

Vinegar also removes hard water deposits from shower heads. Mix a half and half solution of hot water and vinegar, and soak your shower head in it, either by taking off the head, or putting the vinegar solution in a bag and putting the bag over the shower head. *WARNING: vinegar is an acid and might dull some metal finishes, particularly if left in contact with them for an extended length of time.* Check after 15 minutes and see if the deposits are dissolved. Here at the homestead we dulled the finish around the edge of our nickel finish bathroom faucet by forgetting we had a bag of vinegar on it for...oh, about 12 hours.

Mirrors And Shiny Fixtures
Spray with your 50/50 vinegar and water mix and wipe clean. Dry the mirror to avoid spots. If you're cleaning for company and want everything extra-shiny, try using vodka. Just dampen a rag with it and wipe.

Drain Cleaner
To keep drains clear of greasy build-up, every so often put a cup of baking soda down your drains, followed by a couple of cups of boiling water, or a cup of vinegar. Now, if your drain is actually clogged, it is too late for baking soda. Hair is

the source of most clogs, and so if possible, put one of those little mesh baskets in your drains to catch hair and prevent clogs in the first place.

The best way to unclog a drain or a toilet is with a device called an auger. The ones for sinks or tubs are called crank augers, and the ones for toilets are called toilet (or closet) augers. They both have a long flexible metal rope called a "snake." You twist this snake down your pipes to physically break up the clog. The two kinds of augers are not interchangeable—a toilet auger has a snake inside a protective tube which allows you to run the business end into the toilet without damaging the bowl's porcelain.

It is far better to use these simple tools to manually remove a clog than to send caustic drain openers into our water supply, or to pay for an expensive plumber's visit. In fact, we learned about toilet augers from our plumber, who said as he cranked a toilet auger down our clog-prone toilet, "You can get yourself one of these, or you can call me out to do this for you for a hundred bucks a pop." Both kinds of augers will run in the $30 range.

Window Cleaner

Rigorous scientific studies here at our urban homestead have revealed a surprising truth: hot water and a rag works better than anything else at removing the combination of smog and dog snot on our windows. The key to window washing is not so much in the washing, it seems, but in a thorough drying.

Vinegar and water works too. Whether plain water or vinegar water works better might depend on what's dirtying your windows. If you keep a 50/50 mix of vinegar and water around for general cleaning, you can just use that for quick touchups. But you can dilute the mix more if you are mixing it up special for windows. A bucket of steaming hot water with about a ¼ cup of vinegar in it would be a good mix for a big job.

If you get streaks when you try using vinegar on your windows, it is probably because you have a wax build-up from using commercial window cleaners. Add a squirt of soap to your vinegar mix, and it should cut through the wax. After that, you can go back to just plain vinegar.

Carpet Freshener

Sprinkle a generous cloud of baking soda over your carpet, then use a broom to brush it into the fibers. Let it sit for at least 15 minutes before vacuuming it up. If you wish, you can scent the baking soda first with essential oils by mixing a few drops of oil with the baking soda and shaking them together in the box or in a bag. Baking soda also makes your vacuum bag smell better.

Furniture Polish

Dusting and wiping with a just barely damp cloth to remove any grime does a whole lot toward maintaining wood. Only furniture polish manufacturers expect you to polish every week. But if the wood looks thirsty, you can mix up a little salad dressing: three parts olive oil to one part vinegar and rub that on sparingly with a rag.

Too easy, Martha? This is an advanced furniture polish recipe given to us by our Montreal-based urban homesteading friend, Severine:

Lemon furniture polish:

1 ounce beeswax
8 ounces jojoba oil (or other light oils such as grapefruit oil)
¼ teaspoon lemon essential oil
¼ teaspoon orange essential oil
¼ teaspoon grapefruit essential oil
⅛ teaspoon thyme essential oil

1 Measure the beeswax and jojoba oil into a Pyrex measuring cup and place the cup into a bath of boiling water. When the wax is nearly melted, remove the cup from the water and stir the ingredients to thoroughly combine.
2 Allow the mixture to cool for about one minute.
3 Add the essential oils next and stir well to combine. Pour into a wide-mouthed jar so you can easily dispense it. Let cool completely for a few hours, best overnight.
4 To use, apply the mixture a little at a time to clean furniture surface using a soft wool or cotton cloth. I like to use worn dish towels because they are very soft and pliable.

Laundry Soap

Try using ¼ to ⅓ cup pure liquid castile soap to wash your next load of laundry. It may feel slightly transgressive. "What? No cleaning crystals? How's this going to work?" It works surprisingly well. Castile soap works fine for cleaning jeans, t-shirts and dark cotton knits, especially when boosted with baking soda. It also works well for lingerie and other delicates. But it is not fantastic for whites. Over time whites washed in soap can take on a grayish cast. So for them use an eco-brand laundry detergent supplemented with oxygen bleach.

Laundry Boosters And Rinse Aids

Increase the cleaning power of your soap by tossing in ½ cup of baking soda along with your soap (or any detergent) as the washer fills. Be sure the soda has a chance to dissolve before you add your clothes, otherwise you might end up with white soda residue on your laundry. One cup of straight vinegar can be used in the rinse cycle in place of fabric softener. A vinegar rinse also helps deodorize stinky laundry.

Laundry Bleach (Chlorine Alternatives)

For bleaching purposes, you are best off using one of the chlorine-free bleaches sold by the green cleaning folks. As a class these products are called oxygen bleaches. At heart they are basically hydrogen peroxide, and are quite safe for you and the environment.

The thing to understand about oxygen bleaches is that they are really best for preventive whitening: you add a little to every load of whites to keep them white. If your whites are already yellow or grey, they are probably beyond the reach of oxygen bleach.

The Power Of The Sun

A really simple way to keep your whites fresh, at least in the summer, is to hang them out in the sun. Sunlight is a powerful bleaching agent. You may have discovered this if you've ever left something like a beach towel or t-shirt lying out in the sun for a few days. Even if you don't have a laundry line, you can drape your wet laundry over shrubs. Just give the foliage a hose-down first to make sure the leaves aren't coated with city smog.

Extreme Measures

Ellen Sandbeck, author of our favorite book on green cleaning, *Organic Housekeeping*, makes an interesting suggestion for saving any white item that seems hopelessly grungy or stained. She recommends that you treat it with something called a color remover, also known as a reduction bleach. Found in craft stores, hardware stores and some drug stores, color removers are used to strip color from fabric before dyeing. The well-known dye company, Rit, makes Rit Color Remover and Rit White-Wash, but there are other brands too. The active ingredient in color removers, sodium hydrosulfite, is what the paper industry uses as a less toxic alternative to chlorine bleach.

Stain Removers

Stain removal is an art — what will remove blood won't remove coffee. If you want to keep sweat stains from setting in the armpits of your favorite shirt, try spritzing your shirt with vinegar. Protein-based stains respond very well to a little presoaking in a strong solution of any commercial oxygen bleach (which is safe even for colored fabric). Follow the instructions on the container. Soap lifts grease stains, which makes sense, but it actually sets tannin stains, like wine or tea, so never try to spot clean those with soap. Instead, do as much as you can just flushing those with water, and then launder with detergent—any cleaning agent which does not contain plant or animal oils.

GREYWATER REVOLUTIONARIES: If you are recycling the water from your washing machine, you have to do business differently than directed above. Castile soap, vinegar, and baking soda are not so great for your soil. Nor are most commercial detergents, even the green ones. All of these substances are easy on the public water supply, and on aquatic life, but are not so good for terrestrial plants. You must use a product specifically formulated for greywater use, like Oasis Biocompatible laundry detergent.

Less Toxic Ways To Deal With Unwelcome Critters

Pantry Moths

If you frequent bulk bins, you'll get moths. One way to prevent them is to freeze anything you bring home for four days, or just keep all of your bulk grain and flour in the fridge or freezer all the time. If you open your cabinet and a moth flies out, don't ignore it. Kill it, and find out where it came from. At least one item in your cupboard is infested. Check the cereal first—oatmeal containers are a big favorite. They also like flour, corn starch, nuts and sugar, but won't turn their noses up at pasta. Look for larvae and webbing or strange clumping or crumbling.

If you catch the outbreak in time, you might get away with just throwing away that one source of infestation, but if you continue to see moths, you have trouble. Then you have to throw away everything in your pantry that is not canned. They can get into *anything*, all plastic bags and boxes, even some kinds of lidded jars. Jars have to have threaded screw tops or rubber seals to keep them out. After you've emptied your pantry, clean the shelves with straight vinegar, being sure to shoot vinegar into all the cracks and crevices where their eggs are hiding.

Ants and Roaches

Prevention first. Keep surfaces clean, and food in sealed containers or in the fridge. Put away cat and dog food. Get a garbage can with a tight lid, like one of those snazzy ones than open with a foot pedal. If you are under siege, keep everything in the fridge.

Boric acid is a low-toxicity mineral that is a much safer solution to ant and roach problems than poison sprays. That said, keep it out of reach of kids and pets, and follow the safety precautions on the label. Use it by dusting the powder in crevices and inaccessible areas where ants and roaches travel. You can also make an ant bait by mixing a little sugar with the boric acid. Look for boric acid in the pest control section of a hardware or drug store, where it will be sold in squeeze bottles under the label "ant and roach powder." You can also add about a tablespoon of boric acid to a bucketful of whatever you use to mop your kitchen, and mop as usual. Don't rinse. The thin layer of dust it leaves behind will not be dangerous to you or your pets, but it will clog the breathing tubes of your bugs.

Hazardous Waste Disposal

Once you make the switch to non-toxic cleaning, you might be left with a cupboard full of potent chemicals that you never intend to touch again. Don't let them sit, because they change over time and may eat their own bottles, and please don't flush them down the toilet. Dispose of them safely, and for free, by taking them to the hazardous waste facility nearest you. To find out where your hazardous waste drop-off point is, contact your city government.

A Homestead Of Your Own

Wherever you are now—that's your homestead. Never put off homesteading because you think you are in the wrong place. Even if you live in a windowless box, or in the most tight-assed planned community ever conceived by a black-hearted developer, there are ways to homestead. Even if you can't grow food in your own backyard, you can forage for edible plants, tend a plot in a community garden, preserve and ferment foods, whether they are from a farmers' market or a dumpster dive. You can lessen your dependence on the car, or build community in your neighborhood. The homestead is about much more than just growing food.

That said, if it is moving time, it makes sense to keep gardening in mind as you search for a new apartment, look for a house to buy, or plan to build your dream home. Everyone has certain preferences that guide their house hunt. You have to have wood floors, for instance, or you have to be near a certain school. You might want to add agricultural concerns to your list as well.

If You Are Looking For An Apartment

Search for an apartment with a south-facing balcony or patio for outdoor gardening, or at least banks of south-facing windows for indoor growing. Look for complexes with little bits of undeveloped land that you might be able to colonize. Look for ground floor units with little patches of soil around the front door.

Talk to the building manager, and see if they'd be cool with you festooning your public spaces with lots of potted plants. Check the other units out. Is there any kind of conformity standard at work, or is everyone sort of doing their own thing on their porches and balconies? Ask about roof access, too. Could you keep "a few" plants up there?

Renting Or Buying A House

Whether you rent or buy, the basic considerations for choosing a house are the same, though of course as a renter you must get permission for your farming endeavors. Enlightened, or at least negligent, landlords do exist who will not mind if you start a compost heap, keep chickens, or grow food on their property. If they are uneasy about you digging in their yard, propose that all of your growing be in raised beds. At least you will not be digging holes in the ground, and theoretically the entire thing could be thrown away when you leave.

Take Note Of These Things As You House Hunt

How big is the backyard? How is the sunlight back there? Is it shaded out by neighboring buildings or trees? The best situation for the garden is the south side of the house, so that the plants get the maximum amount of sunlight. Western and eastern exposures are second best, but north-facing yards are to be avoided, because they probably won't get enough light to grow food.

If the light or space in the back is poor, how's the light in the front yard? Are there side yards that you could plant in, too? Would the neighbors have a conniption fit if you replaced the front lawn with a vegetable garden? Is there a neighborhood ordinance again line-drying clothes? How about chickens?

Check out the current landscaping, or lack thereof. Mature fruit trees and good soil are a big plus, if you are lucky enough to find a property so blessed. If not, concentrate on avoiding big negatives. A backyard sheathed in concrete, for example, is a big negative. Yes, you can rip it out, but then you have to start building your soil from scratch.

For your own comfort and pleasure, look for mature shade trees planted where they will cool the house but not shade your vegetable garden. A big deciduous tree can do a lot to cool a house in the summer, but unlike a big pine tree, it will not make the house shadowy and chilly in the winter, because its leaves will be gone.

The Ecology Of The House

Look for homes that have access to good cross ventilation and ways to deal with the heat of the summer without resorting to air conditioning. Houses like this might have windows protected by awnings or deep eaves so the sun doesn't heat up the house in the summer, but can shine in the windows in the winter. They might have sleeping porches and screened porches for the summer, and sun rooms for the winter. Good insulation is a definite plus. If you're considering converting to solar, look for property where either the roof or the yard has good exposure to the sun. And remember, the most efficient way to conserve energy is to choose to live in a smaller space.

Water Harvesting

If you are interested in harvesting rainwater or using greywater, look for these things:

- A house where the garden is lower than the plumbing in the house so that you can use gravity instead of pumps and tanks to bring greywater to your garden. Look for ways that rainwater flowing from your roof, from any slopes on the property or from your neighbor's yard, can be redirected toward the yard to water your crops.
- Accessible plumbing. Some houses sink the plumbing into a concrete slab, others put it in damn unpleasant, nearly inaccessible, crawlspaces. The ideal setup is a house with a basement where you can standup straight, and all the pipes are exposed.

Location Location Location

Proximity To Culture

When you choose your house, imagine you don't have a car. How would you get around? Can you walk to anything from your hypothetical house? Draw a circle with a one-mile radius on a map with your home in the center and consider what falls into that circle. It is especially nice to have a few restaurants close at hand, as well as a market. And at the risk of sounding like a couple of lushes, we enjoy having a dark and cushy bar a few blocks from our house. That way we can go out, have a couple of martinis, and not have to worry about the drive home.

Also consider the house's proximity to public transportation, and the quality of the bikability of that neighborhood. Is it possible for you to walk, bike or take public transport to your job? To the places you like to shop? To your gym, yoga studio, or school?

Neighborhood Character

Take a walk around your prospective neighborhood and look for signs of life. Is it one of those professional ghost towns inhabited only by housekeepers during the day, or are the residents out and about—on the front porch, working the garden, or playing with their kids. Are there any fellow gardeners in the neighborhood? Conversely, do you see any weedy, ill-kept yards? Yards like that mean it's more likely that you'll be able to get away with revolutionary schemes in your own yard. All in all you are searching for a neighborhood that is lively, and diverse, and not uptight. In such a neighborhood you'll probably fit in well and find some good neighbors.

Building a Homestead

Nowadays the style sections of newspapers and magazines are full of profiles of spacious and sleek "green" houses made with novel eco-materials by famous architects. Eco-design is the wave of the future, these articles promise, it is going to save us all. This is all very glamorous, but the truth is that if you want to take the truly environmentally conscious route, you can do two things: renovate an old house instead of building new and live in the smallest place you can, whether you rent, buy or build.

Tearing down an old house is wasteful; the craftsmanship and materials used to build old homes cannot be replicated today. More than that, the construction of a new house—any type of house—generates three to five tons of waste that goes straight to the landfills. We urban homesteaders suggest that you revitalize a house instead, a home in the dense urban core, somewhere central where you can walk and bike around. Your footprint will be much smaller than someone who builds a "green" house on pristine land at the edge of the city and has to get in the car and drive for miles just to get a carton of milk.

There is much to be said for living in a small place. It seems counter to the American dream to suggest that we downsize. The size of our homes has been growing steadily since World War II, and along with it our home energy use and our personal debt. We have to stop thinking big, at least when it comes to material things.

When you live small, you'll be living in a more ecologically sustainable way. Small homes are significantly easier to heat, cool, light and maintain. Apartments, even more so. Nothing trumps size in terms of energy efficiency. But more compelling than energy savings is life savings. A small home supports you and allows you to do what you want to do, rather than burdening you with debt, worry and upkeep.

When We Say Small, We Mean SMALL

Living in California, we dream about a lot covered with lush crops and fruit trees, but which contains no central house at all. Instead it would have a small trailer or micro-house for sleeping, sheds for offices, and a sheltered deck for

For the past five years I've lived on top of a sandstone bluff in a territory overlooking the confluence of the number 2 freeway and the number 5 freeway. I live in the middle of a dense garden in a 26-foot trailer that I purchased sight-unseen near the Mexican border some seven years ago. The trailer came to me complete with critters and a rotting floor—an investment which seemed questionable to me at the time, but in hindsight, the greatest material gift that has entered my life thus far. This trailer has not only served as my shelter and work space for the past years—but as a kind of entry into another understanding of what life (and specifically life in a massive city) can be. I am surrounded by a small group of brilliant, lovely people I get to call neighbors, and collectively we grow food, build spaces, sew clothing—live on and enjoy this plot of land in which we are all so completely invested. By living in a small space, in a more or less rent-free scenario, I have been able to shift the locus of my life energy and imagination to tasks and work which are for me ultimately meaningful and nourishing.

I am convinced that a first step towards emancipation from the pressures and brutality of meaningless work (perpetuated cyclically by rent/bill-paying slavery) can be found by living in smaller spaces, or trailer-like spaces—and slipping into the cracks. The benefits of living in a trailer/small space are endless, some of the possibilities being: minimizing major expenditures in your life; learning about and inventing living systems (such as understanding where your source(s) of energy and water come from) with the very real possibility for employing alternative energies and "off-grid" technologies; living more autonomously, experimenting with indoor/outdoor living situations which might allow for the transformation of a tiny living space into an expansive environment to share with others, learning how to fix and maintain a variety of household systems: plumbing, electrical, hot water, refrigeration (when you live in a small space, the scale of these such systems are far more manageable and basic); inventing alternate ways to "pay" for a place to park your trailer or build your small abode—barter, work exchange, etc., building tents, tree houses, outhouses(!), living more simply, consuming less—creating more!

The downsides to living in a small space (in my understanding) are very few. At times there can be hassles or inconveniences, such as running out of propane and having freezer meltdowns...or strange brushes with the Department of Building and Safety. No matter where you live, there is a set of sacrifices or payment for shelter, space, and infrastructure. Choosing to live in a trailer or small space is a deliberate and conscious effort to take on a slightly different set of sacrifices, which lead to a more expansive, liberating, and productive life. In these uncertain times, when the default, standard modes for living are becoming harder and harder to maintain (both physically, and spiritually), you can invent alternate methods, which can be energizing and transformative for your well-being, as well as the lives of people who surround you.

Eva, Los Angeles

gathering and entertaining and outdoor cooking. Our friends would live with us, in their own tiny houses. The entire setup would be so energy-wise that we could go off-grid. It would be a village within the city.

We've been experiencing fantasies like the one above ever since we discovered The Tumbleweed Tiny House Company (tumbleweedhouses.com). The founder of the company, Jay Shafer, builds perfectly planned, exquisitely crafted tiny houses, and also sells plans for them. What sets his designs apart from playhouses is their perfect planning. Not an inch of space is wasted, or ill-considered. His houses are so small they do not even qualify as dwellings fit for residences in many cities, therefore his houses are often fit with wheels so that they qualify as "trailers."

Tumbleweed House

Alternative Living Strategies

Anybody who is willing to live a compact domestic life is freed up financially to follow their dreams. We know of urban homeowners who have bought a tiny house or trailer and parked it at the back of their own property. They rent out their big house as an income source. That way, they don't work for their property, their property works for them.

Other people might live in a guest house, or in a trailer on someone else's property, or they might be gypsies, or they might park their trailer behind their business and call it an "office," and so be able invest their housing dollars into doing what they love.

Unfortunately, at this time, city officials take a dim view of people "camping out" in trailers, so to avoid hassles you need to keep your trailer behind a legitimate house or business, so that it can reasonably be argued to be an office, or a recreational vehicle.

Chapter Six
Be Your Own Utility: Water And Power For The Homestead

Be Your Own Utility:
Water And Power For The Homestead

The bricoleur, says Levi-Strauss, is someone who uses "the means at hand," that is, the instruments he finds at his disposition around him, those which are already there, which had not been especially conceived with an eye to the operation for which they are to be used and to which one tries by trial and error to adapt them, not hesitating to change them whenever it appears necessary, or to try several of them at once, even if their form and their origin are heterogeneous.
— Jacques Derrida, *Writing and Difference*

Dealing with water and power on the urban homestead means dealing with technology, everything from high-tech solar panels to low-tech composting. On our urban homestead we're neither Luddites nor tech-heads. We believe in flexibility, taking the simplest option first and searching for small opportunities to make a big difference in our overall consumption. Just as some parties call for Mai Tais and some call for hauling out a cheap bottle of bourbon, different problems call for varying responses, some high-tech, some low-tech.

But for us, the most compelling motive to tweak the power and water utilities on our living spaces is taking the joyous and rewarding path of the *bricoleur*, the tinkerer, or what our technological age has termed the hacker. While advanced *bricoleurs* with backgrounds as electricians might wire up their own solar system, we've emphasized low-tech projects so that everyone can participate. Just because a project is low-tech does not mean that it lacks innovation. Non-profit organizations such as the Apervachio Institute and the university departments such as MIT's D-Lab have developed simple but clever adaptations of existing materials to improve lives in developing countries. We can take some of these same ideas and apply them in the first world.

What follows is a set of ideas and projects that anybody willing to do a little work with their hands can execute.

Harvesting Water

In all likelihood most of your water right now comes from one place—the tap. If so, you're missing out on two free and abundant water sources: rainwater and greywater.

There are many reasons to catch that water that would otherwise flow out into the sewer. Global warming and the resultant radical changes in weather patterns have triggered water shortages in many parts of the world. According to scientists at the National Center for Atmospheric Research, between the 1970s and the early 2000s the area of the earth stricken by drought doubled. And increased temperatures cause higher evaporation rates, meaning we need more water than ever to grow our food. (Source: *USGS, Estimated Use of Water in the United States in 2005.*)

One sobering statistic to keep in mind: the average American uses between 80 and 100 gallons per person per day, with the higher consumption coming from residents of the desert southwest. The average African uses five gallons a day. Americans consume seven percent of the **world's total energy supplies** just in the pumping and treating of our water. (Source: Center for Sustainable Systems.) The good news is that by tweaking your plumbing, you can dramatically reduce the amount of water you use as well as create an oasis around your house even in the driest of places.

You can do this by learning to take control of both your plumbing and your rainwater whether you live in a suburban house in Phoenix or an apartment in Manhattan. By reducing our dependence on city water, we'll prepare our homesteads for possible water uncertainties on the horizon. Even those who live in rainy cities can put all that rain to good use, reduce their dependency on municipal water and sewage services, and send the water back to the land.

Water Principles For The Urban Homesteader

1 Rain is a resource, not a problem

Yes, catastrophic floods can ruin everything from a basement to an entire city, but that's no reason to treat rainfall as a problem that must always be contained. There are simple ways to use rainfall as a free resource. True, water needs to be kept away from building foundations, but instead of sending it straight to the gutter it's possible to direct it to where it will water your plants. Around our own urban homestead we've shifted our initial fear of water, to an awareness of where water flows when it rains, and have worked on simple ways to channel it to where it will be more useful. Living in Los Angeles, in a dry, Mediterranean climate prone to long periods of drought, makes this shift in water consciousness—from problem to resource—especially important.

2 Water can be recycled

The water that flows out of the shower, bathroom sink, and washing machine, known as "greywater," can be put to use in the gardens irrigating crops rather than just going down the sewer. Just as with rainwater, by reusing "waste" water a former problem becomes a resource instead.

3 Water-saving strategies should be simple and cheap

Around our own urban homestead we've kept the rainwater and greywater strategies simple and low-tech — we've skipped the pumps, filters, and high-priced consultants. Putting in a greywater system that costs thousands of dollars and requires constant maintenance makes no sense from an economic or environmental perspective. Is our system up to code? No. Is it functional, ecologically sound and inexpensive. Yes.

Conserving Water

Outside of a few urban revolutionaries who have figured out how to shower with rainwater, the vast majority of city dwellers are dependent on municipal water for our in-home water needs. In your garden, however, you have options for how to water.

The obvious option, turn on the faucet, is not the most sensible option. Watering your yard — or your balcony garden — should follow a three-part sequence. First, you allow the rain to do its work. This includes channeling and saving rainwater, as well as minimizing hard surfaces around your house so that the rain has plenty of chances to find its way into the soil. When that first step does not suffice for your water needs, the next step is to use greywater for irrigating your plantings. If both rainwater and greywater do not keep your plants green, then turn on the faucet and tap into the municipal water supply.

This approach is common sense. What does not make sense is to direct bountiful rainfall down the streets, into the sewers and out to the sea, or to send only slightly used shower water down the drain. Our urban water tables are starved by the paving over of cities and need recharging. In short, the best place for water is the soil, not the street.

The ease of using rainwater or greywater will vary greatly depending on where you live and how your home is situated. What follows are series of suggestions of different complexity and ambition to suit different tastes and needs. The first step is conservation, which is within everyone's means.

How To Play Water Detective

The easiest way to collect water is to save water. It's the old "penny saved is a penny earned" principle. But please do not fall into tortured imaginings of once-a-week showers and itchy sackcloth vestments. Conservation of water is not about giving anything up. Rather, it's about spending a few afternoons tinkering around to increase the efficiency of our homes.

First let's take a look at our current water needs, and ways we can increase the efficiency of the systems we've already got in place.

We like water guru Brad Lancaster's (author of *Rainwater Harvesting for Drylands*) concept of assessing your water budget, which is the amount of rain that you could theoretically collect on the land you occupy, the water allowance given to you by nature. The equation below calculates how much water falls on your entire property, roofs, driveways and soil combined.

$$\text{collection area (total square feet of your property)} \times 0.6 \times \text{annual rainfall (inches)} = \text{gallons per year}$$

Data on both yearly and monthly average rainfall for your area can be found on the National Oceanographic and Atmospheric Administration website: ncdc.noaa.gov/oa/climate/online/ccd/nrmpcp.txt

The number you come up with is your "water budget." Of course, you'd never be able to catch it all since much of this water will be lost to runoff. But it will give you perspective when you compare this number with your water bill. For many of us, particularly those in dry places, the discrepancy between the two numbers will come as a big shock.

Where Does All That Water Go?
In the typical American home, it breaks down like this:

58.7% Landscaping
10.8% Toilet
 8.7% Clothes washer
 6.8% Shower
 6.3% Faucet
 5.5% Leaks
 0.6% Dishwasher

Let's take a look at what we use our water for and see if we can do some tweaks to boost efficiency.

58.7% Landscaping Water
In most homes, the majority of water use is for "landscaping." Landscaping is just a code word for lawns. Lawns and non-native decorative plants suck water like nobody's business, which is one reason we advise against them. Our strict rule bears repeating—if you gotta water it, you gotta be able to eat it. As an urban homesteader, your outdoor irrigation concerns are going to be centered around watering your crops and trees. Depending on where you live, you're probably going to need some kind of outdoor irrigation system.

Drip systems are not only water-wise but good for lazy people too, because you don't have to stand around with a hose or drag a watering can around. Later we'll describe ways to direct rainwater and greywater to your yard, so that you rely even less on municipal water for irrigation.

10.8% Toilet

We'll assume you already have a low-flush toilet—they've been standard issue for years. If you are stuck with an old toilet, put a plastic water bottle full of stones in the tank to displace and thereby reduce the amount of water used to flush (don't use a brick for this purpose since it can kick around and damage the flushing mechanism).

Toilets are also the number one culprit for water leaks, most often in the form of a faulty flapper. To learn how to keep that toilet of yours in high performance mode, consider becoming a "toiletologist." Following the extensive self-guided lesson plans on the website toiletology.com will turn every urban homesteader into a knowledgeable toilet geek with the ability to proudly maintain a leak-proof throne.

If you want the ultimate in a water-conserving toilet, consider a composting toilet, which not only uses no water whatsoever, but also creates compost for your yard.

8.7% Clothes Washer

Washing machine water can be recycled and sent outside to irrigate your landscaping. If you are in the market for a new washer, seek out one that qualified for an Energy Star. To qualify for the Energy Star label, a washer has to use 18–25 gallons of water per load, as opposed to the 40 gallons used by a standard machine.

6.8% Shower

Beyond the obvious, such as switching out old showerheads for low-flow heads, consider running the shower waste line outside to your garden. Or build an outdoor shower near plants that need irrigation. See pages 246 and 267.

6.3% Faucet

Make sure your faucets aren't leaking. Just 60 drops per minute will equal 192 gallons per month. Another simple step is to turn off the water while brushing teeth, washing dishes or shaving.

5.5% Hidden Leaks

You can track down hidden leaks in your house by using your water meter. Your water meter will be found where your utility company's water pipes meet your

Water Meter

house's pipes. It's the thing the meter reader guy (or gal) comes to look at once in a while. Many water meters have a triangular red flow indicator. To check for a hidden leak, turn off all taps in your house. If the red flow indicator shows that water is still moving, you've got a leak somewhere. If your meter does not have a flow indicator, simply turn off all water taps in your house for a period of three hours and note the reading at the beginning and ending of this period. If your meter reads higher after the three-hour period, you've got a leak.

If your meter has a flow indicator, you can use it to troubleshoot your plumbing system. Go around your house progressively shutting off plumbing fixtures and sprinkler systems, assuming they have separate shutoff valves, until you isolate the part of your system that is leaking. Shutoff valves can be found under your sink and toilet. Likely leak candidates include toilets, sprinklers, as well as badly-executed pipe-fitting jobs.

0.6% Dishwasher

The "greenness" of dishwashers is a controversial topic—a study conducted by the University of Bonn in Germany concluded that dishwashers use half the energy, one-sixth the water, and less soap than handwashing. On the other hand, the resources used to manufacture these complex machines might, according to some environmentalists, eclipse their benefits. We're not purists—we've got one, and it has probably saved our marriage. Green or not, you'd have to pry it out of our cold, dead fingers.

Harvesting Rainwater

After conservation, the second step toward water independence is harvesting rainwater. The number of ways you can go about this might surprise you.

Six Ways To Harvest Rainwater

Rainwater harvesting is an easy and positive course of action for people in nearly every climate in the world. Living in a dry place such as the desert southwest may make it seem more urgent, but no matter where we live, rainwater harvesting is a positive step toward changing our attitude toward the water that falls for free from the sky. Rainwater can be sent to where nature intended it to go—to the soil.

The most important step in formulating a rainwater harvesting strategy is careful observation of present conditions. Where does water flow when it rains? Rainwater harvesting expert Brad Lancaster suggests working from the highest point in your yard to the lowest point. For most of us the highest point will be the roof of the house, but other high points could include sidewalks, decks, outbuildings, or your neighbor's driveway. Observe where water goes in a rainstorm or when the neighbors overwater their lawn and ask yourself if there is a way to direct this runoff to where it will percolate into the soil and water your plants.

Rainwater Harvesting Technique 1
Become A Radical Depaver

Our first concern is to minimize the impermeable surfaces that prevent rain and earth from meeting. Your initial step in harvesting rainwater has nothing to do with barrels or pipes. Instead, you're going to pick up a sledgehammer. In so doing you will eliminate, as much as you can, every impermeable surface that prevents rainwater from getting into your soil where it belongs.

Paving is convenient, but not healthy for the earth. Consider alternatives for any concrete or asphalt that is on your property: wood chips, un-motored brick, decomposed granite, anything that lets water seep through. These surfaces are more pleasant to walk on and look at than concrete, and they free up soil for planting. For instance, a driveway needs only twin tracks of stone, brick or concrete for the car wheels. The rest of it can be gravel or low-growing plants, and the edges of the drive can be lined with garden beds or trees. Less hardscaping in your yard means more water will percolate into the soil, and down into the water table.

Most concrete work will yield to a few swings of a sledgehammer. For densely-poured concrete you may need to rent an electric-powered jackhammer from a tool yard. A jackhammer is an easy tool to use despite its intimidating looks. Cradle it lightly in your hands (keeping it in a death grip will vibrate the hell out of your joints) and direct the chisel end at a slight angle so as to dislodge the outermost portions of the concrete that you are trying to remove. Using either a sledgehammer or a jackhammer, work from the outside of the concrete inwards towards the middle. Loosen broken concrete with a crowbar and pull it aside. If you have asphalt paving to remove, follow the same technique. It is softer, and so easier to pull out.

If you've got concrete poured next to your foundation you will want to leave some of it in place to prevent water from getting under your foundation or into your basement and causing expensive damage. To make a clean break between the concrete you are removing and a portion you may want to keep, you'll need to cut a line in it. To cut concrete you have to rent a gas-powered concrete saw fitted with a diamond-edged blade. Your local rental yard should have one of these in either a hand-held or walk-behind version. You have to be careful to make sure that the blade does not go all the way through the concrete and into dirt. Dirt will strip off the diamonds and the rental yard may end up billing you for the replacement of the blade that can run into the hundreds of dollars. A concrete saw is a noisy and aggressive tool that needs to be hooked up to a hose to keep the blade cool. It makes a big mess and you'll need to make sure to wear plenty of protective clothing—including eye and ear protection. There's no shame in hiring someone if you don't feel comfortable cutting concrete.

Chunks of broken concrete, sometimes called "urbanite," can be used to make excellent raised beds and retaining walls. When breaking up your concrete, think about what projects you would like to use the urbanite for, and size it accordingly as you break it out.

One reason you should consider recycling your concrete is that it is expensive to get rid of it. You'll have to pay to have it taken away in a special dumpster called a "lowboy." The other reason is that the company that carts off the lowboy will do one of two things with your broken concrete: either stick it in a landfill or recycle it into yet more pourable concrete, exactly what our cities don't need.

Any depaving at all is a step in the right direction. Nothing is more depressing than the millions of acres of concrete and asphalt that cover our urban environments, but at least we can deal with the little bits of concrete that we are responsible for.

Rainwater Harvesting Technique 2
Smart Gutters And Downspouts

Our roofs are another impermeable surface. We can minimize the surface area by living in as small a house as possible and trying to maximize open ground. At our own compound we've even gone so far as to remove an ugly addition, increasing the backyard space of our home. So-called green roofs, which have soil and plants growing on them, are an option for the wealthy, but at present are still rare in the U.S. Most of us will be dealing with conventional roofs.

Hopefully your roof has gutters. If yours doesn't, it's time to put some on. Gutters on the urban homestead channel water away from your foundation, and toward your crops. This is a job to hire out, as putting up a gutter can be challenging, especially when your roof is high up and professionals can fabricate seamless gutters, which are less prone to leaking.

Downspouts are the up-and-down pipes usually attached to the corners of a house that bring water from the gutters on the roof down to the ground. Having more than one downspout around your house will lessen the chance that any of them will get overloaded and will increase the possibilities for evenly distributing rainwater to your landscaping.

The bottom end of a downspout can be hooked up to a drainage pipe which carries the water away from the foundation and out to the yard. You can run these pipes above ground or below ground to anywhere you want water—to a mulch basin with plantings, for instance, which is described below. Drainage pipe is a white plastic pipe that comes in multiple sizes, with the most commonly used being 4". There are a variety of fitting options for connecting them to your downspouts. You can find drainage pipe at home centers and lumber yards. See ndspro.com for examples of drainage pipe fittings.

Building codes requires that downspouts take water a minimum of ten feet away from a structure and this is a good rule of thumb to ensure that water doesn't undermine your foundation.

Keeping It Clean

While we're big believers in sloth and idleness, one task that absolutely must be performed at least once a year is to get up on a ladder and clean out the gutters. Otherwise, you will be attempting this task, as we know from experience, during a downpour at midnight, after the downspouts have clogged up sending a cascade of water over the damned-up gutters.

Two simple bits of technology can make gutter cleaning easier. We have inexpensive strainer baskets made out of ½" hardware cloth in each of the downspouts to keep them from clogging up. You may wish to consider leaf guards which run along the top of the gutter to keep out leaves and other debris. The problem with leaf guards is that in order to clean out your gutters you must tediously remove the guards along the whole length of the gutter while balanced precariously on a ladder. While leaf guards catch large leaves, smaller stuff can still get through, so unless your leaf drop is monumental, you might as well just stick with the strainer baskets.

Rainwater Harvesting Technique 3

Earthworks

Earthworks are a simple, elegant way to ensure that rainwater gets to your plants rather than flowing out into the street. With an earthwork you shape the soil to catch and direct the rainfall into the ground. To build an earthwork all you need is a shovel and a sense of purpose. Basically what you are trying to do is to channel the water from roofs, sidewalks, driveways, steep hillsides, and other impermeable or semi-permeable surfaces to where that rainwater will nourish the roots of your plants. You do this by digging trenches and building up low earth walls to direct the flow of water.

The best way to design your earthworks is by careful observation of existing conditions. Even the most neglected of places will have plants growing where water naturally flows and collects. For instance, the drip lines of build-

Illustration of water flow from roof through a series of earthworks

ings, or low points near streets and sidewalks will often support a lush weedy landscape. Use these areas as your starting point. As a clever rainwater harvester your role will be to "hijack" rainwater and direct it to your plants.

Rainwater Harvesting Technique 4

Mulch Basins

One of the best ways of dealing with the sudden flood of water that a storm sends off a roof or that a washing machine ejects in a rinse cycle is with a mulch basin. Mulch basins are simply shallow trenches with raised walls that are filled with wood chips. You can direct rainwater or greywater in their direction via pipes, hoses or earthworks. They hold the water in one place until it can sink into the ground. The wood chips (the "mulch") are there to help keep runoff from getting stinky, prevent evaporation and keep mosquitoes from breeding. Anything planted in a mulch basin will receive a good deep watering every time it floods, whether by act of man or nature. Mulch basins are particularly good places to plant trees.

If you're clever and have slightly sloped land you can channel the overflow from one basin into the next so that when the first basin begins to overflow the water will spill into the next and so on. In other words, you will have a chain of basins.

An exception to mulch basin building is for people who live in excessively moist places. In these climates you will sometimes need to do the opposite — plant in mounds to keep roots from getting waterlogged.

HOW TO SIZE AND PLANT YOUR GREYWATER MULCH BASIN

Size the mulch basin to accommodate the amount of water that the greywater source that feeds it usually generates (i.e., how many gallons you use per shower, how many gallons your washing machine holds, etc.).

Some trial and error may be necessary to get the correct size of the mulch basin. One thing to take into consideration is your soil type, i.e. sandy vs. clay. Water percolates into clay soil more slowly than sand, so to prevent overflows, it might be necessary to dig a clay soil basin with wider and more shallow dimensions to encourage absorption. All that is important is that it is sized correctly to hold the periodic floods you will generate—too big is better than too small.

The addition of an outlet chamber made out of an upside down bucket with holes in it, and placed within the mulch basin, will enhance water infiltration, particularly in heavy clay soils.

What to plant in your greywater mulch basins: greywater tends to be alkaline in nature, due to the salt contained in soaps. Thankfully,

Greywater
Mulch Basin

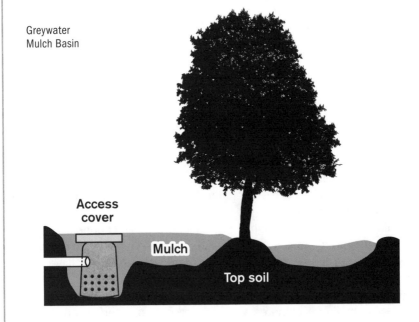

Access cover

Mulch

Top soil

there are a number of plants that tolerate alkaline conditions including bananas, citrus, blackberries, elderberries, currants, loquat, pineapple, guava, and many other fruit and nut trees. Plants to avoid are acid lovers such as blueberries, ferns, and shady forest dwellers. Another thing to take into consideration is the water needs of your plant, and how much greywater you are going to be able to offer it. Bushes and trees are the best candidates for a greywater mulch basin, simply because they are big enough to not be bothered by the periodic flooding. In addition, their edible parts are well above ground, keeping them safe from any greywater splash-up.

Terracing

If you have a hill on your property, water will cascade straight off it, and find its way to the street before it has time to sink into the soil. Slow the flow by cutting stair-stepped terraces into the hill. Support each "step" with a retaining wall made of stone, broken concrete or wood beams.

Slopes with terraces and retaining walls act as a water storage system. Rain penetrating the soil at the top of the slope forms a lens of water which over time migrates down through the hill. Plants with deep roots can reach into this lens and support themselves though extended dry periods. Plant drought-tolerant plants toward the top of the slope, and more water-needy plants toward the bottom, where the water tends to accumulate for longer periods.

My wife and I live in a drought-prone climate that occasionally gets torrential rainfalls. During those downpours a great deal of our neighbor's runoff used to race across our backyard, down our driveway, into the street and right down the sewer—completely wasted because it didn't have time to be absorbed by the earth. To make better use of that rain-water in our garden and to reduce moisture-related foundation problems, we recently built a simple rainwater collection system and also sculpted the land with berms and swales.

In the yard, we created berms and swales to redirect rainwater away from the house and capture it in pools around the garden beds where it has time to soak into the ground. For those who don't know, a berm is a mound of dirt and a swale is a depression in the ground. My wife designed the berms in attractive shapes and locations for growing plants. The swales surround the berms. After a rainstorm, the swales hold water that slowly soaks into the berms over several days—long after the rest of the yard has dried out. We also bermed dirt close to the house so water would stay away from the foundation to reduce those problems. All the dirt we needed to build the berms we got from digging out the swales, so we didn't need to import any dirt. Incidentally, we learned about the usefulness of berms and swales at a free "Intro to Permaculture" lecture which you may find in your city, too.

Our roof collection system is as basic as it gets: a 20-foot section of gutter, a flexible plastic downspout, a big plastic barrel, a brass spigot, and standard garden hose. I got the gutter parts at Habitat for Humanity's ReStore, a non-profit that sells donated building materials at bargain prices. I got the used barrel at an ecological retailer in my town, although some cities provide free rain barrels. The spigot and hose I bought at a hardware store.

To install the spigot I drilled a hole in the side of the barrel near the bottom and screwed the male thread of the spigot into the hole. The other end of the spigot is the correct size to accept the upstream end of a garden hose. I raised the barrel on a platform of cinder blocks to increase the water pressure at the end of the hose, then attached the downspout to the gutter and directed it to an opening on the top of the barrel. Now, when we want to water the garden, we turn on the spigot and get a gentle flow of water from the barrel. In the future we're going to direct the outflow from our nearby clothes washer into the barrel for additional water savings.

Ken and Lorie Marsh, Austin, Texas

Rainwater Harvesting Technique 6
Rain Barrels And Cisterns

If you've got more rainwater than your earthworks can handle or if you want to bridge gaps between rainfalls, one strategy to consider is using rain barrels to store water. A rain barrel doesn't just collect water like a big bucket, it has fittings which allow you to hook up a garden hose to the barrel, so you can use your rainwater on whatever you wish, whenever you wish. You can purchase commercial rainwater barrels, or make your own.

How To Make Your Own Rain Barrel

The ubiquitous 55-gallon plastic drum makes an excellent rain barrel. The trick is figuring out a way to hook a hose up to the barrel. Often this is done with what is called a bulkhead connection, made by cutting a hole through the barrel and fitting a threaded pipe through it. The thing is, improvised bulkhead fittings have a tendency to leak. To make our rain barrel, we used instructions from a company called Aquabarrel which showed us how to use common PVC fittings available in any hardware store to hook a garden hose securely to

the barrel. Aquabarrel also sells kits for a little more which come with all the fittings and a DIY video at aquabarrel.com.

With the Aquabarrel system you use the preexisting threaded bunghole fittings on the top of the barrel to hook up your garden hose, so be sure to get a "two bunghole" model when you're buying your barrel. Once you've got the fittings installed, all you do is turn the barrel upside down on top of a couple of cinder blocks or similar for clearance, hook up a garden hose, and you're ready to rock.

Another thing we like about the Aquabarrel design is the large overflow pipe and how easy it was to put together. You can even string several barrels together to increase storage capacity.

Rain Barrel
The garden hose coming off the bottom allows you to use collected rain to water your garden at will. The big, flexible pipe coming off the top is the overflow pipe. The pipe coming into the barrel from above is connected to a downspout from the roof.

TIP: If it's time to replace your roof, and you are thinking about rainwater collection, consider roofing with metal, which, unlike asphalt shingle, doesn't shed undesirable stuff into your water. Metal roofs will last a lifetime and also reflect the heat of the sun, thereby keeping your house cooler in the summer.

HOW MUCH WATER CAN I HARVEST FROM MY ROOF?

To figure out how much water could be harvested from the roof, first you have to know how well the kind of roofing material you have sheds water—we'll call this the "collection efficiency factor."

Efficiency Factor by Roof Type

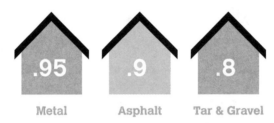

.95	.9	.8
Metal	Asphalt	Tar & Gravel

Next, measure the outside perimeter of your roof—you need not take into account the pitch or slant of the roof, since this does not affect the amount of water collected. Multiply the width by the length of your roof to figure out its square footage. If your roof is irregularly shaped, just break it down into pieces, figure out the square footage for each, then add it all up.

Finally, go to the National Oceanographic and Atmospheric Administration website: ncdc.noaa.gov/oa/climate/online/ccd/nrmpcp.txt to find out the annual rainfall in your city.

Plug the figures you collected above into this formula:

collection area (square footage of your roof) × 0.6 × collection efficiency factor × rainfall (inches) = gallons per year

For our house in Los Angeles, we have a collection area of 992 square feet, an asphalt shingle roof and an average of 15.06 inches of rain a year. So the average amount of rain we could collect in a year would be: 992 x 0.6 × 0.9 × 15.06 = 8,067.34 gallons.

If we transported our house to Atlanta, where the average annual precipitation is 48.6 inches per year (except in recent drought years!) we could theoretically collect 26,034 gallons of water a year.

Of course, in most places, rain falls bit by bit throughout the year, and you're always using it anyway, so you don't need to size your barrel or cistern to hold an entire year's worth of water at once (26,034 gallons would be a huge tank!), all you need to do is bridge the dry gaps between rainstorms. To do this, figure out monthly rainfall statistics, also available on the NOAA website, using the same formula above. That way you can anticipate how much rain you get each month rather than in a whole year.

With these numbers in mind, you can begin to answer if rainwater collection makes sense for your climate and water needs and you'll know how many rain barrels to string together or how big a cistern you'll need.

Intermediate Bulk Containers

For greater rainwater storage capacity in a more space-efficient square form, permaculturist David Khan suggests what is called an Intermediate Bulk Container or IBC for short. IBCs come in 275-gallon and 330-gallon sizes and are made out of plastic with a metal reinforcing cage. Dimensions vary, but most IBCs will fit within the same footprint as a shipping pallet, roughly 40 by 48 inches in North America. Some are stackable. IBCs run around $140 to $250 depending on size and whether you want a new or reconditioned one. The nice thing

Intermediate Bulk Container

about IBCs is that they already have a drain at the bottom so there is no need to do any cutting and fitting, making them a good option for folks who don't want to tinker.

A Really, Really Big Water Barrel: Rainwater Cisterns

A potable rainwater harvesting system suitable for storing drinking water is a big step, and due to the space necessary is one rarely made by urbanites. But if it works in your situation, we'd really encourage you to think about it. Building a household cistern for potable water ain't rocket science but it's a topic worthy of a book in itself such as Suzy Banks' *Rainwater Collection for the Mechanically Challenged*. A more likely option is a big cistern for outdoor irrigation. If you won't be drinking it, you can skip the filters, pumps and complexities. Inexpensive polypropylene tanks are probably the easiest and cheapest option for a large cistern and can be purchased from tank, farm and ranch suppliers. They come in sizes ranging from 300 to 10,000 gallons. Just remember that all that water is heavy, 8.34 pounds per gallon to be exact, so you need to make sure that your tank is placed on stable ground and well away from your house's foundation.

Greywater

So you've enacted a few conservation measures around the house and taken steps toward directing and harvesting rainwater. Now it's time to see if you can harness even more water by reusing your greywater.

Let's be clear about what we mean by "greywater." Greywater is the fluid that goes down the drain of your shower, bathroom sink, and washing machine. "Blackwater" is the stuff that comes out of your toilet and kitchen sink. You might think kitchen sink water is not nearly as foul as toilet water, but the tiny bits of food waste it contains make it go septic very quickly, and so it should not be harvested.

There are two basic ways to deal with greywater. One is to use it to water plants, and the other is to simply dispose of it by sending it into the ground, instead of into the sewer. To send greywater into the ground, all you need to do is dig a big hole far enough away from your house's foundation so as not to cause damage, and back fill it with enough gravel so that water never pools or runs off. To use greywater on plants, you'll need to follow a few precautions that we'll describe in detail.

Our philosophy for dealing with greywater is to keep your interventions simple and economical. Complex filtering systems, pumps, and underground irrigation drip tubing simply aren't cost-effective or even ecologically sound since these kinds of setups mean a lot of plastic and maintenance. Unfortunately, many municipalities require filtering and put up other expensive impediments to greywater use. We suggest you become a water pirate, keep those inspectors at bay by being discreet and nobody will ever know.

In order to create a simple greywater system, your plumbing must be easily accessible, that is, not embedded in a concrete slab. Also, in an ideal world the destination being watered (e.g. your garden) should be lower than the source of the greywater (e.g. your shower drain) so that you can let gravity do the work of carrying the water out to your garden to avoid having to rely on a pump. For these reasons, greywater is highly context-specific and so may not work out for everyone.

Greywater collection also does not make a lot of sense in very wet climates or for those who only have a small patch of land to irrigate. That said, if the pipes are easily reached, go for it. And if you happen to be doing a bathroom or laundry room remodel and the plumbing is exposed, that is the perfect time to route those pipes out to somewhere useful.

By far the most informative source on greywater that we have found is Art Ludwig, author of *Create an Oasis with Greywater*, a must-read for the greywater revolutionary. He also maintains an extensive website at oasisdesign. net. Ludwig takes a balanced stance on the topic and has a range of advice from the simple to the complex that can be used by everyone from renters to homeowners to folks living in undeveloped countries.

Greywater Precautions

The dangers of greywater have been greatly exaggerated by public health and building inspector types. Ludwig says that nobody in the U.S. has ever gotten sick from exposure to greywater. The plumbing codes in this country are overly cautious in their restrictions on greywater use, as the Man, quite simply, wants you to throw perfectly good water down the sewer. But the existence of E. coli reminds us we that we do need to be careful. So here are some general safety rules to follow when using greywater:

1. Definitely do not apply greywater to crops that you will eat raw, such as strawberries, carrots or lettuce. Greywater is fine for edible plants such as fruit trees where the crop is far from the ground and the risk of direct contamination by contact with contaminated water is low.
2 Do not apply greywater to lawns or directly onto the foliage of any plant as this can cause a microorganism growth party. Remember that greywater is purified by moving through soil.
3 Do not distribute greywater with a sprinkler as you don't want any potential bad stuff to become airborne—or to coat plant leaves. Greywater is for the ground only.
4 Do not use the water from your washing machine if you are washing diapers (gross!).
5 Do not allow greywater to stand around as it will quickly become the perfect habitat for anaerobic bacteria which will quickly turn your wash water into a stinky, mosquito-infested pool of sewage. Plan a system that will use your greywater immediately.
6 Do not use the sort of detergents and soaps that are not plant-compatible.

Detergents And Soaps For Greywater

If you start to harvest your greywater, you might have to make some changes to the kinds of soaps and detergents you use around the house. With a greywater system, those substances go straight to your plants, so they have to be plant-compatible. This is different from "bio-degradable." The natural, phosphate-free soaps and detergents you might already be using are great for the environment as a whole, but may not be appropriate for greywater use. Just because it is an eco-friendly product does not mean it's good to water your garden with.

Most shampoos are compatible with greywater irrigation schemes, but you should switch from bar soap to liquid soap in the shower.

Most laundry detergent, however, is not good for greywater use. Even common non-toxic laundry additives like baking soda and borax will kill your plants. Baking soda, washing soda, borax, and the various mineral salts used in eco-friendly laundry detergents all cause salt to build up in your soil and they will damage plants. The big brand detergents contain many additives and chemicals that you don't want in your soil, particularly chlorine bleach. The phosphates in those products, which are so damaging to our oceans and rivers, might actually be beneficial to your soil. So it is not the "no-phosphate" label that you are looking for when choosing a detergent to use in conjunction with greywater. Phosphates aren't your problem.

The State of California Department of Water Resource's *Greywater Guide: Using Greywater in Your Landscape* lists the following ingredients as *unsafe* for greywater:

- chlorine or chlorine bleach
- peroxygen
- sodium perborate
- sodium trypochlorite
- boron
- borax
- petroleum distillate
- alkylbenzene
- "whiteners"
- "softeners"
- "enzymatic" components

In addition, we suggest avoiding powdered soaps and bar soaps. In the end it comes down to this: The laundry detergent you use must be specifically labeled as being greywater-compatible. If it is not labeled so, you can assume it is not. We use Oasis Biocompatible detergent available at bio-pac.com.

Non-Invasive Greywater Methodologies

Bucket Flushin', Tub Siphoning And What To Do With Your Bathroom Sink

Bucket flushing is for those who don't want to start cutting pipe. It's a cheap and easy greywater recycling idea that even those living in apartments can do. Simply keep a bucket next to the shower and collect the water that you run before the shower gets hot. Since you haven't even stepped into the shower this water is fresh and clean, and not even technically greywater. You can use this water on house plants, outdoor plants, or to flush the toilet manually by pouring it directly into the bowl.

Another simple greywater strategy is to siphon bathtub water out the window with a siphon obtained at an auto parts store. A third idea is to disconnect your bathroom sink from the sewer and let the wastewater drain into a five-gallon bucket that you keep under the sink. You can use this water for plants or to bucket flush your toilet. **Around 25 kids drown in buckets every year in the U.S., so don't leave buckets unattended if you have little ones.**

Highly Invasive Greywater Strategies

Greywater Plumbing 101

The Hack: For those without the means or courage to start cutting into drain pipes, don't despair, just stick with the aforementioned bucket flushing and bathtub siphoning. But if you want to be a greywater hacker, you'll be working with your home's drain pipes which are also called the DWV or drain-waste-vent system.

For those not familiar with basic plumbing, the drain pipes (the ones that take water out) are the big pipes which are made out of either plastic, or in older homes, cast iron. The supply pipes (the ones that bring water in) are much smaller and are made out of either copper, galvanized steel, or in some new houses out of flexible or rigid plastic.

The drain pipes slope horizontally out to the sewer and are also connected to vent pipes that run vertically and admit air into the system to allow the waste water to flow downwards. Your plumbing system also uses u-shaped pipes called "p-traps" that hold a small amount of water to prevent sewer gases from venting into your living spaces. Look under any sink, and chances are you'll see a p-trap.

Tapping into conventional plumbing, with its vent stacks and p-traps requires plumbing knowledge, especially in a large house with a complex tangle of pipes. If you screw it up, you could send blackwater (sewage) into your greywater, or worse, into the house, and then it would be time to make an embarrassing call to the plumber. So to keep things simple we make our greywater connections downstream of the vents and traps. We like what Ludwig calls "radical plumbing," which is simply bypassing your conventional plumbing altogether and running drain lines directly from the drain of your shower, bathroom sink and/or laundry machine and out to the garden.

Working with ABS and PVC plastic pipe: Post-1950s houses usually have waste lines made out of either white plastic PVC or black plastic ABS pipe. Older homes that have been remodeled may have plastic pipe as well. To keep things simple, and to avoid having to use different cements (ABS and PVC aren't glued together with the same cement), we suggest not mixing ABS and PVC pipes together. So when you make additions, match the new pipe to the existing pipe.

Both ABS and PBC pipe are easy to use. This is how you join together plastic pipe:

1 Cut plastic pipe with a hacksaw and clean out the burrs with a file or knife so the cut is smooth. Assemble the pipes the way you want them but don't glue them just yet—this is called "dry fitting." Dry fit only three or four connections at once, since the dimensions may change as you work.

2 Make sure that you slope all pipe downwards ¼" for every foot of length. Less and you'll risk a backup.

3 Once you're ready to start gluing, clean the connections off with a towel and rub the appropriate cement (your hardware store will carry both ABS and PVC cement—they are not interchangeable) on the inside of the fitting and the outside of the pipe end. If you are working with PVC pipe, you will also need to use a special primer before you apply the glue. Once the glue is applied, hold the pipes together for around 20 seconds and you're all done.

Cast Iron Pipe—Not For Wimps

All of these projects work the same whether you have plastic or cast iron waste lines. Altering plastic drain lines is well within the abilities of everyone with the will, but cast iron waste pipes are more tricky. Those with cast iron pipes may wish to hire a plumber to cut it and help you make connections to plastic ABS or PVC pipe. Extra-intrepid urban homesteaders who want to cut cast iron pipes themselves need to take precautions. Cast iron pipe is very heavy, so make sure that waste lines and vent stacks are supported before you start cutting. You don't want it falling on your head, or your foot.

We recommend that you read Michael Litchfield's book *Renovation: A Complete Guide* before you begin more complicated projects. It has a lengthy section covering plumbing basics among many other topics on home repair useful to all urban homesteaders.

How the Greywater Guerrillas Learned to Plumb from *Dam Nation: Dispatches from the Water Underground*

I wanted hands-on skills. Since I knew literally nothing about plumbing, I decided to sign up for a residential plumbing class offered by the local community college. After two plumbing classes and a Sunday afternoon greywater conversation, I was ready with my partner-in-crime, Cleo, to make the first cut. So we did. This rental house was blessed with a genuine slumlord. Every winter we made a phone call to tell him it was raining inside our bathroom and kitchen. Every winter he put up a small blue tarp, which immediately blew away. We had no qualms about cutting pipes in this house. Giggling down to the basement with a saw and flashlight in hand, we found the shower drainpipe and promptly severed it. That jagged slice through two-inch ABS pipe cut the mental umbilical cord of fear, uncertainty, and apathy that had tied me to modern sewer infrastructure.

Greywater Guerrillas, Oakland, CA

SHOWERS TO FLOWERS

Along with your bathroom sink, your shower has the least dirty water and makes an excellent source for irrigation. One of the best greywater strategies is hooking up a pipe that runs directly from the bath or shower drain out into the garden. That way you'll avoid all the complex plumbing issues that come when you tap into that tangle of waste pipes under your house. Your shower is a great candidate for running straight out. If your shower drain is higher than what needs to be watered, give this a try.

How To Run Your Shower, or Any Greywater Source, Directly Outside:

1 Go under your house and locate the waste line from your shower. Measure the distance to the garden so you can get all the pipe, fittings and cement you'll need to make the run to the garden.

2 Using that measurement, confirm that your shower waste line is higher than the point you are watering. The minimum fall for waste pipes is ¼" per foot—any less and you'll risk a backup. That means that you have to measure how many feet it is between shower and garden, and multiply that number by .25. If it is 12 feet to the garden from your shower drain, the garden must be at least 3" lower than the shower drain (12' × .25 = 3") to drain properly.

3 Choose plants whose watering requirements match the amount of water coming out of your shower by estimating how many showers and how much water you use per week. Odds are that the best candidates for Showers to Flowers will be water-hungry and alkaline tolerant plants such as blackberries or banana trees.

4 If you just want to do a good deed and recharge the water table with your showers, all you have to do is dig a ditch big enough to absorb the longest shower you and your housemates might take and backfill it with gravel. Drain all the water there.

5 Assuming your drain lines are plastic, cut your shower line using a hacksaw. Dry fit your run of pipe with the appropriate fittings out to the garden, remembering to maintain at least a ¼" per foot drop. Glue up the pipe with cement when you are sure all is well.

6 Put a screen over the outdoors end of the pipe to prevent rats and other critters from climbing up the pipe and surprising you in the shower. Keep the destination of the pipe at least ten feet away from your house's foundation.

7 Use only liquid soap, not bar soap for showers. Most shampoos should be fine.

Or what about just showering outside? If you don't want to reroute your shower water, you can take the entire shower outside and create an outdoor bathing paradise. To do this, run your plumbing outside or construct an independent solar-heated shower like the one in our solar heating section on page 267. Landscape around the shower to take advantage of the water and to create a living privacy screen.

PROJECT

RECYCLING YOUR SUDS

One of the simplest greywater projects is routing your washing machine water out to the garden. Because of the easy accessibility of your washing machine's waste line and the fact that washing machines have a built-in pump that pumps the water out from the machine, it's even a strategy that renters can take on. After the shower and bathroom sink, the next cleanest source for greywater is the washing machine. Here's three ways to do it:

PVC Pipe

The easiest way to get water from your washing machine to your yard is simply to hook the drain hose of your washing machine up to a length of flexible 1" PVC pipe. Flexible PVC pipe is something that you'll find at pool and spa supply stores, on the Internet and at large home centers. With flexible pipe you can run the greywater out to different areas of your yard just like you would with a garden hose. But you must use flexible pipe that is at least 1" in diameter—garden hose is not big enough and will burn out your pump, especially if it gets a kink.

The built-in pump contained in your washing machine makes it possible to send water both uphill and a reasonable distance horizontally. Unfortunately, washing machine pumps are not designed with this in mind, so you run a slight risk of burning out or decreasing the life of your washing machine's pump should you attempt to pump the waste water uphill. There are, however, ways to minimize the risk of pump burnout. Whether you use flexible 1" pipe or glue up a permanent run of ABS or PVC remember the following things to preserve your pump:

1 The pipe you use, flexible or not, must be at least 1" in diameter. Smaller pipes risk burning out the pump.

2 Most washing machines empty into a vertical pipe behind the machine called a stand pipe. Use this height at which the washing machine hose pipe meets as a reference point. You don't want to pump your water up any higher than this point or you will risk pump burnout.

3 You also need to take into account the length of the run. The longer the run, the more stress it will put on the pump. According to Ludwig, each 50' is the equivalent of about 10" of vertical rise. Add up the length and height of the run and compare it to the height the washing machine hose used to meet the stand pipe.

4 For a more permanent installation, consider installing a three-way valve at the standpipe to send the water to the sewer when you need to. This is necessary if you wash diapers, because the water shouldn't be sent to the garden.

5 It's best to get the pipe up to its highest point early and then run down from there even though it is possible to run pipe up, down and up again (since the water is under pressure). Having sections of pipe where water will stagnate, however,

run a slight chance of causing the water to get smelly, and risk burst pipe if it freezes.

Installing a swing check valve (a device that prevents water from flowing backwards in the line) close to the washing machine will prevent water from flowing back into the machine should you happen to move the flexible hose above the level of the machine.

Remember to use only detergent specifically made for greywater use such as Oasis Biocompatible detergent.

6 In freezing weather you'll need to revert to sending washing machine water back to the sewer to prevent a burnout of your washing machine pump caused by frozen water in the pipes running out to your garden.

Tricking Out Your Washing Machine With Multiple Stand Pipes

With plastic pipe so easy to work with, you can also make several permanent runs out to the garden each with their own labeled stand pipe next to the washing machine. To do this you rig up multiple stand pipes each with their own separate run out to different places in the garden. Each time you do your wash you could choose the "citrus tree" pipe or the "banana tree" pipe, switching your machine's outlet between them and allowing you to become a greywater disc jockey.

Make A Surge Tank For Your Washing Machine

Another way to use your washing machine's greywater is to construct what is called a surge tank with a 50-gallon plastic drum. A greywater surge tank is pretty much the same as a rainwater collection barrel — you could even combine the two. All you need is a 55-gallon drum with a garden hose connected to the bottom. As discussed previously, our favorite method of hooking up a hose to a 55-gallon barrel can be found at aquabarrel.com.

Draining your washing machine into a 55-gallon drum rather than sending it out directly into the garden has multiple advantages: it allows hot water to cool, prevents siphoning mishaps and washing machine pump burnouts. Hooking up the surge tank to a garden hose allows you to use the hose around to water different plants. Here's how to adapt your rainwater harvesting barrel to become a washing machine surge tank:

1 Direct your washing machine's drain hose into the barrel. The hose must first go above the top of the machine before going down into the tank in order to prevent the machine from draining accidentally. Also, don't make this connection airtight—the washing machine needs an air gap, normally provided by the loose connection to the standpipe to prevent wastewater from siphoning back into the machine.

2 You must use the water in the tank within 24 hours to prevent the water from going septic. Standing greywater goes bad quickly.

3 Use a nylon sock as a filter to catch lint and other debris coming out of the washing machine. Stretch it over the pipe coming out of the washing machine at the point where the pipe enters the top of the barrel.

4 Remember to only use greywater-compatible detergent such as Oasis Biocompatible.

PROJECT

ARRANGING A TWOSOME OR THREESOME —USING DIVERTERS

In some situations, rather than sending a pipe straight out to the garden it might be more convenient to shift your greywater back to the sewer system such as during an extended rainy spell or during the winter. If you want to use your washing machine, but have to run loads of diapers, you must have one of these to send the diaper water to the sewer where it belongs.

There are two ways to do this. The "Cadillac" option is a piece of plumbing known as a three-way diverter valve which will allow you to switch back and forth between sending your water out to the garden and sending it down the sewer with the simple turn of a handle. Three-way diverter valves are a bit exotic and probably won't be found at your local hardware store. Instead, you'll have to seek out a pool and spa supply shop. Art Ludwig sells one through his website (oasisdesign.net/greywater/divertervalves.htm) in the $50 range. If you think you'll need to constantly switch back and forth, this valve should be placed in an easily accessible place. There are electronic remote controls for such valves but they cost around $250, which violates our "keep it simple and cheap" rule.

The cheap alternative to a three-way diverter valve: two ball valves used to switch between sending your water out to the garden or to the sewer.

For a cheaper way to divert water back to the sewer, water activists the Greywater Guerillas suggest rigging up a set of two ball valves that every hardware store should have. These are the plumbing equivalent of an on-off switch: turn the two-way valve and the line will close. Position them as shown in the illustration to divert water either to your garden or to the sewer. Just remember not to shut off both valves or your waste line will back up.

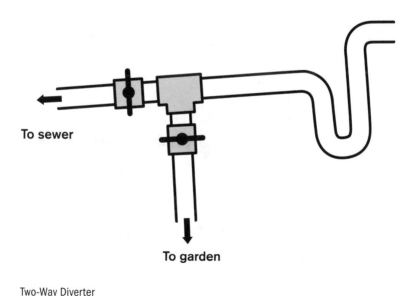

To sewer

To garden

Two-Way Diverter

MAKE A GREYWATER WETLAND

PROJECT

As we've already stated, our approach to greywater must be kept simple and away from the prying eyes of building inspectors. One way to improve the quality of the greywater, while avoiding complicated and expensive filters, is through the construction of a greywater wetland. Wetlands are nature's way of purifying water, and the water treated by a wetland can be used on plants that don't tolerate untreated greywater. Aquatic plants take oxygen from the air and release it through their roots, helping to break down and treat both greywater and even blackwater. A greywater wetland will give you both a water garden and a way to further improve the water quality of your greywater. If properly constructed, a greywater wetland can even purify blackwater from your toilet, though amateurs should probably stick to greywater.

Excellent instructions for constructing a simple greywater wetland can be found on the website of the San Francisco Bay Area Greywater Guerillas at greywaterguerrillas.com. Their method involves routing greywater to a pair of 30- to 50-gallon containers. The first tank serves as a surge tank and the second, containing sand, filters out the soap scum. After passing through these tanks the greywater is sent to a set of salvaged bathtubs. Depending on how much greywater you produce and how much you want to purify it, you can use anywhere

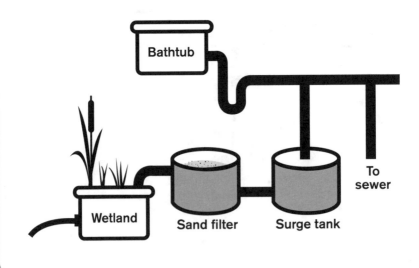

Bathtub

To sewer

Wetland   Sand filter   Surge tank

from one to three bathtubs that drain into each other. The system the Greywater Guerrillas use consists of two bathtubs containing ¼" to ¾" pea gravel planted with aquatic plants such as cattails. On top of the gravel, there's a layer of wood chip mulch to decrease evaporation and smells. The third tub contains water hyacinths that finish off the purification process.

Greywater wetlands will work best in mild, moist places. In desert areas your wetlands may evaporate faster than you can use the water. In these cases, simply routing your greywater directly to the garden and choosing greywater-tolerant plants may the best option. Additional resources for greywater wetlands: frogs.org.au/frogwatch/greywater.php

So what can you do with all that blackwater from the toilet that we've so far told you to send down the sewer? The answer is the most extreme of our water projects:

PROJECT

THE COMPOSTING TOILET
AND HOW TO POOP IN A BUCKET

Radical urban homesteaders can do away with the flush toilet altogether and opt for a composting toilet. With a composting toilet, not only will you eliminate the water that you waste on flushing, but you'll also be saving all that useful organic matter that can help build your soil.

Composting toilets come in commercial and DIY versions. The best-known commercial system is the Clivus Multrum (clivusmultrum.com) which sends your waste into a large basement composting chamber. Smaller, self-contained systems such as those manufactured by Sun-Mar rotate and dry waste in place. With both Clivus Multrum and Sun-Mar toilets you need to periodically empty and distribute the finished compost.

Composting toilet revolutionaries can save a lot of money by following the DIY advice of Joseph Jenkins, author of *The Humanure Handbook* which is available both in book form and as a free download at jenkinspublishing.com. Jenkins' "humanure" method amounts to using a five-gallon bucket with an attached toilet seat as your new throne—infinitely cheaper than the aforementioned commercial systems. After you leave a deposit in your bucket you cover it with a layer of carbonaceous material such as sawdust or peat moss to prevent odor. When the bucket is full you take it outside and put it in a compost bin (separate from your regular compost) and, just as you do with the bucket in your bathroom, you make sure that each new layer added to the pile is thoroughly covered with carbonaceous material. Jenkins adamantly suggests that you never turn the pile. When your humanure bin is full you start another pile and let the first one sit for at least a year to thoroughly decompose. When the pile has decomposed you can use the compost on trees and non-food plants.

In most urban places, dealing with your own sewage will make you an outlaw in the eyes of building inspectors and your local health department, so if you try humanure be discreet and responsible—read Jenkins' book for the details of the process.

You Will Always Have a Pot To Piss In

Even if the thought of becoming a humanure revolutionary is a little much for you at the moment, it's good to know that you can use five-gallon buckets as toilets in the event the sewage system fails. You don't need to dig a latrine, use scary blue chemicals, or wait in line for the Port-A-Potties, just set up a bucket in your bathroom. When you fill up the bucket, put a lid on it, set it aside and start a new one. Those buckets will act like mini-composters and in a year or so they will no longer be yucky inside.

If you have the space, stash away an old five-gallon bucket with a lid, filled with sawdust or peat moss, just for this sort of event. It might be difficult to find a sawdust source while simultaneously fighting off zombie hordes.

Luggable Loo Composting Toilet

Pooping in the Bedroom and Proud of It!

Well, I finally just realized that nothing was stopping me from composting my humanure, except my own fear and inhibitions. There's a certain awkwardness to get past with this system. It's not conventional, and many people don't know what to make of it at first. My husband was one of those people. Well, talking about it warmed him up, but the only way to get him used to it, was to do it!

So I've done it! Not surprisingly, my husband has come around. He assisted me in building the toilet (which was a great sign), and has been using it more and more. It's only been four days! He's commented several times that he's impressed and proud of me for going through with it. This from a man who was adamantly against it originally! I now have my husband's full support. In fact the tension about the decision dropped away the minute he realized he couldn't talk me out of it. He's been positive about it ever since!

I've wanted to do this for years, but have let other people's negativity hold me back. The recent catalyst for me was about three weeks ago, when a new friend of mine said she was planning on building one, even though her partner "thinks it's disgusting." I thought, wow, she's going to do it anyway...Why not?

Now I've done it, and it's already inspiring another friend of mine to build one. Good ideas catch on! By the way, I live in a rental apartment, and we had to put the thing in a corner of the bedroom! I think pooping in the bedroom took more getting used to than pooping in the bucket!

Walking lightly on the Earth and proud of it,
Amy, Massachusetts

Power To The People

It seems, there is almost no activity or product that, in the course of our daily lives, does not owe its existence to fossil fuels, oil, natural gas or coal. All of our energy needs, our transportation, heating, and lighting, as well as the myriad petrochemical-derived products such as plastics and the chemical fertilizers that grow our supermarket foods, owe their origin to fossil fuels whose extraction in our lifetimes is becoming increasingly expensive. As the balance between supply and demand tightens with the expanding industrialization of countries such as China and India, concerns about energy security and future supply make clear the necessity of seeking energy efficiency and self-sufficiency on our urban homesteads. In addition, the climatic implications of our dependence on fossil fuels leaves many folks who stumble out of a screening of Al Gore's *An Inconvenient Truth* wondering what exactly they can do in an increasingly desperate situation.

Optimists, such as Amory Lovins of the Rocky Mountain Institute, predict a new economy based on the production of innovative forms of alternative energy. Peak oil pessimists believe the world's petroleum reserves are rapidly approaching a point where extraction will soon take more energy than it is worth, the result being economic disaster and the collapse of modern society.

Between these two extremes, waiting for some technological miracle or collapsing in despair, we propose a pragmatic third position: Keep your living space small, and tweak what you've got through low-tech, simple and small solutions aimed at maximizing the energy you use. Some high-tech miracle may come along, but in the meantime we'll be doing what we can and having fun while we do it. Together, the simple projects we propose in this chapter will add up to a dramatic reduction in your environmental footprint and a big step toward energy independence. Energy independence is an accumulation of small opportunities—not grand strategies.

Principles

Our "keep it simple" energy plan takes a cue from the laws of thermodynamics that are inescapable in our universe. To oversimplify, the laws of thermodynamics basically state that you can't get something out of nothing and secondly, that entropy or decay will guarantee that all energy in all its various forms ultimately decays. Or as author and scientist C.P. Snow put it, "you cannot win" and "you cannot break even." So what we've got, we've got to use wisely and efficiently, leading us to our energy principles:

1 **Energy systems we use should produce or conserve more energy than they took to make.** In technical terms this principle is called "energy return on energy investment" or EROEI for short. A proven technology such as photovoltaic cells, which generate electricity from the sun, when properly made and installed will over time generate more power than it took to create them, giving us a positive EROEI. Though there is considerable controversy on this topic, some consider Ethanol that is produced from corn or soybeans to be an example of a fuel that takes more energy, in the form of fertilizers and transportation costs, than it produces.

2 **Energy generation and conservation technologies on the urban homestead should be simple, long-lasting, and low-maintenance.** Photovoltaic panels fit this description, as do bicycles and solar ovens. We like technologies whose parts and functions are readily understandable, standardized, and interchangeable. We don't like complex contraptions with no proven history, with parts that can't be replaced, and with promises too good to be true.

3 **Energy systems should benefit the people they serve.** Just as we do in our gardens, in energy production we seek out mutually beneficial arrangements, We search for techniques and technologies that enhance rather than drain our lives. If we can generate our own power, what do we use it for? We use it to create positive and enriching experiences.

4 **Neither Luddite nor geek.** Our tinkering ethos is pragmatic and extends to the way we generate and use energy. We do what we need to do to get by, as long as it is ethical and produces a net energy gain. Urban homesteaders are not Luddites. Any technology that has a proven EROEI and greatly reduces our emissions we'll happily use. At the same time we must be skeptical of new alternative energy schemes. Recent history is replete with examples of ridiculous gadgets, fads, and frauds that simply don't work other than to enrich hucksters looking for a quick buck.

Household Energy Use

Before we can get to tinkering with things like solar panels, we've got to increase the efficiency of the systems we currently have. And by starting with efficiency, renters and apartment dwellers who might not be able to take on the more radical projects will still have a way to save on those utility bills and make a contribution to keeping the globe cooler.

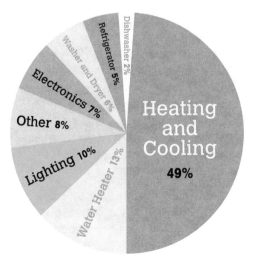

Household Energy Use

Heating and Cooling 49%
Water Heater 13%
Lighting 10%
Other (stoves and small appliances) 8%
Electronics 7%
Clothes Washer and Dryer 6%
Refrigerator 5%
Dishwasher 2%

Source: Residential Energy Consumption Survey, 2001

This chart gives us a visual understanding of where we should direct our priorities in both conservation and innovation. What follows is a series of projects and suggestions to help you both increase the energy efficiency in your home and explore alternative technologies, arranged in order of energy costs.

Heating 49%

According to the last U.S. census, most homes are heated with gas, with smaller percentages heated with electricity, fuel oil or kerosene. Alarmingly, natural gas, which was once abundant and cheap, now faces an uncertain future as domestic supplies dwindle and demand increases. The same supply-and-demand problems also face the small percentage of homes that use fuel oil and kerosene. Right now, heating with gas is still cheaper than heating with electricity, but both will definitely rise in cost in coming years.

Strategy 1: Insulation

As with all projects relating to energy we first suggest increasing efficiency, which in the case of heating and cooling means making sure that your urban homestead is well insulated. Insulation is a complex (not to mention dull) subject and frankly, we have yet to follow our own advice, and live in a hastily built 1920s bungalow that's basically a wood and plaster pup tent that offers merely symbolic resistance to wind and rain. When we get around to the task of sealing all those drafty cracks we'll first consult *Insulate and Weatherize* by

Bruce Harley, an excellent resource for information on insulation matters. It's one of many books published by the Taunton Press, our go-to source for all home repair and construction questions. Taunton also puts out the informative *Fine Homebuilding Magazine*. There is a Taunton book on almost any construction or remodeling topic and all are thorough and well researched. Even if you're hiring out the job, Taunton publications are a great way to educate yourself on getting the details right, and in the case of insulation, the devil is definitely in the details.

The Energy and Environmental Building Association also has an online checklist that you can go through to make sure your house is well sealed and insulated: eeba.org/resources/publications/hec.

Bubble-Wrap Your Windows

Windows are a huge source for heat loss. Admittedly this is not the most elegant solution, but it works, and it's a cheap and easy way for anyone to cut heating bills in the coldest months.

Simply cut sheets of bubble wrap so they are sized to fit your windows, apply some water to the window with a spray bottle and before it dries, stick the bubble wrap on the glass. It will stay put. While you can buy special bubble wrap designed for greenhouses, regular bubble wrap will probably work just as well. If you number the pieces you use and keep a key on what piece goes where, you can stick the same wrap up again next year with less work.

Strategy 2: Gathering Solar Heat

Passive Solar Heating

Passive solar heating refers to heating that comes about through the design of the building itself, where both the materials and the configuration of the home are designed with the intention of catching and keeping the heat of the sun in the home, and so lessen the need for fuel-based heating. It is an ancient technology. Greek and Roman homes were set up to take advantage of the heating power of the sun's rays. In ancient Greece, entire communities were laid using sophisticated passive solar design principles.

Few of us are able to design our homes from scratch, but when it comes time to rent or buy a house or apartment we can seek out inadvertent passive solar assets, such as south-facing windows, or make little changes around our present homes to enhance solar heat.

Some passive solar tips: If you're searching for an urban homestead in a cold climate, try to find one with south-facing windows and a long wall on the south side that will collect heat. Clear obstructions that shade your south-facing windows. You want that sun to come on in. The south side of the house is a good place for deciduous trees (trees that lose their leaves in the winter).

These provide shade in the summer and let in sunlight in the winter after the leaves have fallen off in the fall.

When it's time to replace the roof, choose dark-colored roofing materials, which will absorb the heat of the sun. Tile and masonry floors in sunny rooms absorb sunlight, and hold that heat into the night.

Solar Air Heating

The principle of solar air heating is identical to the solar dehydrator that we describe on page 174. We're not talking about photovoltaic panels here—no electricity is being generated or used. A solar hot air collector is an insulated box topped with glass or plastic, inside of which you put dark metallic material such as metal screen to absorb the light of the sun. It sits outside of your house, but is connected to the interior of your house via a vent. The sun heats the black metal and the resulting hot air rises up the length of the collection box and is vented into your living spaces. In most places a solar air heater won't completely replace your conventional heating, but it can help augment it, and greatly reduce your power bills. Solar hot air will work best in cold places that get a lot of sun in the winter, like Colorado.

DIY solar hot air collectors come in different forms. The simplest version involves constructing a collector box, and feeding it into a window of your house, the same way you would stick a cheap air conditioner in a window. Detailed instructions for building window-mounted solar air heater like this can be found in the archives of *Mother Earth News* at motherearthnews.com/Green-Home-Building/1977-09-01/Mothers-Heat-Grabber.aspx.

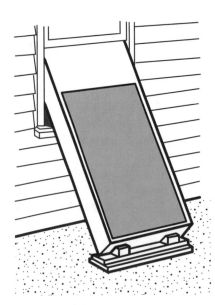

Solar Hot Air Collector

Between The Studs

Another approach is to integrate a solar air heater into the wall between the studs of your house. Retired aircraft engineer Gary Reysa has an impressive design that he says will pay for itself in heating costs in just a year's time. Rather than taking in cool air from the outside like the design above, Reysa's solar heater passively recycles inside air, resulting in greater efficiency.

Other than the fact that the intake vents are inside rather than outside, the basic design is essentially the same principle as the food dehydrator described on page 174. Detailed instructions for how to build Reysa's solar heater can be found at in the October/November issue of *Home Power Magazine* and on the Build it Solar website at builditsolar.com/Projects/SpaceHeating/SolarBarn.pdf.

Commercial Versions

You can also purchase commercially-made solar hot air heaters that work just like the DIY versions. Commercial solar hot air systems often have an electric fan to help circulate hot air and may also have a thermostat. They come in both roof- and wall-mounted versions. The solar cost calculator at findsolar.com can help you figure out if buying a solar hot air system makes economic sense where you live.

Strategy 3: The High Mass Rocket Heater
The Limited Fuel Use Option

In many places in the world, heating is provided by wood, but unfortunately this practice can lead to massive deforestation. Rocket stoves (which we'll describe in detail in our stove section) allow for high-efficiency burning of small materials such as twigs and wood scraps and are therefore much more energy-efficient than regular wood-burning stoves. A high mass rocket heater uses the same principle as the rocket stove to heat your house. Ecologist and author Ianto Evans has written a DIY book entitled *Rocket Mass Heaters: Super Efficient Woodstoves You Can Build* that details how to construct your own rocket heater.

Cooling 49%

Chill: Easy Passive Cooling Strategies

Just as with heating, it's entirely possible to cool your house with simple and inexpensive passive measures. Remember that air conditioning did not come into widespread use until the 1950s and somehow we all managed to survive.

- Plant the things you water most (veggies, flowers, fruit trees, etc.) close to the house, that way they'll help cool your living spaces through the water evaporating from both soil and leaves (as well as making it easier to grab food when you want it).
- Plant deciduous trees on the south side of the house to provide shade in the summer and sunlight in during the winter.
- Create inviting outdoor living spaces, preferably on the north side of the house, and spend your time outside on hot evenings.

- In hot climates, it's a good idea to paint the exterior of your house with light-colored paint to significantly reduce heat absorption from the sun. For the same reason, choose light-colored roofing material if you don't need winter heat.
- Observe where prevailing winds come from and do everything possible to enhance cross ventilation in your house.

HOW TO MAKE A LIVING AWNING OR SHADE

For south-facing windows, an awning or horizontal window trellis will shade your living space in the summer months and let the sun shine in during the winter. If you grow edible vines over your window trellis, not only will they give shade, but they will also give you food and the moisture evaporating from their leaves will cool the house more than an awning.

We really like the idea of being able to reach out the window to retrieve dinner.

Window trellises can be ordered, scavenged or, for those with carpentry skills, improvised. All they consist of are two supports, like shelf brackets, on either side of the window. Across those you lay something for the vines to cling to. That might be a piece of lattice, or several narrow pieces of cedar, or bamboo poles, or copper pipe.

Choose a deciduous, perennial vine (like a squash, maybe?) and you'll have shade in the summer and sun in the winter. Just remember to keep vines neatly trimmed to prevent them from working their way into the walls, where they might do damage.

How do you know how deep the trellis should be? You could wing it—it's fair enough to say that any sort of awning helps. But the best way to tell would be to take a ladder and a long stick, a yardstick would be nice, but any stick will do, to your window on a sunny day at noon around the summer solstice: June 21. Climb up the ladder and position the stick so that it is poking out perpendicularly from the wall of your house, just over your window (i.e. the spot where you'd install the trellis). You'll see the shadow of the stick fall across the window. Run a finger along the stick until you can see the shadow of your finger at the lower edge of the window. That point, the place your finger is on the stick, indicates the ideal depth of your trellis. See, this is where having a yardstick comes in handy! But if you have a plain old stick, just mark that magic point and go measure the length of your stick to that point.

Living Curtains

A less formal approach than a trellis is to rig up a living curtain right in front of your window by providing vertical supports for climbing vines. Some thin wire or concrete reinforcing wire (find it at home centers in 3 ½' by 7' sections), the same stuff we use for tomato cages, can provide a temporary support for annual vines. Tomatoes, pole beans and cucumbers are the types of plants that are good candidates for a living curtain. The greenery will cool your house and provide a privacy screen.

If you don't have any soil beneath your window, plant your vines in big self-watering containers.

Living Awning

Whole House Fans

Imagine your bathroom fan on steroids and you'll have some idea what a whole house fan looks like. Whole house fans are usually placed somewhere in the center of the house in the joists between the ceiling and the attic. The fan points up into the attic. Fire it up, and the air flow it generates will suck cool air from the outside of the house, move it though the living areas and push hot air out of the attic.

A whole house fan is good for exactly one thing: cooling the interior of your house to the temperature outside. It won't work in places where the nights are sweltering, but very useful for cooling down your house in the evening if the days are hot but the nights are reasonable.

In order for a whole house fan to work the attic itself must be adequately vented to exchange air with the outside. Screen material over your attic vents decreases air flow, so if your vents are screened, replace it with ½" hardware cloth to both keep critters out of the attic but allow the air to move.

Whole house fans come in different sizes depending on the square footage of your house with the smallest ones priced around $200. Installation will probably involve cutting ceiling joists so hire a carpenter if you feel uncomfortable sawing a giant hole in your ceiling. You can also make a low-rent whole house fan by jamming a large floor fan in your attic access door.

NOTE: If you have AC, do not use the whole house fan at the same time the AC is on or you'll be sucking the expensive refrigerated air you are paying for straight out of the house.

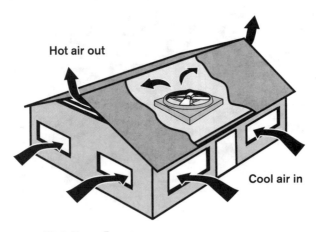

Hot air out

Cool air in

Whole House Fans

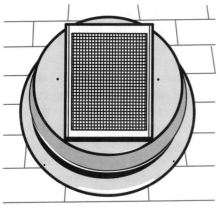
Solar Attic Fan

Solar Attic Fan

Though not as effective as a whole house fan, attic fans, which are mounted on top of the roof, can help evacuate hot air out of your attic and that in itself will keep your house cooler. To be clear, the difference between these and whole house fans is that attic fans have nothing to do with sucking hot air out of your living space — only your attic. But a hot attic makes for a hot house, so they are worthwhile.

There are a few solar models available and installation is as simple as cutting a hole in your roof and installing the unit. In order for an attic fan to work properly the attic should have some intake vents, often placed under the eaves of the house, so that the attic fan can pull cool air from the outside up and then out of the attic.

One possible strategy is to run an attic fan during the hot parts of the day to keep the attic from heating up, and the whole house fan during the cool hours of the evening.

Ceiling Fans

Ceiling fans are an excellent alternative to conventional air-conditioning — they keep the airflow in a room moving, they are inexpensive and easy to install and don't use a lot of energy. The only drawback to them, in fact, is an aesthetic one. For some reason, ceiling fan manufacturers adhere to a saloon-whore-house-meets-cheap-Chinese-slave-labor look. While very expensive designer models exist, the urban homesteader can pimp out most ceiling fans with some paint and creativity to cover up the factories' unfortunate attempts at ornamentation. You can also switch out the ugly lampshades that seem to always come with these things.

Water Heater 13%

Pimp My Hot Water Heater

Treat your water heater like teens treat their Hondas — as a source for self-expression and optimized performance. If you're going to attempt solar water heating it's especially important to boost your conventional water heater's efficiency.

- First, make sure that your water heater's thermostat is set at the lowest agreeable setting. While thermostat settings of any kind are a potential source of spousal/roommate conflict, there is no sense heating water to dangerous temperatures.
- The next step is wrapping your water heater in a insulating blanket. Insulating kits can be purchased at your hardware store for around $20 and they will pay for themselves in a few months. Follow the kit instructions precisely.
- Finally comes the less than scintillating annual task of water heater draining. That gurgling sound you might hear after taking a shower is the result of sediment from your municipal water supply that builds up in the bottom of the tank. As this sediment builds up, it prevents the water in the tank from being heated efficiently. We recommend draining your water heater once a year, but some plumbing experts suggest doing it more often. To remind yourself to do this task, pick a significant date like the summer solstice or your birthday and throw a water heater draining party.

How To Drain The Tank

1 Turn off the cold supply to the tank. If it's an electric water heater shut the power off to the heater—if you don't you'll burn out the heating element. If you have a gas heater shut off the gas at the heater.

2 Hook up a garden hose to the drain pipe that you will find at the bottom of the tank.

3 Open up the hot water side of any faucet in your house.

4 Open the drain valve on the water heater and kick back—it will take a while to drain the tank. Send it to a kiddie pool for a low-end hot tub party—after all, it is your birthday, remember? Make it a nude hot tub party.

5 After the water has drained, shut off the drain valve and turn on the cold water supply to the tank to loosen more of the sediment. Let the tank fill partially and then drain it again. If you've got a lot of crap in the tank you may need to do this several times.

6 To finish up, shut off the drain valve and let the tank fill up completely. You'll know the tank is full when water starts coming out of the hot water faucet you left open in your house. When the tank is full turn the power on again or, if it's gas, turn it on and light the pilot light.

If all of this seems a little wearisome, it might be time to consider a tankless water heater. Popular in Europe for a long time, tankless heaters heat on demand, and might use less energy depending on where you live and how many folks live on your homestead. The big drawback right now with tankless systems is the expense, but you'll never have to drain one.

Alternatives To The Gas-Heated Shower

The Sunshine Shower
We're not suggesting you take all of your showers outdoors. But outdoor shower/tub situations have been all the thing in fancy home mags of late, and though we lack the budget, we don't see why we can't have the pleasure of showering with the birds on a warm summer day. It's cheap and easy to install a solar shower. You'll have fun with it, and whenever you use it, you'll be saving energy, and watering your yard.

Plant things around your shower that can take advantage of the water-rich environment. Line the floor of your shower with gravel to keep your feet out of the mud. The shampoo and soap you use will be of small enough quantities that they should not harm the plants, but it couldn't hurt to use very mild, natural products in your outdoor shower.

The principle behind the solar-heated shower is simple—fill a black container with water, let it heat up in the sun, and take your shower in the afternoon. Here are three ways to construct one:

Camping Shower
First off is the camping shower in a bag concept. The principle is simple—you fill a black bag with water, leave it out in the sun, and hang it somewhere for your very brief shower. You can buy one of these things for around $20 or, better yet, you can improvise one with a truck tire inner tube.

Plumb the truck tire with a ½" plastic pipe coupler, a male hose connector, a small clamp, and a nozzle. See our bibliography for a pointer to instructions at motherearthnews.com. Create a stall for your shower out of scrap wood and put the tire on top.

Camping Shower

Garden Hose Shower

Another option that makes for a longer shower is simply to coil up 200' of black garden hose and put it somewhere sunny, like the top of a shower enclosure, or the roof of your house. For temperature control, add a "Y" connector to blend in cold water from a second hose. These connectors are found next to the hose section at the hardware store.

ABS Shower

Inexpensive black ABS (plumbing) pipe can also be used to make a solar shower. You get this stuff at any home center. All you have to do is glue it into a squarish configuration using the cement that is sold for this purpose, connect a shower head to the lowest part of it. Fill it with a hose, leave it out in the sun to heat. Your shower lasts as long as the amount of water contained in the ABS pipe, meaning use more pipe for longer showers. You could also construct a sort of trellis-roof out of ABS for the top of your improvised shower stall. This will provide greater privacy if your city has as many police helicopters as birds.

Solar Water Heaters For General Household Hot Water

Heating water for general household use is one of the most promising applications for the light of the sun. And the good news is that creating your own solar water heating system is within the means of the ambitious do-it-yourself urban homesteader. Note that with solar water heating we won't be using photovoltaic panels—those are for generating electricity. Instead we'll be using sunlight to heat water directly.

Solar water heating is an old and proven technology with the first patent for a solar water heater, which consisted of a black water tank on the roof, dating to 1891. Solar water heaters fall into several different categories. The type you choose will depend on your climate and whether you want to do the work yourself. With most urban installations you'll probably keep your conventional gas or electric water heater as a backup.

The simplest solar water heaters that you can build yourself closely resemble the 19th-century versions (yes, there was a solar craze in the 19th century!), and consist of a black tank, often a scavenged old water heater, contained in a insulated, glass-topped box. These simple systems are known as batch heaters or "integral passive solar water heaters" (IPSWH for short) since the collection and storage of your hot water takes place in the collector itself. The Build it Solar website has a detailed 100-page book on how to design and build batch heaters by David Bainbridge called *The Integral Passive Solar Water Heater Book* that you can download for free: buildilsolar.com/Projects/WaterHeating/ISPWH/ispwh.htm

Another slightly more complicated solar water heating method is called thermosyphoning. Thermosyphoning is the most common solar water heating method in the world. Just as with air, hot water rises and thermosyphoning takes advantage of this principle with a separate solar collector through which water is circulated. As the water heats, it rises up to a separate hot water storage tank. The advantage of this system over the batch heater is that the hot water ends up in a separate tank which can be insulated and housed indoors to make hot water available for a longer period of time after the sun goes down.

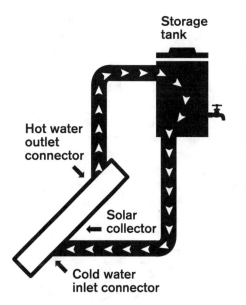

Storage tank

Hot water outlet connector

Solar collector

Cold water inlet connector

Thermosyphoning Diagram

Closed Loop Systems For Freezing Conditions

To operate a solar hot water heater year-round in a cold climate there are additional considerations to take into account. The solar hot water heaters we just described are called "open-loop" systems—the water in the tank or collector is the same water that you'll use in your house. In cold climates, where water could freeze and burst the pipes, you have two choices: either drain the system for the winter and rely on gas, or upgrade to a "closed loop" system which circulates an antifreeze solution such as propylene glycol though the collector instead of water. The antifreeze solution heats your water through a heat exchanger, which usually consists of a pipe with the antifreeze surrounded by another pipe containing your household potable water. For most, this kind of system is going to be store-bought and professionally installed.

Other Options

Besides open-loop and closed-loop there are additional kinds of solar collectors for heating water such as flat plate collectors, which are a network of pipes in a glass covered insulated box, and efficient evacuated tube collectors which have pipes surrounded by vacuum-sealed glass tubes. With evacuated tube collectors the vacuum creates a highly efficient insulation around the collector pipes making these expensive collectors a good option for cold places. Even on a cloudy day, an evacuated tube collector can heat your water.

For more information on commercial solar hot water systems and to determine if they are economical for you check out findsolar.com. For DIY solar hot water projects go to the Build it Solar website: builditsolar.com.

Lighting 10%

Light Bulbs

It should be old news by now that compact fluorescent bulbs are where it's at—we'll assume you've already gotten rid of the energy-wasting conventional light bulbs in your house. One thing to note is that the quality of compact fluorescents varies widely. It's best to stick to the big brand names, as off-brand or generic bulbs may not last as long and may have unappealing hues.

While there will no doubt be a bright future for LED bulbs, right now, compact fluorescents are still more cost-effective if you consider the ratio between cost and the amount of light they put out. It's not entirely fair to compare compact fluorescents to LED lights, since LED bulbs have a more directed light, making them better for certain applications such as bedside reading lights, where you don't want to bother a dozing partner. LEDs also have an exceptionally long life—upwards of 60,000 hours. LEDs just don't, at this point, work so well in situations where you need general dispersed lighting, such as in a floor or ceiling lamp. This will change soon as the lighting industry continues to develop new kinds of LED bulbs.

Tubular Skylights

Tubular skylights are an easy and simple alternative to lightbulbs that will bring sunlight into your home during the day without installing an expensive and potentially leaky skylight. Tubular skylights consist of a collector that you mount on the roof and a tube that snakes down through the attic and through the ceiling, allowing filtered sunlight to pass from the sky into your house. These "light tubes" are a godsend for dark bathrooms, hallways, and kitchens. The light they create is pleasant and diffuse. Best of all, a light tube means you can keep the light switches in your home in the "off"

Tubular Skylight

position until the sun goes down. Installing a tubular skylight is well within the means of a DIY urban homesteader. The most well-known brand name in this field is Solatube (solatube.com).

Stoves and Microwaves And Small Appliances (8%)

The uncertain future of natural gas makes finding alternatives for conventional stoves essential. And a word on anything that uses electricity to heat—don't use it if you can help it. You are better off cooking and heating with gas or with the alternative means described below. Electric heating elements, which can be found in things like coffee makers and toasters, are an inefficient and expensive way to cook.

An Overview Of Solar Cookers

One of the most promising alternatives to cooking with gas or electricity is solar cooking. While solar cooking can take more time than a conventional oven, one nice side benefit is that with the lower temperatures it is impossible to burn anything. Put your food in the solar oven in the morning and in a few hours you'll have a hot lunch or early dinner. Food can be removed any time after it is done.

There's definitely a solar cooking season with most solar cookers, since sunlight is diminished when the winter sun hangs low on the horizon. In most places solar cooking season is the time of year when your shadow is shorter than you are.

There are three basic types of solar cookers, and all can be improvised with scavenged materials.

- **Panel cookers** are the simplest and can be made with a cardboard box, aluminum foil, and a black pot.
- **Box cookers** are more efficient and consist of an insulated box, some glass, and reflectors to increase the amount of sun going into the box.
- **Parabolic solar cookers** are the fanciest of all. They consist of mirrors focused on a tight spot—they are the most difficult to build but will produce temperatures so high that you can deep-fry with them.

Panel Solar Cookers

The simplest kinds of solar cookers consist of nothing but a black pot and a piece of cardboard covered with aluminum foil. The extraordinarily useful Solar Cooking archive (solarcooking.org/plans/default.htm) has a large number of designs that you can download and build for next to nothing. To make a panel cooker all you have to do is take a piece of cardboard, spray-glue some aluminum foil

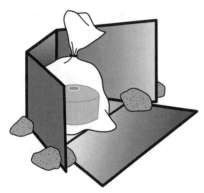

Panel Solar Cooker

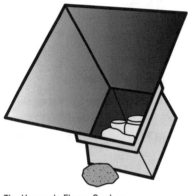

The Heaven's Flame Cooker

on it, and bend it into the shape you see in the illustration and point it at the sun. Your pot should be black to absorb the heat better, and efficiency can be further increased by putting the pot in a clear plastic bag (oven cooking bags are great for this purpose since they won't melt in high heat).

Box Solar Cookers

Box cookers are our favorite type of solar cooker for day-to-day use, and the best do-it-yourself design we've seen is the Heaven's Flame. Search this name for free construction plans from a number of sources. It consists of a smaller cardboard box placed within a larger cardboard box, with the space between the two stuffed with rags as insulation. You cover the opening with a piece of glass and affix a set of panels around the top to bounce more light into the box.

The Global Sun Oven

The readymade alternative: If you think you'll be doing a lot of solar cooking, and want something sturdy, or just don't want to make one yourself, you can buy a solar box cooker called the Global Sun Oven for around $200. The Global Sun Oven has a convenient tilting tray to put your pots on, a temperature gauge, thick insulation, and is sturdier than a cardboard box.

Parabolic Cookers
A Hybrid Parabolic-Panel Cooker

Arranging your cardboard panels into a parabolic shape (that means shaped like a satellite dish for those of us who have forgotten our geometry) will increase efficiency and generate more heat. The Parvati Solar Cooker, developed for use in India where shortages of cooking fuels are a serious problem, is one example of an easy-to-build parabolic panel cooker. Search Parvati Solar Cooker for free plans. Plans also exist on the Solar Cooking Archive website.

Purely Parabolic

Genuine parabolic cookers are more difficult to make because of the complex shape, but they generate heat well. We've heard of people roasting coffee beans in them. There are a number of clever designs out there, including one by Marc Ayats called the Paracuina solar cooker, which is made from an umbrella. Plans for the Paracuina cooker can be downloaded at solarcooking.org/plans/paracuina.pdf. Some folks have built parabolic cookers from repurposed satellite dishes.

The Built-In Solution: A Wall Cooker

One drawback to solar cookers is that you have to take them and your food outside. For greater convenience in cooking you can build a solar box cooker into a wall or window of your house so that you have indoor access to your solar oven. All you do is make an insulated plywood box with a slanted top to catch the sun, on which you put a piece of glass. Caulk everything carefully with silicon to seal in the heat and create an access door in the wall or window of the house. Affix the box to that opening.

The downside to wall cookers is that the oven cannot be aimed at the sun, so it must be installed on a sunny wall, and you must time your cooking to coincide with the hours the sun is on that wall. Barbara Kerr has a nice design that can be accessed at solarcooking.org/bkerr/DoItYouself.htm

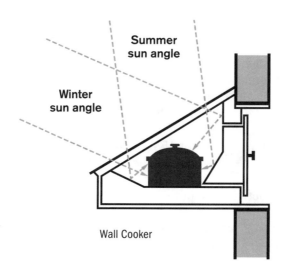

Summer
sun angle

Winter
sun angle

Wall Cooker

BUILD A ROCKET STOVE

The rocket stove was designed by Dr. Larry Winiarski of the Aprovecho Research Center, a non-profit organization that develops "appropriate technology" (which they define as "technology that can be made at an affordable price by ordinary people using local materials to do useful work"). Rocket stoves are an efficient way to cook using only twigs and small wood scraps, not logs. They are twice as efficient as conventional wood-burning methods. There are a number of different designs, but most consist of a heavily-insulated L-shaped metal pipe, at the bottom of which you burn a small, hot fire. The super-efficient transfer of heat from the wood to the pot is facilitated by the chimney effect.

To make a rocket stove you'll need:
- **Square five-gallon metal cooking oil container** (ask a restaurant for one of these),
- **Stove pipe**
- **Stove pipe elbow**
- **15 oz. can**
- **Small metal grill** to rest your pot on

Wear gloves while you're making this so that you don't cut yourself on the sharp pieces of metal.

1 Fit the stove pipe into the elbow snugly so that no heat leaks out.
2 Cut a circular hole low down on one of the sides of your five-gallon metal container for the elbow to stick out of. This is where you feed the fire.
3 Take both ends off your 15 oz. can. Cut it lengthwise and flatten it out so that it becomes a rectangle. Cut the metal into a T shape so that the tail of the T will fit into the elbow sticking out the side of the can to form a shelf for the firewood.
4 Cut out a circular hole for the top of the stove pipe in the lid of your oil can. Then cut off the edges of the lid so that it will fit down a few inches into the five-gallon container.

5 Assemble the elbow, stove pipe and shelf. Pour ashes into the five-gallon container so that they surround the stove pipe, filling the container entirely to provide insulation for the stove pipe. Tuck the lid of the can a few inches down into the container, so that it rests on the bed of ashes.

6 Put the grill on top of the container and you're ready to cook.

7 To use the stove, select small pieces of kindling and start a fire with some newspaper. Feed the kindling slowly into the stove across the feeding tray, pushing it bit by bit as it burns.

The Aprovecho Research Center has developed a number of other rocket stoves that you can build for your urban homestead. You can download plans and watch instructional videos on the Aprovecho Research Center's website at aprovecho.org. Particularly useful is their publication "Capturing Heat": weblife.org/capturing_heat/pdf/capturing_heat.pdf

Place an old grill on top of oil can to hold the pot

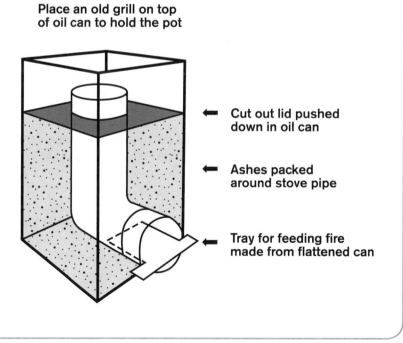

← **Cut out lid pushed down in oil can**

← **Ashes packed around stove pipe**

← **Tray for feeding fire made from flattened can**

TOMATO CAN STOVE

This is a little outdoor hobo stove that works on the same principle as a charcoal chimney starter and the rocket stove described above. It burns twigs, so it's easy to fuel. Best of all, it's extremely simple to build.

A cheap little stove is a good thing to have on hand for emergencies. Sometimes it's just nice to be able to have a hot drink or heat up some soup while you wait for the power/gas to come back on. In more extreme situations, it could be used to boil water for drinking.

You need:

- **A 28-ounce can**, or similar.
- **Heavy wire**. Coat-hanger wire is a little flimsy for this project. About 3 feet of it.
- **A drill with a 1/4 inch bit and a 1/8" inch bit.** (You could do this with a hammer and awl, too.)

1 Turn the can upside down and drill a bunch of 1/8" holes in the bottom. No particular pattern or number, but don't be shy. Make it into Swiss cheese. These holes will allow air to draw through the fire. The more holes the better.

2 Measure down about ¾" from the upper rim of the can. Using a pen, mark eight evenly spaced holes around the perimeter of the can. Drill at these points using the ¼" bit.

3 Do exactly the same thing at the bottom of the can. Mark ¾" up from the bottom rim and make eight ¼" holes. Make sure these holes align with the ones above.

4 Cut three equal pieces of wire to serve both as legs and to elevate the cooking surface. This sounds strange at first, but it's actually simple. You're going to thread three longish pieces of wire through the top and bottom holes of your can at equal intervals, forming tripod legs for the can. However, those same pieces of wire are going to extend over the top

edge of the can as well, forming three prongs that you can balance a pot or kettle on.

So cut the wire with a mind to how far you want the can off the ground, and how far you want the cooking surface elevated. You should have an extension of at least two inches off the top and bottom to allow for good air flow. The total length of your wire = the height of your can + (at least) four inches.

On our tomato can, which measures 4 ½", the total length of each piece of wire is 8½", allowing two-inch extensions top and bottom.

5 Thread your first piece of wire into the can by pushing it through one of the bottom holes from the outside. Run it up the inside of the can and back out of the matching ¼" hole at the top. Do the same with the other two pieces of wire, spacing them at even intervals to form a tripod base.

Yes, there are eight holes top and bottom and you're only using three. The others are for air.

6 Bend the wire and fiddle with the legs until it stands sturdy. Do the same with top, shaping the prongs until they'll balance an empty pot.

7 To use the stove, gather a bit of newspaper and a bunch of pencil-sized and smaller twigs. Wad a little newspaper on the bottom, and then pack the can tightly with twigs that you've broken up into one- to two- inch pieces.

The idea is to create a slow, controlled burn with a minimum of soot and smoke. The looser you pack the wood the faster it will burn, which is not as good. Light the newspaper through one of the bottom holes. The twigs should catch fire easily. You can add a squirt of starter fluid if you're having trouble.

You'll get the feel of it. Play with your stove prior to an emergency, just for fun. That way when you really need it, you'll be comfortable with it.

HEAT ON THE CHEAP: BUDDY BURNERS

A buddy burner is an easy craft project for the family survivalist, which we learned from the brilliant '70s Mormon classic, *Roughing it Easy* by Dian Thomas.

Think of it as a homemade Sterno can for camping or emergencies, made entirely of recycled materials you're likely to have around the house.

Completed, a buddy burner is simply a tuna can packed with cardboard rolled in a sweet-roll configuration. The cardboard is saturated with wax, making the whole can flammable. It can be used as cooking fuel, light, or a heat source. It will burn for 1 ½–2 hours, and can be recharged and reused.

What you need:

- **A clean tuna can**
- **A piece of cardboard**
- **A bunch of candle stubs** (You knew you were keeping them for a reason!)
- **Some kind of double boiler setup**, e.g. a soup can and a small sauce pan

Part 1: Cut your board and pack your can

Begin by cutting the cardboard into strips as wide as the can is deep. It doesn't matter how long they are, but longer strips are easier to work with.

Cut across the corrugation—across the ridges—so that when you look at the edge of the strip you see the open channels. You are going to coil the cardboard in the can, so you will need maybe three or four feet of cardboard total. Roll your strips of cardboard up like a sweet roll, starting with your longest strip. Tuck it in the center of the can, and coil the rest of the cardboard strips around it until the can is filled with cardboard. It doesn't have to be tight, but it should be pretty full.

Part 2: Melt your wax and pour it in

Pile your candle stubs next to the tuna can to get a sense of how many you'll need to melt. The wax soaks into the cardboard, so you always seem to need more than you expect. Don't worry about the wicks, dust, soot, or those little metal tab things. The purity of your wax doesn't matter.

Melting wax directly over a flame is dangerous, because if it reaches high temps it could catch fire. Therefore it is safest and best to use a double boiler. All this means is that you're going to put your candle stubs in a clean soup can. Then you're going to put the soup can in the center of a pot of gently simmering water.

Keep your eye on it, and give it an occasional stir. The wax will melt eventually. As it melts it will liberate bits of old wick. Fish these out first and tuck two or three in a standing position between the cardboard coils to act as starter wicks for the burner. Then pour the hot wax slowly into the tuna can. It will fill up fast at first, then the wax level will sink as the cardboard soaks it up. Keep adding wax a little at a time—you want to be sure the can is absolutely full of wax and the cardboard completely saturated.

Cooking with your buddy

To cook with your buddy burner, all you have to do is figure out how to elevate a cooking pot above it. You could use a fondue setup, or stack up some bricks on either side of the can, or fashion a base out of wire.

To start the burner, light the wicks that you tucked into the cardboard and turn the can up on its side so that the cardboard catches fire, too. The cardboard is a huge wick. That inferno effect is what you want.

Control the size of the flame by making a damper out of a piece of aluminum. Fold the foil into a rectangle as wide as the can, but much longer so that you can use the excess as a handle. Slide the foil back and forth to expose or repress the flame as needed.

To recharge the burner, place chunks of wax on top of it while it's burning. The wax will melt down and refuel it. The wax will always burn at a lower temperature than the cardboard, so the cardboard should last a long time.

Safety note:

Unfortunately, these days, most "tin" cans are coated on the inside with plastic. The plastic leaks estrogen-mimicking compounds into our food. It also makes heating up food directly in cans problematic, ruining a whole school of outdoor cooking. You're not eating out of the buddy burner, but it might release some plastic fumes during use. We've never smelled anything, but they're probably there. To prevent this, you might want to toss your empty tuna cans on an *outdoor* fire and burn off the plastic coating before you begin the project. The cans will blacken, but may easily be scrubbed clean.

We do not have any DIY substitutes for the electronic toys that fill our homes short of learning to play a musical instrument and putting on your own plays, but we can use our electronic gadgets as efficiently as possible.

Hunting The Phantom

Electronics are the most insidious source of so-called phantom loads, a colorful way of describing how certain appliances drain electricity even when they are not in use. Anything with a transformer, those plugs with big annoying plastic cubes at the end, are the first place to hunt phantoms.

Transformers—we prefer calling them "wall warts"—take household current and step it down to the level that your answering machine, laptop or cell phone charger uses. Unfortunately transformers consume power even when you've turned the appliance off. Plug all such electronic gadgets into a power strip, that way when you're done using them you can cut off the power at the strip and stop those phantom loads.

Also look out for any appliance that has a clock, because a clock is an energy drain. If you don't need the clock, like the one on your microwave, for instance, put the appliance on a powerstrip and turn it off when not in use. Phantom load meters with punning names such as the Kill-A-Watt and Watts Up, can help you figure out if an appliance is draining power while "off," but these things cost between $40 and $100, meaning you'd probably be better off just assuming they do, and investing in a few power strips.

Computers

Some computer folks will tell you that computers will last longer if you keep them on all the time. True, the power supply may last longer, but it doesn't justify the electricity costs; and people tend to replace computers long before the power supply will die. For reducing power loads, consider a laptop computer that uses a lot less power than a desktop model.

The Boombox: Your New Home Stereo

Big stereo systems draw a fair amount of power. An energy-saving tip that many off-grid rural households take advantage of is to replace the home stereo with a much smaller "boombox" or a small dockable desktop iPod speaker system. Plug it into a power strip and you'll also be able to kill any phantom loads when not in use.

Plasma TVs Are The New Hummers

Bad news for those with a jones for gargantuan TVs—some new plasma screen TVs consume more power per year than your refrigerator even if you only have them on for a few hours a day. According to the *Wall Street Journal*, a 60-inch plasma screen will cost you around $120 worth of electricity to run for a year compared with $60 for your refrigerator. Add on the fancy surround sound, game consoles, DVD players, set-top boxes and digital recorders and you're looking at a veritable fiesta of energy-sucking plugs.

Washer & Dryer 6%

The Solar Clothes Dryer

The solar clothes dryer, otherwise known as a clothesline, is probably the simplest solar power application that virtually anyone can use. Why air-dry your clothes? In terms of energy savings the economic benefit doesn't seem all that impressive at first. In our urban homestead at our current natural gas prices we figure we're saving about 17 cents per load. If we had an electric dryer the cost would be considerably higher—44 cents per load. But if you live in an apartment and use a coin-operated dryer you'll have an even bigger savings since you won't be pumping quarters into the machine.

Of course if we figure in the cost of the dryer itself, those loads would cost quite a bit more. But the greatest savings over time may be that air-drying is simply better for your clothes. They'll last longer and smell fresher than machine-dried clothes.

Simple retractable clotheslines as well as clothespins are available at your local hardware store. Those with limited space may want to consider a rotating collapsible design especially made for small spaces. There are also drying racks made for use both indoors and outdoors. The smaller racks can be moved around to take full advantage of the sun.

KELLY SAYS: Homesteader is not a synonym for martyr. I have to be honest here and say that we have a dryer as well as a laundry line. Erik is advocating that we do not replace the dryer when it finally shakes and sputters its way off to dryer heaven, but you can bet there will be some bickering here when that day comes. Laundry lines are great, but they do require that you plan your laundry days. Time spent hanging laundry can be calming, meditative, wonderful, but sometimes you want to—have to!—do laundry at night, or when it is raining. So I'll retain the option to machine-dry, and save the suffering for when the zombies come, thank you very much. Then I will out to hang laundry with an Uzi strapped to my shoulder.

ERIK SAYS: Planning when to hang laundry is one of those activities, like growing food, that connects you with nature. You've got to watch the weather! That's what the National Oceanographic and Atmospheric Administration website and the Weather Channel are for—I'm not a Luddite after all! That being said, we live in Los Angeles where the weather is almost always sunny and warm, so if we lived in Seattle and I had to deal with an armful of soggy laundry during a rainy spell, I might feel differently.

Refrigerator 5%

Refrigerators are the single biggest power-sapping appliance in your household, and they have a depressing history of bad design. Back in the days of cheap electricity, manufactures increased the interior capacity of refrigerators by reducing the amount of insulation and then adding *heaters* to deal with the moisture that developed on the outside of the fridge because of the lack of insulation. This resulted in refrigerators so inefficient (1950s refrigerators were four times more efficient than 1970s models) that California stepped in with regulations in 1976, with the federal government following in 1993. There is still room for improvement and the most innovative and energy efficient refrigerators made today are to be found in the world of off-grid solar living.

We are particularly fond of our ConServ Refrigerator made by the Vestfrost company. While more expensive than a comparable-sized refrigerator it will, over time, make up the difference in lower electricity bills, and its high efficiency is especially important if you want to power your kitchen with solar. Another added benefit of this refrigerator is its very small footprint—just two by two feet making it an ideal appliance for old kitchens that have no room for modern refrigerators.

The easiest way to take energy consumption down is to use as small a refrigerator as possible. Some folks may be able to get away with a bar-style fridge. As Shay Soloman, author of *Little House On A Small Planet*, told us, big refrigerators are usually filled with nothing but the two C's: condiments and compost.

Dishwashers 2%

The good news about dishwashers is that a study conducted by the University of Bonn in Germany concluded that dishwashers use half the energy, one-sixth the water, and less soap than hand-washing.

Generating Your Own Power

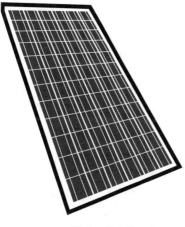

Photovoltaic Panel

Since all power on earth ultimately originates with the sun, it makes sense to go straight to the source. Generating electricity from sunlight is the most promising way for urban homesteads to achieve energy independence. Systems can range from the simple, such as a photovoltaic solar panel hooked up to a laptop for emergencies, a tiny trailer wired for a solar-pimped version of Thoreau's cabin, to a full-blown system for all of your household needs installed by a licensed electrician. Lets first look at some of the components involved in generating electricity with sunlight and then take a look at some examples of how these individual components might be put together.

Electricity From Solar Power—The Components

Photovoltaic Panels

Photovoltaic Panels (PV for short) convert the light of the sun to electricity. PV panels come in a wide variety of sizes from small panels you can use to charge batteries or run a laptop, to multiple panels chained together to run your urban homestead. They are sized according to how much power they generate, a figure measured in "watts," though in the real world they won't quite generate their rated power. Photovoltaic panels are modular and can be hooked together to provide more watts of power.

Panels should ideally face south with an unobstructed view of the sun. Just a little bit of shade across the panels can dramatically reduce their electricity output. Panels also need mounting hardware so they don't blow away in a storm, and so they can be tilted at the optimal angle.

Prices for PV panels are beginning to fall dramatically and whatever your feelings about our international economy, low-cost manufacturing of PV panels in China may spark a solar revolution. Recent manufacturing breakthroughs have included panels that can double as roofing or siding material allowing them to be easily integrated into most any building.

Inverters

PV panels output direct current (DC) electricity. Direct current is the kind of power that batteries put out and it's the power that you'll find in cars and boats, but not in a conventional house. So with a solar power system you have two options — use DC appliances, like the kind found in the world of recreational vehicles, or convert that DC to AC. There is a whole world of DC appliances, but they tend to be more expensive and limited, so most urban household PV systems make use of a device called an inverter which converts DC to regular household AC, meaning that you can use all your normal electronic devices. Inverters take away some of the power in converting DC to AC, but not as much as they used to.

Off-Grid vs. Grid-Tied, Or, When The Sun Don't Shine
During the evening hours, or during an extended stormy spell, you'll have to decide whether to go completely off-grid, by using a battery backup, or if you'll stay tied to the utility grid ("grid-tied") and use city power to keep the lights on at night.

In an off-grid system you store your electricity in batteries that the solar panels charge up during the day. The advantage of this system is that you are energy-independent—power outages will have no impact on your homestead. The disadvantage is the additional expense and maintenance of a whole bank of batteries and the added cost involved in having enough photovoltaic panels to completely cover all of your electricity needs. To go off-grid you will definitely need to trim down your energy usage by adopting many if not all of the conservation techniques we've already discussed.

The most common photovoltaic power installation in urban areas is a grid-tied system where you stay hooked up to your utility company. During the day, when your PV panels are collecting electricity, your power meter will run backwards if you are generating more power than you are using, and you'll be selling electricity back to your utility company. Your power company will credit you for the power you have fed back into the grid. At night, since you are still hooked up to the grid, you'll use your utility company's power.

Batteries
Advanced DIY types who want to experiment with small-scale solar systems need to know a few basics about batteries. Car batteries, for instance, are designed for brief periods of discharging when starting the car followed by a long period of slow charging, when the car is running. If you try to run your light bulbs off of a car battery it will quickly become impossible to recharge, and you'll end up with a toxic doorstop.

The cheapest battery option for solar systems is six-volt golf cart batteries — string them together in pairs and you'll have the 12 volts you'll need to power your typical small DC system. Lead-acid golf cart batteries need periodic maintenance, which consists of adding distilled water so that the internal lead plates stay immersed in a chemical stew. Fail to do so and the battery can smoke, catch fire and/or explode. These types of batteries can also produce hydrogen gas which is why they should be vented to the outside. Placing your batteries on a concrete floor, or concrete backer board, used for backing tile, is also a good idea in case of acid spills.

One way to avoid these maintenance hassles is to purchase the more expensive gel or absorbed glass matte batteries (AGM). These batteries are completely sealed and do not need to be topped off with water and you don't need to construct a vented enclosure, though it's always good to keep the terminals in an enclosed box or covered in some way to prevent accidental electrocution.

Charge Controller
If your system uses batteries you'll need a charge controller. A charge controller's electronics monitor your batteries charge level and prevent overcharging.

Safety Disconnect
As required by code, properly installed photovoltaic systems will have a disconnect switch to allow for safe troubleshooting of electronics. Just like the juice flowing from your power company's wires, your solar system can fry you and light your casa on fire if you get careless.

Fuses
Fuses prevent electrocution, fires and damage to equipment in the event of a short circuit. All solar systems, even really small ones, need fuses.

Solar Systems: Small, Medium And Large
Most discussions of solar electricity use revolve around large systems installed by a professional that provide all or part of the energy needs of your household. We will briefly discuss what such a system would look like. But solar systems can also come in small and medium forms—you can use them to power a few outdoor lights, or to provide backup power to a tiny house or a home office.

Entry-Level Solar

Simple entry-level solar gadgets such as battery chargers, cell phone chargers, outdoor lights, while probably not economical, can provide a cheap solar thrill as well as give an introduction to basic solar electronics.

Tiny Kit For A Laptop

A kit is probably the best way to put together a small system. Kits such as this one, which includes a PV panel, battery and inverter, available from Sundance Solar, could be used to power a light or laptop,

Ted Kaczynski Solar:
Systems For Small Homes, Apartments, And Emergency Backup

While even a small solar photovoltaic system is expensive, anyone can put together a simple panel and battery combo that could power a home office or an extremely frugal household. To see detailed examples of small systems that renters have put together see issues 93 and 96 of *Home Power Magazine*, available at your library or online for a small fee. Both of these examples consist of a couple of PV panels on the roof hooked up to an inverter and batteries all contained in a small plywood box. The cost for such a small setup will be in the low thousands—expensive, but keep in mind that when you move, you can take it with you.

It's tempting in such small systems to skip the inverter and run everything off DC power; however, the cost of the larger wires, and more exotic appliances you need with DC make it impractical for all but the tiniest applications.

Going All The Way

For homesteaders who can afford it, a grid-tied system installed by a licensed contractor with an economic assist from government incentives and tax breaks will be the most sensible path.

If you own your own homestead, there are many federal, state and municipal incentives for installing solar photovoltaic systems. These incentives are constantly in flux so you'll need to check findsolar.com and use their online calculator to help determine the cost of a full-scale installation and whether it makes economic sense. Findsolar's calculator will also tell you if your local utility company has a net metering plan that will let you sell power back to the grid for a further reduction of your costs.

Some Precautions

While we're bullish on solar power, beware of too-good-to-be-true claims which the alternative energy industry is full of. Get references from any contractor and watch their work carefully. One persistent problem with solar contractors is carelessness when mounting the panels on your roof which can lead to leaks and mold. You'll also need to make nice with the neighbors to make sure they don't plant trees that will eventually shade your panels.

Self-Contained Solar

It takes years for a solar system to pay for itself, and that fact keeps many people from investing in one. Why pay for an expensive installation when you're likely to move before it pays off? One solution is to buy a self-contained solar system (both off-grid and grid-tied versions are available) in which the panels, inverter and other electronics are all mounted together in a big box. All you do is plop it down in the sun somewhere in your yard and hire a licensed electrician to hook it up to your home's electrical panel. Because it is not affixed to the roof, when you move, you just take it with you.

In 2004, after doing some work on our home, we decided to purchase a small-scale solar unit to provide some of the power used within our home. Over the previous years we had reduced our lifestyle to demand just one car, and numerous bicycles, but the continued wringing of our hands over the world's energy situation was getting old. We decided to make an investment. Our intent was multi-pronged: we wanted to support the solar energy industry, take advantage of plentiful sunlight that was falling on our property every day, contribute to the power grid, rather than just take from it, and be somewhat self-reliant in regards to the power we used in our daily lives. To us, a small investment in the future was the way to go. Someone needed to start building the alternative energy infrastructure of the 21st century so we volunteered.

We settled on the Bluelink 960 (960 Watts DC) after talking with company CEO, Naoto Inoue. Bluelink, a partnership of Talmage Solar, Solar Market, and Two Seas Metalworks, makes affordable "plug-n-play" systems that are fully assembled and ready to go (think washing machine that sits in your backyard and generates electricity). We went small because we didn't want half of our investment to go into the system's installation. Bluelink's system really fit our needs so it was an easy choice. Spending a little over $9,000 on the system, we received a rebate of $2,200 after completing a mound of paperwork for the California Energy Commission's Renewable Energy Program.

A year and a half into the system's use, we've been quite pleased with how our 960 functions. Bluelink claims that our system will work better during the winter months, but our problem is the surrounding trees in the neighbor's yard that keep the sun's rays from hitting our BP panels during a considerable portion of a day. Fortunately, that's only during the colder months: November through March. In the warmer months, the system generates anywhere from three to five kilowatt-hours. On average, we use about seven kilowatt-hours per day and this is mainly due to the fact that we live in Southern California, spending virtually nothing to heat or cool our house. We've installed a very energy-efficient Lennox heating and air conditioning system that is probably in use for about one month of the year. The rest of the time we use either sweatshirts or fans, depending on the extreme. The other crucial component of our energy system is the array of trees, plants, and other biomass, that further reduce our need of energy to make our home comfortable.

In the coming years, we plan to expand our system onto our garage roof. We've started another "solar fund" for this effort. Another converter will be needed as will an installation team. California's progressive energy policies will hopefully make it easier for us, and for others, to take energy production into their own hands. Growing your own power is a great thing. We walk out to take a look at the converter every day to see what we've generated and this has really impacted how we use energy. Frugality is the key to the future, and though the sun is an abundant energy source, we found that using solar energy has only pressured us to use less. Energy is not something to squander. It is something to be thankful for, and every day the sun comes out we are just that, thankful.

Deena Capparelli and Claude Willey, Altadena, California

Wind Power

For most urban dwellers the odds are that wind power won't be a viable option, largely because buildings inhibit the flow of wind. Wind turbines need to be mounted as high as possible, at least 30 feet above the nearest building—any lower and it's like putting a solar panel in the shade. Because of the tower requirements, wind power is generally a better option for folks in the suburbs and country.

Of course you also need wind, so to find out if wind power will work where you live, Southwest Windpower has links to wind maps across the U.S., showing the most promising areas.

Wind maps: skystreamenergy.com/skystream/will-skystream-work/local-resources.aspx

Microturbines

For folks living in a windy area in a tiny house, so-called microturbines, scaled-down version of the ones that power a big house are an option, especially when combined with photovoltaic panels.

Microturbine

Chapter Seven
Transportation

THE JOURNEY IS THE JOURNEY

Transportation

Revolutionary urbanists will not limit their concern to the circulation of things and of human beings trapped in a world of things. They will try to break these topological chains, paving the way with their experiments for a human journey through authentic life.

—Guy Debord, *Situationist Thesis on Traffic*

Transportation for the urban homesteader means much more than getting from point A to point B. Transportation can be a joyous experience, a tool for a radical re-envisioning of the urban environment and a means by which we form deep connections with our surroundings. Our means of transportation should enhance our awareness of ourselves and connect us with our neighborhoods. Most of all, our transportation should be fun.

Axe-Grinding Alert

Be warned, we're biased toward human-powered transit; specifically, we're bike-obsessed (at least one of us is). By all means, stay in your hybrids, or buy those carbon offsets (the Papal Indulgences of the 21st century), if you please, just know that you're missing out on all the fun.

Transportation Principles:

1 The Journey Is The Journey

Our daily journeys should be a source of joy rather than aggravation. The forms of transportation we choose are those wherein the journey is a joyous end in itself. Why can't commuting be recreational?

2 Transportation Should Be Low-Tech

Ideally, you should be able to repair your means of transportation yourself. Automotive technology has surpassed the ability of the average person to make repairs. The bicycle is simple and elegant. J.B. Jackson said of the bicycle, "It is the kind of machine that a Hellenistic Greek might have invented and ridden."

3 Your Transportation Should Give You Exercise

Combining exercise with transportation is a great time-management strategy. Public health officials have begun to realize that the plague of obesity and the related Type 2 diabetes are directly related to time spent sitting in cars. If your commute is your daily exercise, you not only save time, but you also replace the mind-numbing grind of the treadmill with authentic, real-life experience.

4 Transportation Should Promote Community

Traffic Circulation is the organization of universal isolation. In this regard it constitutes the major problem of modern cities. It is the opposite of encounter, it absorbs the energies that could otherwise be devoted to encounters or to any sort of participation.

—Guy Debord

Our walking, biking and mass transit alternatives are not only more exciting, but also lead to richer connections with our fellow travelers. Communities form when we get out of our metal boxes and meet each other face to face. Pick a form of transportation that increases the likelihood of human contact and you'll soon be surrounded by new friends. Walking and biking especially help us form new communities. Humans are social creatures. The more of us that walk and bike the more we improve our neighborhoods. Urban spaces become dysfunctional when nobody knows each other, when people are isolated, when streets are deserted. We were never meant to spend great chunks of our lives all alone, trapped in a metal cage behind the wheel of an SUV with no company other than bad radio. Walking and biking directly transform our streets into inviting and dynamic living spaces.

The Urban Homestead Transportation Triangle: Walking, Biking, Mass Transit

Walking

We're embarrassed to admit that we used to drive to our local ATM, which is only a half mile away, and then on to the local diner, which is just two blocks further. The average American walks less than 400 yards a day according to a study by the Robert Wood Johnson Foundation. That's a shame, because more than any other form of transit, the fine level of discernment that comes with walking leads to serendipitous discoveries and unexpected pleasures. We meet our neighbors, see the changes in our neighborhood, feel the transitions of the seasons. At the same time, we can also move within, and spend contemplative time alone, because walking is at once a mode of travel and a means of getting in touch with the world.

As Henry David Thoreau once said, "It's a great art to saunter," and thankfully it's an easy art to master. All it takes is a shift in mindset from our car-centric ways. New Yorkers, Parisians and San Franciscans are used to walking, and their cities are made for walking, but that does not mean you can't walk in your city. All it takes is a map and a willingness to try something new.

If you're not already a walker, draw a circle on a map around your homestead. Everything within a mile is an easy walk. Don't use the car to get anywhere in that circle, as strange as that might feel at first. Eventually you will become so accustomed to walking that distance that like us, you will be amazed that you ever went through the trouble of driving such a short way.

Our perception of walkable distance was dramatically shifted by a 26-mile walk we once took across Los Angeles to benefit a charity. While the full 26 miles nearly killed us, we learned on the way that 10 or even 15 miles is a reasonable distance to cover in a day. It also opened our eyes to the city's topography in ways we never considered, and changed our relationship to the city permanently. We encourage all urban homesteaders to devote a Saturday or Sunday to a cross-town perambulation. Not only will your perception and tolerance of long walks change, but you're guaranteed to discover neighborhoods you've overlooked.

Naismith's Rule

Hikers use something called Naismith's Rule to figure out how long it will take to go somewhere on foot. Naismith estimates that the average person can walk a mile in 20 minutes (you add a half hour for each 1,000 feet of elevation gain, though it's doubtful you'll need this adjustment in urban situations). Naismith's rule is a handy way to figure out how long those longer walking trips will take, though with practice you might find you walk somewhat faster than Naismith anticipates.

To measure distances on a map for walking and cycling, nothing beats Gmaps Pedometer (gmap-pedometer.com), which allows you to use Google Maps to measure out and plan routes. Gmaps pedometer combined with Naismith's Rule will give you a good idea of how long it will take to walk to your destination. We also use it to send favorite bike routes to friends.

Cycling

Riding a bike allows a person to pack more life into a day. As Americans, we know all too well that the car driver often finds himself caught in a void, a void of dead space and time. The time spent driving to the store, to work, caught in traffic, attention vaguely drifting from the road ahead to the radio and back, is so nondescript, so forgettable, it is lost forever. Did the driver really live these minutes spent in motorized transit? Technically. On the bike, it is vastly different. This is actual living. Blood and oxygen pumping, muscles straining. There is a sense of being a true part of the world, a participant in one's own life, rather than simply watching it pass by on a big screen.

—Robert Hurst, The Art of Cycling

Every ride on a bicycle is an adventure, the closest thing to flying, with each trip a magical journey through the city. You never have to worry about parking, and you weave effortlessly through the congested streets. Cycling is living what Aristotle called "the examined life," or what our contemporary pop culture might call "taking the red pill."

KELLY SAYS: Erik is the bike activist in the family. I haven't taken the red pill on this one yet, and it is not that I love my car. I'd prefer to live in a dense city where I could rely entirely on walking and public transport, and you can bet if I lived in Holland, I'd ride my bike everywhere, joyfully. But I live in L.A., which is not a bike-friendly city. Basically, I just don't have the balls to share the roads with distracted actors who are driving their SUVs while text messaging, and drinking a latte, and looking over a script, and wondering whether they should switch to a more fashionable yoga studio.

What I do is walk a lot. I like my neighborhood, so I sort of pretend that the rest of L.A. doesn't exist most of the time. I frequent shops, cafes and restaurants which are close to where I live. I like doing this, it gives me a grounded sense of community in the middle of a huge megalopolis. I take public transport when it is reasonable, but not to the point of martyrdom (the L.A. transportation system invokes metaphors like that). I carpool, condense my errands and just try to be thoughtful about when and how I use my car. And you know what? Sometimes Mr. Bicycle himself comes along for the ride.

ERIK SAYS: I could point out that statistically, depending on who you believe, cycling is as safe or slightly safer than walking per mile traveled and that motoring is more likely to get you killed. Cycling in traffic may seem scary the first time you dive into it, but you get used to those latte-sipping SUV drivers after awhile. Plus it's just plain bitchin'.

How To Ride In Traffic

Riding a bike in the city takes some time to master, but it's not as scary as it might seem at first. Eventually you will develop a jones for the adrenaline-pumping thrill of it. The intricacies of how to ride are well beyond the scope of this book—all we'll say is please ride with traffic, not against it, stay out of the door zone (around 3 ½' to 4' from a parked car) and ride in the street, not on the sidewalk. These rules are logical for some but counterintuitive for others which is why we recommend seeking out the following three excellent resources for getting the hang of urban cycling.

The first place to start is Michael Bluejay's excellent and concise "How to Not Get Hit by Cars" at bicyclesafe.com which goes over some basic common-sense rules for riding safely in traffic. Read it before you head out there.

For a more hands-on experience, seek out the adult safety class "Road 1" taught by the League of American Cyclists (bikeleague.org), which usually consists of an evening class followed by a weekend practicing a few emergency handling skills and some time out on the road to go over how to ride in traffic.

By far the best book on urban cycling techniques, a must-read for any urban cyclist, is the phenomenal *The Art of Cycling: Lessons from the Street* by Robert Hurst. Hurst offers advice on every situation you'll encounter, from uneven road surfaces to inattentive motorists, while expressing the sheer joy and wonder of negotiating city streets on a bike. This book has saved our asses many times over, with superb advice on virtually any situation you'll encounter.

Bike Fit
A bike is an extension of the body, what the writer Alfred Jarry called his "external skeleton." Finding the right bike is like finding the right shoe. Above all other considerations, your bike should fit your body. Instructions for proper bike fit can be found on the internet and in books, but nothing beats having a knowledgeable person take the time to make sure that you have the right bike and that it is adjusted properly. Even if you know how to do this yourself, it really helps to have a second set of eyes.

Saddle Sore
One of the biggest complaints from new riders is, specifically, pain in the ass. Some discomfort in your sit bones, which is the part of your derriere that should be in contact with your bike's saddle, is to be expected when you first start out. Work gradually into riding and you'll lessen this problem, largely by building strength in your legs, which takes the weight off of your butt's contact points with the saddle. Bike mechanic Sheldon Brown reminds us that bikes have "saddles" not "seats" for a reason—a saddle is meant to carry some, but not all, of your weight.

Persistent discomfort or numbness somewhere other than in your sit bones is an indication that pressure is being put on the space between your sit bones. This can be due to a saddle that is too narrow or, counterintuitively, a saddle that is too soft. Soft saddles are one of the big causes of discomfort since your ass tends to sink into them, thereby putting pressure on the space between the sit bones. Many new bike saddles have a cutout section in the middle to relieve pressure on the prostate and genitals (an endless, and in our opinion, overblown source of fear and controversy), but it's still more important to make sure that your sit bones are carrying your weight. Additionally, a seat that is too wide can cause chafing, the equivalent of running a cheese grater across your inner thighs—ouch!

The fact is, we are all shaped differently and we ride different kinds of bikes so a saddle that works for one person may not work for another. In addition, seat height, front-back position, and seat angle also play a big role in comfort level, yet more reasons why you need to have a skilled person fit your bike to you and help you choose the right saddle.

Finding A Bike

There are two places we'd suggest beginning your search for a bike. The first is a bike co-op. Many large cities have some form of bike co-op where you can put together a used bike or repair the one you have. The other option to consider is a small independently-run bike shop. With either source, try to go on a weekday when you can find a volunteer or salesperson who will spend time with you to assure proper fit, the seat set at the right height and the handlebars the right width and height.

You are the engine of your bike, so you can't buy performance with money, as you can with a fancy sports car. Your speed, grace, and endurance depend on you actually getting out and riding. No multi-thousand-dollar carbon fiber road bike will make you Lance Armstrong. And anyway, this is urban riding, complete with signals, stop signs, potholes and drifting SUVs, not the Tour de France. So whatever you do, don't run out and buy an expensive bike for commuting. On the other hand, this is your transportation, so don't get some cheap Wal-Mart piece of crap either. You want a dependable, solid bike—start out with something neither too expensive nor too cheap, probably in the $500 to $1,000 range. For short hops to a transit station or workplace where you might need to leave a bike locked up all day, add a cheap (less than $100) beater to your fleet. And don't fall for new gimmicks. It's hard to improve on something as perfect as a bike—that's like trying to innovate on the design of a fork or a pair of chopsticks.

You also don't need 99% of the accessories and clothing sold in bike shops. That said, if you bike, you should have the following things with you at all times:

1 **The means to repair a flat tire**—a patch kit, spare tire, tire levers and a small pump
2 **Helmet**
3 **Water bottle**
4 **Front headlight, rear taillight and side reflectors mounted in the spokes**
5 **Spare change for the bus** in case you can't repair your bike

Bike Clothes

You don't need special cycling clothes to get around the city! Lycra is for folks trying to shave a few milliseconds in the Tour de France. You're not racing. Whatever's comfortable works. Bright clothes are always better for the sake of visibility, but even if you are dressed from head to toe in fluorescent pink don't assume that drivers see you—generally they don't see anything beyond the keypad of their cell phones.

The time you may want to invest in some cycling-specific clothes is in cold weather. Dress in layers, with a base wicking layer such as thin wool, a fluffy middle layer (wool or fleece), and a waterproof shell. You may also want a balaclava to keep your face and head warm under your helmet, even though it will make you look damned scary. Remember that you will warm up considerably once you get moving, so you should be cold when you first head out the door—otherwise you'll be soaked in sweat by the time you reach your destination.

I have been riding a bicycle in New York City for almost 30 years! For transport, not for sport. At first there were only a few of us. Loners, losers, maniacs and nerds. Some of the members of Talking Heads used to make fun of me and say I was going to turn into Pee Wee Herman—and they weren't talking about his extensive porno collection. But we knew some pleasures of which other New Yorkers seemed completely ignorant. Pleasures available to all. An exhilarating feeling as the air rushes past and we dodge taxis and New York pedestrians, who still insist on playing in the traffic. A feeling of flying through and around the inevitably stalled traffic. One has to stay alert—if your attention wavers, you're done for. Who needs coffee? Or a morning at the gym? A ride across town gets the adrenalin going as one heads to work or to the studio in the morning. By the time one arrives for a meeting one is fully awake—blood pumping, on alert—having just had three near-death experiences. In the hot New York summers, yes, one can tend to "glisten" when one arrives at an appointment, which is not always appreciated, so I had a shower installed in my office. But, if one pedals at a relaxed pace and stays away from the snarled traffic as much as possible (cars and trucks raise the surrounding temperature) one can arrive more or less dry, but with a healthy glow.

—David Byrne, New York. From his online journal, davidbyrne.com

Route Choice

Many newbies, embarking on their first urban commutes, simply attempt to follow the same exact routes they've been driving in their cars every day. This is ill-advised. The best routes for cars very rarely correspond to the best bike routes.
—Robert Hurst, *The Art of Cycling*

We can't emphasize enough Hurst's admonition to find quiet, peaceful routes when you head out on your bike. It's not always possible, but more often than not you can find alternatives with a little effort and some time spent carefully studying a map. It sometimes means going out of your way, but it's always worth it. It took us a while, but we even have peaceful ways to bisect the notoriously bike-unfriendly city of Los Angeles with relative ease and comfort. And you'll discover places and streets that you never would find in your car.

Some cities and bicycle advocacy groups publish bike maps that can help find the better streets for biking. Like Hurst, we don't think it's necessarily more dangerous to take a major arterial street, but your ride will be more comfortable and less hassled on peaceful side streets.

Cargo Bike

So how do you carry groceries or other big items with a bicycle? The answer is the amazing Xtracycle, an SUB or "Sports Utility Bicycle." You can buy an Xtracycle whole, or purchase a kit which extends the rear wheel base of your own bike so that it has space to hold a set of saddle bags and a wood platform that doubles as a passenger seat. An Xtracycle can easily transport four full bags of groceries, the same amount we used to carry in our car, and it handles well even with heavy loads. The ride is smooth and cornering is just like any ordinary bike.

The Xtracycle's cargo bags, which the company calls "Freeloaders," are designed in such a way that they cinch up the cargo and maintain a narrow profile, essential for maneuvering in city traffic. This narrow profile is the great-

est advantage that the Xtracycle has over bike trailers. The long wheel base of the Xtracycle combined with a load over the back wheel makes the bike easier to brake and it's nearly impossible to flip over the front handlebars. For our Xtracycle we used an inexpensive fully

Xtracycle

rigid (no front or back suspension) mountain bike, which is, in our opinion, the best kind of bike to turn into an Xtracycle.

We put the Xtracycle together ourselves, but those without bike repair experience can have it done at a bike shop. Doing it yourself involves bolting the Xtracycle's frame into where the back wheel used to be, adding on to the chain and extending the rear brake, derailleur and cables.

Other Cargo Options
If you don't opt for an Xtracycle, make sure that the bike you get has eyelets, threaded connections located on the frame of the bike that allow you to attach a rack to it with screws. Once you attach a rack you can hang pannier bags (saddlebags) over your back wheels, giving you the capacity to carry at least two bags of groceries. Pannier bags can be a bit expensive, which is why some savvy cyclists improvise them by strapping two plastic wastebaskets to a rear bike rack.

Backpack Just For Bikes
When out and about on our road bike, we just use a backpack, which will easily fit a few groceries and a change of clothes. Of course, many use messenger bags on bikes, and those definitely look hipper, but we prefer a cycling-specific backpack because they feel more secure on the back and are more comfortable for long rides and heavy loads. Bicycle-specific packs are built low, so they don't block your over-the-shoulder view. We use the commuter backpack made by Banjo Brothers, which is waterproof, fitted with reflectors, and has a place to hang a blinking rear light.

Bike Trailers
While we prefer the maneuverability of the Xtracycle over bike trailers, if you really want a bike trailer, why don't you make your own out of bamboo and a pair of used bike wheels? Full instructions at: carryfreedom.com/bamboo.html.

How To Lock Up A Bike
The sad truth is that bike thieves are always one step ahead of any lock. But there are ways to minimize thievery. We recommend carrying two locks, a U-lock and a cable. Lock the rear wheel and frame with the U-lock to a secure object and use the cable to lock the front wheel and frame, preferably also to something that ain't going anywhere. The philosophy here is that a thief will have to carry two different tools to defeat both the U-lock and the cable. And secure those wheels—thieves and crackheads will make off with those $100 rims if they can't take the frame.

Mass Transit

Ken Kesey said, "you're either on the bus or off the bus," and as much as we love walking and biking, sometimes the bus (or train) is the way to go. When you site your urban homestead, one of the first things you should consider is its proximity to mass transit. The more transit options the better, and the less likely it is that you'll have to rely on a car. Get out the local transit map, and check times and frequency before signing that lease or deed.

While mass transit sometimes takes longer than biking or driving, at least buses and subways allow for true multi-tasking. Take a book, a laptop, an MP3 player, and a cell phone, and take care of all that business while someone else does the driving.

Trip Planning

Mass transit trip planning is becoming easier thanks to the Internet. Most transit authorities have some sort of web presence with maps and trip planners with varying levels of quality depending on how seriously your city takes public transit. Thankfully a growing number of Internet companies are stepping into augment trip planning. As of the time this book was written, the car-centric Google Maps are being augmented with Google Transit (google.com/transit), which now serves 13 cities with more on the way (we hope!). Another source is Public Routes (publicroutes.com), which has transit information augmented with walking directions for 15 American cities, two metro areas, and the city of London.

Combining Bikes With Mass Transit

Public transit and bikes go together like gin and tonic, creating a mobility cocktail that will get you nearly everywhere, even in the most transit-poor city. Too far from the bus stop? Take your bike. Most buses have a rack on the front you can put your bike on. If your town doesn't, agitate until they do. In most places you can also take your bike on the subway. If there are rules against taking a bike onboard, you can purchase a folding bike that you can take anywhere, even when you fly. Popular folding bikes include the Bike Friday (bikefriday.com), the more spendy and deluxe Brompton bike (bromptonbicycle.co.uk), and the moderately priced Dahon (dahon.com). If you need to lock up your bike all day at a bus stop, or subway stop we recommend getting a disposable beater bike that you won't miss if it gets stolen.

MAKE YOUR OWN BIKE LIGHT

Bike headlights are something we like to gripe about. The cheap ones are little more than toys. They don't have enough power to light up the road, and they break easily. The expensive ones are, well, expensive. A decent headlight that will both keep you visible and light up the road (important when dodging the ever-present urban pothole) will set you back at least $100 and possibly as much as $400.

Thankfully, a cheap and powerful front bike light is easy to improvise using a common landscape light, a few parts from the hardware store, and a battery ordered over the internet.

Materials

- **1 Malibu® Halogen Floodlight** such as model CL507 (costs around $11) or an equivalent 12-volt outdoor light.
- **1 Panasonic Sealed Lead Acid Battery LC-R123R4P** (around $20)
- **1 inline cord switch**, like a lamp switch
- **A length of copper wire** that is longer than the distance between your bike's seat and handlebars—we scavenged ours from a disused power transformer from an old answering machine
- **A battery charger** (order from the same place you get the battery)
- **20-watt halogen spot bulb** (Optional— The Malibu® light comes with a floodlight. This will work fine, but you can replace it with any 20-watt 12-volt halogen spotlight for a more tightly focused light.)
- **A saddlebag** large enough to hold the battery
- A way to attach the light to your handlebars (you're gonna have to improvise this one)

Tools

- **Soldering iron and solder** (optional but recommended)

1 Cut a piece of wire long enough to reach between the saddle bag and the handlebar leaving some slack so that you can wrap the wire around the top tube of the bike to keep it

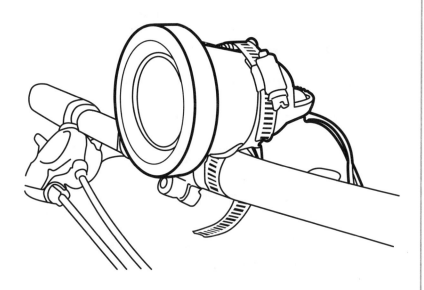

secure and out of the way of your legs. The light will go on the handlebar, of course, and we like to put the battery in a saddle bag firmly attached to the bottom of the seat. It could also go in a pannier bag.

2 Take your Malibu® light and cut off the weird proprietary connectors it comes with—you will be left with two bare wires.

3 Solder in your inline cord switch and add some wire to connect the Malibu light to the battery.

4 Solder the ends of the wire that will go between the seat and the handlebar to the terminals on the battery. Put a piece of tape around the battery to secure the wires to the battery. Leave the terminals exposed so that you can hook them up to the battery charger when it's time to recharge.

5 Flip the switch and test to see if the light works.

6 The hardest part of this project is figuring out how to attach the light to the handlebars. Due to the bumps and vibrations of the road anything you attach to a bike must be solidly secured. We've used the old attachment hardware from busted bike lights as well as hose clamps.

7 Put the battery in your saddlebag and make sure that the bag is securely attached. Wrap the wire a few times around the top tube of your bike and leave enough slack for the handlebar to turn. Make sure that the wire is not dangling where it could get caught in the wheel or some other moving part of your bike. While the battery fits in a water bottle cage, don't be tempted to put it there. Once ours fell out of the bottle cage and swung into our back wheel causing us to skid 30 feet and break a bunch of spokes. For the same reason definitely don't hang the battery anywhere near the front wheel!

8 Your light should run about two hours on a charge, so we usually bring a cheap LED light as a backup if we think we'll be out for a long time. When you're back from your night ride recharge the battery immediately as it will last longer if kept fully charged.

Conclusion: The Future

We don't pretend to know what the future holds. If you frequent thrift stores you'll find plenty of dog-eared books that predicted a doom that never came, and we don't want to be one of those books. All we'll say is that it looks like we are at some kind of historical juncture, caught awkwardly at the end of an industrialization that began in the 19th century, and at the beginning of a technological revolution whose trajectory is difficult to discern. Ominous trends are taking hold—global warming, debt, energy scarcity, a spiritually bankrupt consumer culture, war and fear.

Absent a functioning crystal ball we offer three possible future scenarios:

More of the Same: A continuation of our current paradigm, in which an elite has access to organic produce and solar panels, while the poor eat heavily processed foods, and everyone, rich and poor, tools around in massive oil-guzzling vehicles and entertains themselves by shopping in soulless big-box stores. This is a life where we are defined as consumers rather than citizens, where we are identified by what brands we buy rather than by our actions and ideals.

Apocalypse: Just around the corner may lurk a devastating resource shortage, at which point a many-headed beast of Babylon will shuffle the consumer zombies, sinners, and hipsters off to certain destruction while the righteous ascend into some kind of holy shopping mall/office park in the sky—or descend down into their heavily stocked bunkers.

Consciousness Shift: This is what we hope for, and what the activities profiled in this book are geared to jump-starting—the rise of a new urban agriculture and home economics along with a growing concern about where our food comes from and how we use energy and resources.

The good thing is that if you and your neighbors pick up a few skills in this book you can ditch the crystal ball and be ready for any of these possibilities.

Note the emphasis on neighbors. Intrepid urban homesteaders may attempt all of the many activities in this book and more. However, most of us have jobs, kids and a million other responsibilities. But we can exchange skills and goods with our friends and neighbors. Say I have some land so I grow some food. I trade with a friend who lives in an apartment who makes beer. Together we can swap knowledge, make dinners together, forage for food, bike to work, and agitate for positive change in our communities.

Community building is the next step beyond this book. Share these skills with your friends, family and neighbors. Share your time, your crops, your knowledge—build a community of urban homesteaders.

Build community, and we'll stick our necks out and make a prediction—**everything's going to be all right.**

Resources

www.
homegrown
evolution
.com

Please visit our website www.homegrownevolution.com **for live links and our continually evolving collection of homesteading resources.**

Start Your Own Farm and Projects

Edible Landscaping/General Gardening

Bradley, Fern Marshall, *Rodale's Vegetable Garden Problem Solver*. Rodale, 2007.
Organized by plant as well as by pest/disease—very handy for identifying problems. Cultivation tips too.

Bubel, Nancy, *The New Seed-Starters Handbook*. green-seeds.com/pdf/seed_starters.pdf.
An amazingly detailed free 300 page e-book on everything you could ever want to know about starting seeds, including the science of germination, and timetables for starting different types of plants.

Creasy, Rosalind, *The Complete Book of Edible Landscaping*. Sierra Club Books, 1982.

Flores, Heather C., *Food Not Lawns: How to Turn Your Yard Into a Garden and Your Neighborhood Into a Community*. Chelsea Green, 2006.

Hart, Robert, *Forest Gardening: Cultivating an Edible Landscape*. Chelsea Green, 1996.

Jeavons, John, *How to Grow More Vegetables (and Fruits, Nuts, Berries, Grains, and Other Crops Than You Ever Thought Possible on Less Land Than You Can Imagine)*. Ten Speed Press, 2002.
Presents a program for growing all the calories you need on your own, the problem being that to do this for one person you need 4000 square feet of farming space. Still, it is a useful book in that it actually gives you a plan and timetable on how to plant a garden bed and maintain it throughout the year, which is very useful even if you don't subscribe to his style of gardening.

Kruger, Ann, *Rodale's Illustrated Encyclopedia of Organic Gardening*. Rodale, 2005.
Search for it used—this book has been around in several printings.

Reich, Lee, *The Pruning Book*. Taunton Press, 1999.

Stout, Ruth, *Gardening Without Work: for the Aging, the Busy, and the Indolent*. Lyons Press, 1998.
Originally published in 1961. Ruth Stout is the godmother of the mulch crowd, and this book is a classic on the subject, but it is not a general guide to gardening.

American Community Gardening Association. communitygarden.org
Features a community garden locator.

Plants for a Future—7000 Useful Plants. pfaf.org
Contains a searchable database of 7000 "edible, medicinal and useful plants for a healthier world". An invaluable resource for researching the best plants for your edible landscape.

Meetup Groups.
To find people in your area who share your gardening interests, go to meetup. com and search under keywords such as "organic gardening," "urban gardening"

or specific methodologies that appeal to you, suck as "permaculture" or "Square Foot Gardening."

Guerrilla Gardening

Tracey, David, *Guerrilla Gardening, a Manualfesto*. New Society, 2007.

The Fukuoka Farming Website. fukuokafarmingol.info/fintro.html
Dedicated to Masanobu Fukuoka, the inventor of the seed ball and the "do nothing" method of farming.

"Guerrilla Gardening." Primal Seeds. primalseeds.org/guerrilla.htm
"Armed with trowels, seeds, and vision, the idea is to garden everywhere. Anywhere."

The Guerrilla Gardening Website. guerrillagardening.org
A blog dedicated to acts of "illicit cultivation."

Permaculture

Hemenway, Toby, *Gaia's Garden, a Guide to Home-Scale Permaculture*. Chelsea Green, 2000.
A basic introduction to Permaculture aimed at the backyard gardener.

Mollison, Bill, *Introduction to Permaculture*. Tagari Publications, 1991.

The Permaculture Information Web. permaculture.info

Worm Composting

Applehof, Mary, *Worms Eat My Garbage*. Flower Press, 1997.

Marsh, Lori, *Composting Your Organic Kitchen Wastes with Worms*. Virginia Cooperative Extension.ext.vt.edu/pubs/bse/442-005/442-005.html
How to build your own worm bin and care for the worms.

WormPoop. wormpoop.com
Vermiculture information and supplies.

Worm Suppliers. Urban Agriculture Notes, City Farmer, Canada's Office of Urban Agriculture. cityfarmer.org/wormsupl79.html
A list of worm suppliers in Canada, the U.S., and around the world.

"Worm Your Way Into Composting." Digital Seed.
digitalseed.com/composter/vermicomposting.html. How to build your own worm composter out of plastic storage boxes.

Container Gardening

Mandel, Josh, "Homemade Self-Contained Gardening Systems." 14 May 2007. josho.com/gardening.htm Mandel's updated guide to making self-watering containers with PVC-free design.

Mandel, Josh, *How to Build a Self-Watering Planting Container*. 2007. Seattle Peak Oil Awareness. seattleoil.com/Flyers/Earthbox.pdf
A downloadable guide of his original designs.

ContainerSeeds containerseeds.com
A website that sells seeds selected for container gardens, with tips and resources for container gardens.

Drip Irrigation

Kourik, Robert, *Drip Irrigation for Every Landscape and All Climates: Helping Your Garden Flourish, While Conserving Water!* Metamorphic Press, 1993.

DripDepot. dripdepot.com
A source for drip irrigation kits and parts.

Drip Works USA. dripworksusa.com
A source for drip irrigation kits and parts.

Pest Control

Beneficial Insects in Your Backyard. University of Maine Cooperative Extension.
www.umext.maine.edu/onlinepubs/htmpubs/7150.htm
A guide to beneficial insects and how to attract them.

Manage and Identify Pests in Homes, Gardens, Landscapes, and Turf. University of California Integrated Pest Management Program.
ucipm.ucdavis.edu/PMG/menu.homegarden.html

Pesticide-Free Gardening...Naturally! The Green Pages of the Montréal Botanical Garden, ville.montreal.qc.ca/jardin/en/info_verte/jardiner_sans_pesticides/jardiner.htm
"Twelve rules for an attractive pesticide-free garden."

Urban Foraging

Foraging

Gibbons, Euell, *Stalking the Wild Asparagus.* Alan C. Hood & Company, Inc., 2005. A classic. Many older editions and a field guide available.

Henderson, Robert K., *The Neighborhood Forager.* Chelsea Green Publishing, 2000. Wild food from a gourmet perspective, recipes and medicinal notes.

Hoffman, John, *The Art and Science of Dumpster Diving.* Loompanics Unlimited, 1992. Don't let the comic-style cover put you off. A great book.

Thayer, Sam, *The Forager's Harvest.* Forager's Harvest Press, 2006.
Also see foragersharvest.com

Tull, Delena, *Edible and Useful Plants of Texas and the Southwest.* University of Austin Press, 1987.

Keeping Livestock

Poultry

Buchholz, Richard, "Coturnix Quail." *Mother Earth News*, Sept.–Oct. 1981.
www.motherearthnews.com/Sustainable-Farming/1981-09-01/Coturnix-Quail.aspx
The author mentions raising quail in NYC.

Damerow, Gail, *The Chicken Health Handbook.* Storey, 1994.
A necessity if you have chickens.

Easterly, Allen, "Raising Quail, a Home-Grown Delicacy." *Backwoods Home Magazine*,
backwoodshome.com/articles2/easterly101.html

Henderson, John R., "Henderson's Chicken Breed Chart." Sage Hen Farm.
www.ithaca.edu/staff/jhenderson/chooks/chooks.html

A great chart showing all the chicken breeds with concise information on their characteristics.

Holderread, David, *Storey Guide to Raising Ducks*. Storey, 2000.
    The authority on duck health, housing and breeds. Useful, but not sentimental. You get the feeling he looks at ducks with a knife in one hand and a fork in the other.

Luttmann, Gail, and Rick Luttmann, *Chickens in Your Backyard*. Rodale Press, 1976.
    A classic.

Mercia, Leonard, *Storey's Guide to Raising Poultry*. Storey, 2002.

"Raise Chickens, Build Chicken Coops, Hatch Eggs." BackYardChickens.
    www.backyardchickens.com
    Another general resource for chicken owners, with links, breed info, coop info and its own message board.

Rossier, Jay, *Living with Chickens*. The Lyons Press, 2002.

Ducks. feathersite.com/Poultry/Ducks/BRKDucks.html
    The Feathersite, which is good for chickens too, has a rundown on duck care and duck breeds. A good starting place.

Walbert, David. "Raising Ducks." The New Agrarian.
    newagrarian.com/homestead/ducks/index.html
    A well-written and documented account of one family's flock of Khaki Campbells.

Mad City Chickens. www.madcitychickens.com
    For "questions and concerns regarding all aspects of poultry rearing."

The City Chicken. home.centurytel.net/thecitychicken
    "...a web site to encourage city folks to take the plunge into poultry!" This is a good resource for pictures of coops and runs.

The Society for the Preservation of Poultry Antiquities www.feathersite.com/Poultry/
SPPA/SPPA.html is a great resource for learning about heritage breeds.

Rabbits

Bennett, Bob, *Storey's Guide to Raising Rabbits*. Storey, 2000.
    Covers breeds, breeding, accommodations and how to slaughter and dress rabbits.

Gendron, K., *The Rabbit Handbook*. Barron Educational Series, 2000.

"House Rabbit Society Rabbit Care Guide." House Rabbit Society, rabbit.org

Bees

Backwards Beekeeping beehuman.blogspot.com
    An invaluable resource (with good links) for those interested in back-to-the basics, organic beekeeping.

"Beekeepers, Beekeeping Meetups, Events, Clubs and Groups in Your Area." Meetup.
    Com. beekeeping.meetup.com

Flottum, Kim, and Weeks Ringle, *The Backyard Beekeeper: an Absolute Beginner's Guide to Keeping Bees in Your Yard and Garden*. Quarry Books, 2005.

Langstroth, L.L., *Langstroth's Hive and the Honey-Bee: the Classic Beekeeper's Manual*. Dover Books, 2002.

Revolutionary Home Economics

Canning

Alfred, Beverly Ellen Schoonmaker, *The Jamlady Cookbook*. Pelican Company, 2004. The Jamlady has a jam recipe for nearly every kind of crop, both common and exotic.

Rombauer, Irma S., Marion Rombauer Becker, and Ethan Becker, *Joy of Cooking: All About Canning & Preserving*. Scribner, 2002.

"USDA Complete Guide to Home Canning." National Center for Home Food Preservation. uga.edu/nchfp/publications/publications_usda.html

"Your Complete Source for All Fresh Preserving Needs." Freshpreserving.Com, Ball, freshpreserving.com/pages/home/1.php
Ball makes canning jars. This is their homepage, with tons of resources for the home canner, including step-by-step instructions, canning times, and lots of links.

Solar Cookers and Dehydrators

Delong, Deanna, *How to Dry Foods: the Most Complete Guide to Drying Foods At Home*. Penguin Group, 2006.

Fodor, Eben, *The Solar Food Dryer: How to Make Your Own Low-Cost, High-Performance, Sun-Powered Food Dehydrator*. New Society, 2006.
Fordor offers detailed plans for building a simple solar dehydrator.

Radabaugh, Joe, "Making and Using a Solar Cooker." *Backwoods Home Magazine*. backwoodshome.com/articles/radabaugh30.html
A simple solar cooker made out of cardboard boxes, aluminum foil and a piece of glass.

Scanlin, Dennis, "The Design, Construction, and Use of an Indirect, Through-Pass, Solar Food Dryer." *Home Power,* Feb.–Mar. 1997: 62–72.
We made our solar dehydrator from these plans found in this issue.

Whipple, J.R. "Solar Food Dehydrator." The Farm.
thefarm.org/charities/i4at/surv/soldehyd.htm
Instructions for making a solar dehydrator out of a cardboard box.

The Solar Cooking Archive. Solar Cookers International. solarcooking.org
The best website for information on building your own solar cookers and dehydrators.

Fermentation

Ackland, Tony, "Home Distillation of Alcohol." homedistiller.org
An overview of home distillation.

Buhner, Stephen Harrod, *Sacred and Herbal Healing Beers*. Siris Books, 1998.
A heretical guide to home brewing. Buhner explores the use of herbs in beer for flavoring, medicinal and psychotropic purposes.

"Building a World-Class Home Distillation Apparatus." moonshine-still.com

Fisher, Joe, and Dennis Fisher, *The Homebrewer's Garden: How to Easily Grow, Prepare, and Use Your Own Hops, Malts, Brewing Herbs*. Storey, 1998.
Information on how to grow your own beer making supplies.

Katz, Sandor Ellix, *Wild Fermentation: the Flavor, Nutrition, and Craft of Live-Culture Foods*. Chelsea Green Company, 2003.
> Our Bible of fermentation. A must-have.

Palmer, John J., *How to Brew: Everything You Need to Know to Brew Beer Right the First Time*. Brewers Publications, 2006.
> This book gets way too technical, in our opinion, but does have excellent step-by-step instructions for both extract and all-grain brewing.

Rowley, Matthew B., *Moonshine!* Lark Books, 2007.
> Shows you how to make a couple of different kinds of stills with recipes for distilling your own illegal hooch.

GEM Cultures, Inc. gemcultures.com
> Mail-order sales of soy and dairy cultures and bread leavens.

Leeners. leeners.com
> "Kits and supplies for making everything from beer to bubble gum and wine to cheese."

Cleaning

"Alternative Cleaning Methods." Solid Waste Agency of Northern Cook County www.swancc.org/hcw/alternativecleaningmethods.html
> Many of the best online resources for homemade cleaning supplies come from agencies responsible for waste management.

Hollender, Jeffrey, *Naturally Clean*. New Society, 2005.
> Not a how-to book, but rather a "why" book. Reviews the effects of chemicals commonly used in housekeeping products.

Sandbeck, Ellen, *Organic Housekeeping*. Scribner, 2006.
> This is the how-to book. In fantastic detail Sandbeck tells you how to safely clean every item in your house.

Shelter

Salomon, Shay, *Little House on a Small Planet*. The Lyons Press, 2006.
> An excellent argument for the small house, lots of profiles of people living radically small.

Susanka, Sarah, *The Not So Big House: a Blueprint for the Way We Really Live*. Taunton Press, 2001.

Tumbleweed Tiny House Company. tumbleweedhouses.com.
> Jay Shafer's innovative and beautiful tiny houses are available as plans or as complete units.

Be Your Own Utility

Solar Power

Find Solar. findsolar.com
> A website with a solar power cost estimator. A great way to figure out if solar power will work for your living situation.

Floyd, P.B., Slingshot, slingshot.tao.ca/displaybi.php?0080018.
> How to build a simple solar shower out of plastic ABS pipe.

Meloy, Raymond, "A Portable Solar Water Heater." *Mother Earth News*,
Mar.–Apr. 1980.
motherearthnews.com/Renewable-Energy/1980-03-01/A-Portable-Solar-Water-Heater.aspx
How to build a simple solar shower out of a truck tire inner tube.
The Solar Living Institute. solarliving.org
Located in Hopland, CA, the Solar Living Institute, promotes, "sustainable living
through inspirational environmental education."

Water Conservation/Greywater

Jenkins, Joseph, *The Humanure Handbook*. Jenkins Publishing, 1999.
Available both in book form and as a free download at jenkinspublishing.com
Lancaster, Brad, *Rainwater Harvesting for Drylands*. Rainsource Press, 2006. Also
see his Oasis Design, oasisdesign.net/. Good info. on grey water, rainwater, and
water storage.
Litchfield, Michael, *Renovation: A Complete Guide*. Sterling, 1997.
Bio Pac Inc. Cleaning Systems. bio-pac.com
Greywater-safe laundry detergent

Transportation

Balish, Chris, *How to Live Well Without Owning a Car*. Ten Speed Press, 2006.
Robert, Hurst, *The Art of Cycling: A Guide to Bicycling in 21st-Century America*.
Falcon, 2006.
The bible of how to ride a bike in the city.
Sheldon Brown – Bicycle Technical Information. sheldonbrown.com.
Extensive articles on all kinds of mechanical issues and maintenance.
The Bamboo Bicycle Trailer. Carry Freedom. carryfreedom.com/bamboo.html
Free plans for building one
Xtracycle. xtracycle.com
Manufacturers of our favorite cargo bike.

Our Favorite Magazines

All eminently useful, and all four are available online to one degree or another
Backwoods Home Magazine
Backyard Poultry Magazine
Home Power Magazine
Mother Earth News

About the Authors

Kelly Coyne and Erik Knutzen are the proprietors of the www.homegrownevolution.com blog, a green living resource providing self-sufficiency tips and tricks to urbanites. They live in the heart of Los Angeles on what they like to think of as their mini-farm, along with four chickens and a Doberman with a taste for heirloom tomatoes.

process self-reliance series
Helping urbanites to live sustainably and self-sufficiently in the 21st Century

WHEN THERE IS NO DOCTOR
Preventive and Emergency Healthcare in Uncertain Times
by Gerard S. Doyle, MD

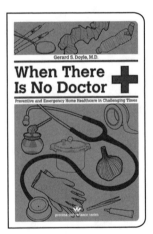

The fifth title in Process' Self-Reliance series offers a practical, sustainable, and cost-effective approach to 21st Century health and home medicine.

When There Is No Doctor is full of medical tips and guidance you can count on. It should be no further than an arm's reach in your household at a time when our healthcare system has become susceptible to strain.

"This is a book about sustainable health, primarily having to do with your health and what you can do to protect it—in bad times certainly, but also in good. I will help you ensure the health of those you love, yourself and, should you so choose, your community, if and when the world changes. World may come to mean your little town or the whole globe. It could change for a few days or weeks, or for a few years. It could change because of a flood, financial crisis, flu pandemic, or failure of our energy procurement, production or distribution systems.

"I will not teach you to be a lone survivalist who anticipates doing an appendectomy on himself or a loved one on the kitchen table with a steak knife and a few spoons, although I will discuss techniques of austere and improvised medicine for really hard times." —from *When There Is No Doctor*

Author Dr. Gerard Doyle teaches and practices Emergency Medicine at the University of Wisconsin, Madison, where he also plans the hospital's response to disasters.

6" × 9" • 200 Pages
ISBN 978-1934170-11-3 • $16.95
processmediainc.com

PREPAREDNESS NOW!

An Emergency Survival Guide, Expanded and Revised Edition
By Aton Edwards

PREPAREDNESS NOW! is the first comprehensive planning and action guide for those who want to be able to protect and provide for themselves in the face of any crisis. This book empowers individuals and communities to take care of themselves and each other in the face of any emergency and build more sustainable lifestyles along the way. Packed with checklists, resources, and step-by-step instructions, *PREPAREDNESS NOW!* has everything from home, office and car preparedness to information on building disaster-resistant geodesic domes.

PREPAREDNESS NOW! is written by one of the most experienced experts in the field. Author Aton Edwards is Executive Director of the NYC-based non-profit organization, International Preparedness Network (IPN). IPN has worked with the Red Cross, Center for Disease Control, New York City Police Department, and other organizations to train thousands domestically and overseas to prevent and respond to emergencies and disasters.

PREPAREDNESS NOW! provides years of wisdom gained from Edwards' first-hand experience and the experience of his extensive network of colleagues. You will learn basic and advanced techniques that will help you make the most informed choices for your own disaster plan–wherever you may live, and whatever your physical abilities and financial means.

This expanded edition has new information in response to the country's current economic crisis, including extensive information on food storage and foraging and a new chapter on preparedness and self-protection in times of civil unrest.

This manual delivers practical advice on:
• Building your emergency kits for home, car and office • Water Quality Control and Storage • Emergency Shelter, Power, Lighting and Heating • Emergency Transportation, Communications and Evacuation • Extreme weather preparedness • Chemical, Biowarfare and Nuclear Preparedness • Defense against Infectious Diseases • Personal Defense and Crime Prevention for the 21st Century Home

6" x 9" • 336 Pages
ISBN 978-0976082255 • $15.95
preparednessnow.org • processmediainc.com

www.ProcessMediaInc.com

www.HomegrownEvolution.com